Teaching
Shakespeare

CAMBRIDGE SCHOOL

Shakespeare

Teaching Shakespeare

Rex Gibson

CAMBRIDGE
UNIVERSITY PRESS

PUBLISHED BY THE PRESS SYNDICATE OF THE UNIVERSITY OF CAMBRIDGE
The Pitt Building, Trumpington Street, Cambridge CB2 1RP, United Kingdom

CAMBRIDGE UNIVERSITY PRESS
The Edinburgh Building, Cambridge CB2 2RU, United Kingdom
40 West 20th Street, New York, NY 10011–4211, USA
10 Stamford Road, Oakleigh, Melbourne 3166, Australia

First published 1998

Printed in the United Kingdom at the University Press, Cambridge

A catalogue record for this book is available from the British Library

ISBN 0 521 57788 8 paperback

Prepared for publication by Paren & Stacey Editorial Consultants

Designed by Richard Morris, Stonesfield Design

Thanks are due to the following for permission to reproduce photographs:

p 10*tl*, Garrick Club/E.T. Archive; pp 10*ml*, 123*l*, Angus McBean/print by Shakespeare Centre Library; p 10*tr*, Alastair Muir; pp 10*b*, 111*tr*, 123*mt*, 146, Donald
Cooper/Photostage; p 15 (RST production at Stratford-upon-Avon 1963), p 111*tl*,
123*tr* (RST production at Stratford-upon-Avon 1969), Shakespeare Centre Library;
p 22, Reg Wilson; p 111*bl*, Douglas Jeffery; 111*br*, Raymond Mander & Joe
Mitchenson Theatre Collection; p 129, 20th Century Fox (courtesy Kabal); p 203*l*,
still from the film Henry V by courtesy of Carlton Film Distributors/print by
British Film Institute; p 203*r*, Renaissance Films; p 215*t*, by courtesy of Shakespeare
Birthplace Trust; p 215*b*, Richard Kalina/print by Shakespeare's Globe. Every effort
has been made to reach copyright holders; the publishers would like to hear from
anyone whose rights have been unknowingly infringed

Contents

> *In order to avoid intrusive detail in the text, full line references for all of the play quotations are provided in an index on page 247*

Introduction

'The play's the thing'

Active methods

Many teachers reading this book will have long experience of teaching Shakespeare. Others will be about to embark on teaching Shakespeare for the very first time. Some teachers will feel confident, eagerly looking forward to renewing acquaintance with a familiar play. Their past experience will have given them a fund of ideas on how to teach Shakespeare to a new class of students. Other teachers will feel nervous, not sure about how to begin, uncertain about how students will respond. They see the difficulties of the play far more clearly than its accessibility.

This book provides help to both kinds of teacher and to all others who fall between these polar opposites. It is a response to requests from teachers for a publication which is rich in practical examples, and which also sets out the theories and principles that inform and direct practice. Readers will find an overview of the current state of Shakespeare scholarship, together with detailed descriptions of practical approaches that have proved successful in a wide range of classrooms.

Teaching is a professional activity in which each teacher makes considered judgements to decide what is appropriate for each particular class of students. Professionals do not seek a universal recipe, a sequenced series of steps to be followed slavishly and exactly. The professional teacher's skill lies in the subtle and thoughtful adaptation of content and method to suit the actual circumstances and the unique nature of his or her own students. The many practical examples in this book are offered in the knowledge that teachers will adapt them in ways suitable for their own classrooms.

One reason why Shakespeare's plays have proved so popular for so long is their infinite capacity for adaptation. As society changes, so do the meanings and significances found in the plays. For 400 years the plays have been interpreted and performed in an astonishing variety of ways. Just as the same play can be performed very differently, so it can be taught and experienced in very different forms. A Shakespeare script is a blueprint from which actors and directors construct their vision of the play. Similarly, teachers and students respond to its multiple possibilities.

Each play works on many levels. It has a surface and a deep structure, literal and metaphoric meanings, naturalistic and symbolic potentialities and so on. Shakespeare can be studied through story and character, themes and issues, language, drama and theatre. As Chapter 3 shows, a Shakespeare play also lends itself to a host of intellectual or ideological concerns. Approaches and interpretations can take different forms and focus: political, historical, gender, psychoanalytic, aesthetic, moral. Each teacher's view of Shakespeare will play a large part in determining the nature of their students' experience and perception.

The commitment of this book is to active methods of teaching Shakespeare. Shakespeare was essentially a man of theatre who intended his words to be spoken and acted out on stage. It is in that context of dramatic realisation that the plays are most appropriately understood and experienced. The consequence for teaching is clear: treat the plays as plays, for imaginative enactment in all kinds of different ways.

Active methods comprise a wide range of expressive, creative and physical activities. They recognise that Shakespeare wrote his plays for performance, and that his scripts are completed by enactment of some kind. The dramatic context demands classroom practices that are the antithesis of methods in which students sit passively, without intellectual or emotional engagement. Shakespeare is not a museum exhibit with a large 'Do Not Touch' label, but a living force inviting active, imaginative creation. Active methods release students' imagination and involve them in speaking and acting. Such action gives focus and substance to the discussion, writing and design work that students undertake. It enables students to gain a sense of theatre and drama in their classroom. It helps them to make Shakespeare their own, as they inhabit the imaginative worlds of the plays through action. Direct experience of Shakespeare's language allows students to feel its distinctive forms and rhythms, and to respond with a real sense of personal engagement.

Active methods dissolve the traditional oppositions of analysis and imagination, intellect and emotion. They encourage informed personal responses which are both critical and appreciative. In active work, students combine critical thought with empathy, confidence with a willingness to suspend judgement. Interpretations do not have to be of the narrowing 'either...or' type but can be the more expansive and imaginative 'both...and' variety.

The varied activities described in *Teaching Shakespeare* acknowledge the value of individual work, and encourage students to work together in pairs and groups of all sizes. Through such participatory and co-operative activity, students both discover and create meaning. They become the agents of their own learning as they take responsibility for their own inquiries and investigations.

Teaching Shakespeare: an overview

Chapter 1 provides a cogent set of reasons for teaching Shakespeare. Chapter 2 sets out the principles of successful active teaching methods, and is illustrated with many practical examples. Chapter 3 reviews recent developments in Shakespeare scholarship, and suggests how these theories and perspectives are related to school and college studies. Together, these chapters offer a coherent rationale and set of principles necessary to any teacher's professional knowledge.

Chapters 4–11 are expressly concerned with practice. They contain a host of approaches that have been successfully used in classrooms. Several activities are given in a good deal of detail, in the knowledge that teachers welcome this occasional wealth of description, and will adapt it to suit their own students. These chapters demonstrate the great variety of activities which comprise active methods. All aim at enabling students to take responsibility for their own learning, and all recognise that the teacher has an essential role in that task. In some activities, the teacher plays a very prominent part in order to progress to student-initiated work.

The material in the practical chapters is presented in the full awareness that it could be differently organised. Chapters 4–8 reflect the major elements of the study of Shakespeare in schools and colleges: language, story, character, theme and dramatic effect. But those elements all intertwine: language *is* character; story and theme are organically part of each other; everything contributes to dramatic effect. It is helpful to treat them separately in a book (or in a lesson), but the aim is to help students realise their essentially interconnected nature, each a part of each other.

The content of each chapter also needs some comment here. While each has its own practical examples, all examples are closely related to those given in Chapter 9 'Active methods'. At the same time, Chapter 9 contains activities which could equally well have found a place in other chapters (for example, the 'sense units' activities would be equally at home in Chapter 4 'Language'). In the same way, teachers of younger students will find their own chapter (Chapter 10) concentrates on dramatic storytelling. They will also find that there are many activities in other chapters which they can adapt for their classrooms. Indeed, every teacher can scale activities up or down, suiting them to his or her own students, and using a vocabulary and style appropriate to any particular group of students.

Teaching Shakespeare can be read straight through to gain a comprehensive overview of Shakespeare in schools and colleges. It can also be dipped into according to need, whether it be for a single lesson on tableau, or for practical ways into a soliloquy, or for a review of recent developments in theory. As with everything Shakespearian, there is no 'one right way', but an openness to many different readings.

Teaching Shakespeare acknowledges the debt I owe to hundreds of teachers and thousands of students. They have allowed me access to their classrooms to share their enjoyment of Shakespeare and the knowledge and insights that such enjoyment brings. All of those teachers faced the familiar problem: 'With a class size of 20–30 or more students, how can I ensure that every student is actively engaged with Shakespeare?' This book is evidence that many teachers have found successful practical answers to that ever-present question. I hope that the descriptions of some of the methods I have seen working in practice will enable other students and teachers to share the joy, satisfaction and understanding that working actively with Shakespeare can bring.

Rex Gibson

Teaching Shakespeare is a companion volume to *Shakespeare's Language*, and to each play in the Cambridge School Shakespeare series. All are published by Cambridge University Press.

Why teach Shakespeare?

'My reasons are most strong, and you shall know them'

An easy answer to the question 'Why teach Shakespeare?' is 'Why not?' After all, many teachers can give examples like the ones below of the intense engagement of their students with the plays.

1 The class of eleven-year-olds who created a thrilling dance–drama of the episode that Prospero relates in *The Tempest* in which Sycorax and her potent ministers imprison Ariel in a cloven pine.

2 The thirteen-year-olds who brought the market square of Verona to bustling life into which the feud of the Montagues and Capulets then violently erupted.

3 The total involvement of the class of fifteen-year-olds who worked out their own compelling version of Macbeth's banquet in which the witches orchestrated the entries of Banquo's Ghost, and the guests echoed snatches of Macbeth's words.

4 The seventeen-year-olds studying *Measure for Measure* who argued passionately over Isabella's refusal to trade her chastity for her brother's life, and who electrifyingly dramatised the Duke's 'Be absolute for death…' in a chorally spoken version intercut with Claudio's 'Ay, but to die…'.

The co-operation that exists in such classrooms, as students work together on 'their' Shakespeare, mirrors the creative, experimental ethos of the theatrical rehearsal room, where individual talents unite in co-operative enterprise. The self-evident commitment of such students, the satisfying sense of pleasure in group and individual achievement, is usually experienced directly only by those who share it. The more public responses to the question 'Why teach Shakespeare?' can be organised under four headings:

- abiding and familiar concerns
- student development
- language
- otherness.

Abiding and familiar concerns

Shakespeare's characters, stories and themes have been, and still are, a source of meaning and significance for every generation. Their relevance lies in the virtually endless opportunities they offer for reinterpretation and local application of familiar human relationships and passions. The plays are peopled with fathers, mothers, sons, daughters, wives, husbands, brothers and sisters. Capulet, raging at his daughter Juliet, is just one of many Shakespearian fathers who fiercely seek to control their daughters' lives (Polonius and Ophelia, Lear and Cordelia, Cymbeline and Imogen, Prospero and Miranda, Duke Frederick and Celia, Egeus and Hermia, The Duke of Milan and Silvia).

Students find the Capulet and Juliet episode in Act 3 Scene 5 exciting to enact. It is recognisable and familiar, if not in every student's real life experience, then in 'felt' knowledge. Female students relish the opportunity to speak Capulet's lines beginning 'Hang thee, young baggage, disobedient wretch!' The scene is an excellent spur to discussion of the nature of parent–child relationships. So, too, is the ambiguous relationship of Hamlet and Gertrude. Even the few lines of Siward on the death of his son, killed by Macbeth, can stimulate discussion of contemporary comparisons and contrasts.

Students of all ages can recognise and identify with such relationships. Similarly, they can explore other relationships of lovers, friends and enemies, masters and servants. All are widely available in the plays: the quarrelling of Hermia and Helena in *A Midsummer Night's Dream*, the dialogues of Romeo and Juliet, Beatrice and Benedick in *Much Ado About Nothing*, Katherina and Petruchio in *The Taming of the Shrew*, or the harsh exchanges between Prospero and Caliban in *The Tempest*. As students transpose these relationships into their own experience, they engage personally and directly with abiding issues of morality, of gender, of control over one's life.

In empathetic enactments and discussion, students gain access to the feelings of Shakespeare's characters caught up in their particular predicaments. The emotions expressed reach across the centuries: love, hate, awe, tenderness, anger, despair, jealousy, contempt, fear, courage, wonder. The settings of the plays may be remote: Caesar's Rome, medieval Scotland, an imaginary island. The dilemmas may be extreme: Juliet fearful of drinking a 'poisoned' potion, a Scottish warlord about to kill his king, an Athenian workman magically transformed into a donkey. But students make immediate connection with emotions and motivations that link with their own feelings and experience. Shakespeare's times were very different from our own, but human emotions are common to all ages.

'O, she's warm' exclaims Leontes in *The Winter's Tale*, as the statue of his long-thought-dead wife Hermione comes to life. The joy of unexpected reunion, of hope that what was lost can be recovered, of the prospect of happiness after sorrow, touches emotional capacities that every student possesses.

It is not only in personal experience, in family relationships and individual emotions, that students find relevance. Shakespeare's plays also explore issues which beset every society: abiding questions of how people should live together, of justice, politics, wealth, war. What kind of places are Hamlet's Denmark, Macbeth's Scotland, Capulet's Verona, Lear's Britain, that they contain such individuals, evoke such behaviour, dispense such kinds of justice?

Students who study *Measure for Measure* are never slow in finding contemporary parallels to Angelo's hypocrisy and Vienna's corruption. The gap that the play reveals between public appearance and private practice, prompts students to identify similar disjunctions today. The sleaze and injustice that hide behind the facade of a seemingly ordered society easily find modern reflections.

In Shakespeare, the private and the public, the individual character and the social world he or she inhabits, are organically interconnected. Students who explore the question 'Why did Romeo and Juliet die?' gain a deeper understanding of the interrelation of individual and society. Their inquiries increase their comprehension of how morality is the product of individual character and cultural and historical context. Responsibility cannot be placed solely upon the lovers, or their parents, or Friar Lawrence, or the patriarchal and violent society of Verona, or even on chance or fate; it is influenced in some way by many such factors. And so with the students' own lives – Shakespeare's concerns are abiding concerns.

Student development

To study Shakespeare is to acquire all kinds of knowledge. It might be increased vocabulary, or an understanding of the Elizabethan and Jacobean stage, or of Shakespeare's life and times. It might be knowledge special to each play. *The Tempest* can motivate students to research into the colonisation of the Americas, or the growth of Renaissance science and literature. The history and Roman plays offer opportunities for developing different kinds of historical understanding.

Beyond such new knowledge, the active study of Shakespeare generates more personal development. Many teachers have seen the growth of confidence and self-esteem that comes from learning a part, however small, and taking part in performance or some other enactment before an audience.

Active methods of teaching Shakespeare are particularly powerful in aiding student development because they accord a greater degree of responsibility to students than traditional ways of teaching. They are rooted in co-operation with others to make some form of presentation. Active approaches to Shakespeare satisfy the creative impulse (How can we stage the shipwreck that opens *The Tempest*?), and offer free play to the imagination (How should *our* Ariel appear, move, speak, vanish?). Such methods are vocally and personally demanding, because they involve students in making presentations of many kinds. They are a source of deepening self-awareness as students find ways to express their understandings and feelings in physical action (How can I overcome my inhibitions about acting in front of others?).

Studying Shakespeare allows exploration of human feelings in ways that give mental, physical and emotional release, but in the safe conditions of classroom and drama studio. Enacting Shakespeare can help students to confront and control their own emotions. The resultant understanding of others can lead to greater empathy. Practical activities involve students' sympathies very directly: what does it feel like to be Ophelia, on the receiving end of Hamlet's verbal onslaughts?

The dilemmas that beset so many of Shakespeare's characters offer students opportunities to argue the moral issues and to exercise judgement and choices. Such arguments do not have to be conducted through traditional essays or class discussion, they can be undertaken in role-play. Students' moral understanding can increase as they explore the moral perplexities of individual, social and political life embodied in the plays. For example, students in role as Capulet and his wife can describe their feelings and hopes for Juliet, their only daughter, and try to make sense of her death.

In such activities, the development of critical thinking accompanies imaginative and emotional growth as students speculate, reason, predict and hypothesise about the actions, motivations, relationships and contexts of characters and communities. To use the language of developmental psychology, Shakespeare can increase students' competence and confidence across the widest range of developmental possibilities. To express it less prosaically, Shakespeare develops the understanding heart.

Language

Shakespeare's language is both a model and a resource for students. In its blend of formality and flexibility it offers unlimited opportunities for students' own linguistic growth. Variety abounds: in *Hamlet*, the immediacy of the opening words 'Who's there?' contrasts with the deeply reflective tone of 'To be or not to be...'. Shakespeare uses many different styles of language, and plays all kinds of language games. His language provides students with rich models for study, imitation, and expressive personal re-creation.

Shakespeare was clearly fascinated by language. He was acutely conscious of its use, power and limitations; every play displays that awareness. Language is action, and Shakespeare's characters reveal themselves through it. Antony uses language to persuade the citizens of Rome against the conspirators. Iago uses it to deceive and destroy Othello. Juliet uses it to express her love; Macbeth to voice his tortured conscience.

The language of the plays is energetic, vivid and sensuous. Its difficulties are enabling difficulties. Students gain a sense of achievement and satisfaction as they respond to its challenge. For example, by understanding Shakespeare's craftsmanship and using it to assist their own writing, students can develop their own voices in writing. As students come to grips with the language in active explorations, they gain insight into the power of language and become enfranchised as readers, writers, speakers, listeners and actors.

Otherness

A powerful argument for studying Shakespeare exists in his extraordinariness, his strangeness, his unfamiliarity. His appeal lies in a unique blend of the familiar and the strange, his relevance and his remoteness. All education is about 'opening doors', extending opportunities and experience. It is concerned that individuals should not be imprisoned in a single point of view, confined solely to local knowledge and beliefs. Education shows that 'there is a world elsewhere' beyond the familiar and everyday.

These educational characteristics are abundantly displayed in the characters, language, settings and issues of Shakespeare's plays. The plays acquaint students with different ways of living, different values and beliefs. His characters are simultaneously familiar and exotic. They often live at the extremes, caught in agonising dilemmas. They express themselves in heightened language, and live in worlds that are clearly not those of today. Shakespeare invites students to develop a deep acquaintance with those characters, to experience their extremes of emotion, to imaginatively inhabit their remote worlds, and to learn from those close encounters with otherness.

Every student is entitled to make the acquaintance of genius. Shakespeare remains a genius of outstanding significance in the development of English language, literature and drama. All students should have opportunities through practical experience, to make up their own minds about what Shakespeare might hold for them.

Principles

'Play out the play!'

This chapter identifies the principles underlying the teaching methods which make Shakespeare accessible and enjoyable to school and college students of all levels of ability. Brief practical examples illustrate each principle. More detailed examples are given in Chapters 3–8.

Treat Shakespeare as a script

Shakespeare wrote his plays to be performed, to be brought to life on stage before an audience. Over centuries, however, generations of scholars have transformed each play into a literary text. That legacy of textual scholarship has weighed heavily on school Shakespeare. It is part of a tradition that is deeply suspicious of enjoyment, that finds it hard to accept that pleasure and learning can go hand in hand. It sees literature as 'serious' and 'work', and drama as merely 'play'.

The notion of 'text' is deeply ingrained in Shakespearian study at all levels, and carries greater status than 'script'. 'Text' implies a desk-bound student who passively reads, rather than enacts the play; it implies authority, reverence, certainty. That implication does its own sad work in schools – it tacitly suggests that studying Shakespeare involves the pursuit of a 'right answer'.

In the clearest contrast, treating a Shakespeare play as a script (and calling it so) suggests a provisionality and incompleteness that anticipates and requires imaginative, dramatic enactment for completion. A script declares that it is to be played with, explored, actively and imaginatively brought to life by acting out. A text makes no such demand. Its privileged taken-for-grantedness conceals its social construction behind a mask of naturalness.

The textual approach is evident in those scholarly editions of the plays which until very recently served as models for school editions. The lengthy academic introductions and extensive footnotes encouraged school editions to mimic, inappropriately, the procedures and apparatus of university scholarship. Such editions promote teaching methods that explain and analyse, rather than enable students actively to inhabit the imaginative worlds that Shakespeare offers. This criticism in no way devalues traditional scholarship. But scholarly editions were not written for school and college students, and their academic approach is unsuited to the classroom. The scholarly model may be suitable for postgraduate study, but it has had a demotivating effect on generations of school and college students.

Macbeth provides a very obvious example of the textual approach. One highly respected scholarly edition begins with fifty-three pages of introduction. Much of that information, of great interest to professional Shakespeare scholars, is inappropriate to school students' needs or interests. When the play begins, the first page contains only four lines of Shakespeare:

FIRST WITCH When shall we three meet again?
            In thunder, lightning, or in rain?
SECOND WITCH When the hurly-burly's done,
            When the battle's lost and won.

These four lines are followed by fifty-two half-lines of explanation and mention of twelve named 'authorities'. The contrast between the imaginative invitation of the language and the sober commentary of the notes, is stark. This is not to denigrate the value of the edition, which is well fitted for the time, purposes and audience for which it was written. It is simply to remark that such considerations are remote from the great majority of modern school and college classrooms.

School students welcome a script approach which invites them to act out the witches' language of Act 1 Scene 1. In groups of three or more, students can create their own version of the supernatural atmosphere that Shakespeare establishes right at the start of the play. It doesn't take long to learn the lines and the students' task is to present the scene as dramatically as they can. There is no 'one right way'. The script requires little explanation other than that witches were believed to have familiar spirits: demons who helped with their evil work. These familiars were usually animals or birds (Graymalkin, a grey cat; Paddock, a toad). Teachers should use their discretion as to how far they resource students' enactment with questions such as the selection set out on page 147.

Treating the scene as a script releases the energies of students and the language. Playful activities (saying everything twice; speaking only vowels and so on) can yield surprising discoveries. A group of ten-year-olds who decided that their witches spoke all their sentences backwards were filled with excitement at finding that line 12 has its own eerie incantatory quality as they spoke it backwards and forwards:

> Fair is foul and foul is fair.

Make Shakespeare learner-centred

Successful Shakespeare teaching is learner-centred. It acknowledges that every student seeks to create his or her own meaning, rather than passively soak up information. The Shakespeare teacher's task is to enable students to develop a genuine sense of ownership of the play. That entails active expression: helping students to ask their own questions, to create and justify their own meanings, rather than having to accept only the questions and interpretations of others.

The recognition that learners actively *make* meaning, has cultural implications. Each student brings his or her own culture to every lesson. That rich variety of culture is a resource that Shakespeare lessons can celebrate and employ rather than dismiss. Such celebration and fruitfulness is evident in the many transpositions of *Macbeth*. The 'Scottish play' has been set in the worlds of medieval Japanese Samurai, Chicago gangsters, a German Walpurgisnacht with Spiderwomen witches, a Hare Krishna-type religious cult, and the leather-clad world of a rock and roll musical.

The consequences of such vividly realised cultural transpositions is obvious. The film *West Side Story* transformed the Montagues and Capulets into the Jets and Sharks of twentieth-century New York;

As these different versions of *Macbeth* show, there is no 'one right way'
to perform or interpret any Shakespeare script.

with audacious panache, Baz Luhrmann's brilliantly successful *William Shakespeare's Romeo + Juliet* locates the feuding families in the mythical Hispanic American city of Verona Beach. In the same way, students should be encouraged if they wish to set *Romeo and Juliet* somewhere other than sixteenth-century England or medieval Italy, or to play *Twelfth Night* in Asian costume and incorporate Hindi and Gujarati speeches, or to develop an Afro-Caribbean *Macbeth* in dreadlocks with many speeches rapped or sung. Shakespeare does not necessarily have to be performed in doublet and hose, or spoken in the received pronunciation (RP) of the English upper class (an accent quite unlike the pronunciation of Shakespeare's time).

Cultural diversity adds to rather than detracts from Shakespeare. A narrowly textual approach imposes strict limits on interpretation and staging. A student-centred script approach encourages variety because it recognises the play's theatricality – its openness to different realisations. Part of Shakespeare's enduring appeal is that new generations and different societies find the plays relevant to their own times, their own cultures. Students are strongly motivated when they realise that they can make *Macbeth* or *Romeo and Juliet* or any other play, their own, something that belongs to them, not to a cultural elite. Every student brings to the classroom his or her own cultural baggage. The interaction of that rich variety of culture with Shakespeare's stories, language, and characters contributes to successful classroom Shakespeare.

Students can draw on their own cultures for settings, costume, movement, dialect, music and so on. They can find their own rhythm for the witches' chant:

> The weird sisters, hand in hand,
> Posters of the sea and land,
> Thus do go, about, about,
> Thrice to thine, and thrice to mine,
> And thrice again, to make up nine.
> Peace, the charm's wound up.

Shakespeare is social

Successful classroom Shakespeare is a co-operative, shared activity. It encourages students to work in pairs or in groups of appropriate size, sharing responsibility. Such practice reflects Shakespeare's own working conditions as he and his colleagues at the Globe rehearsed together to produce a performance. Very obviously, the nature and purposes of a classroom are quite different from those of a theatrical rehearsal, but the analogy is illuminating. Like actors in rehearsal, students work together on the script, helping each other to understand a scene and to find dramatically effective ways of presenting it. The difference between text and script is immediately evident. A script calls for co-operative action, a text carries no such requirement. Scripts are social by nature, requiring active, shared participation.

In addition to preparing for performance of a scene, many other co-operative methods are available. For example, students can work together to share the language of a speech or soliloquy: Macbeth contemplating the murder of Duncan; Juliet filled with fearful thoughts before she drinks the potion; any of Hamlet's soliloquies.

Sharing out a speech by each punctuation mark can be remarkably effective. Pairs (or two large groups) of students work together to insult each other. Each speaks only a word or short phrase at a time, changing over at each punctuation mark:

KENT Fellow, I know thee.

OSWALD What dost thou know me for?

KENT A knave, a rascal, an eater of broken meats, a base, proud, shallow, beggarly, three-suited, hundred-pound, filthy worsted-stocking knave; a lily-livered, action-taking, whoreson glass-gazing, superserviceable, finical rogue; one-trunk-inheriting slave; one that wouldst be a bawd in way of good service, and art nothing but the composition of a knave, beggar, coward, pander, and the son and heir of a mongrel bitch.

Because a soliloquy is a kind of internal conversation, two students can speak short sections, turning it into dialogue. Try it right now on this extract from *King Richard III*, speaking the two voices in your mind. It is early morning, just before the battle of Bosworth. Richard awakes from a fearful dream:

Give me another horse! Bind up my wounds!
Have mercy, Jesu! Soft! I did but dream.
O coward conscience, how dost thou afflict me!
The light burns blue. It is now dead midnight.
Cold fearful drops stand on my trembling flesh.
What do I fear? Myself? There's none else by.
Richard loves Richard: that is, I am I.
Is there a murderer here? No, yes, I am.
Then fly. What, from myself? Great reason why –
Lest I revenge. Myself upon myself?
Alack, I love myself. Wherefore? For any good
That I myself have done unto myself?
O no! Alas, I rather hate myself
For hateful deeds committed by myself.
I am a villain. Yet I lie, I am not.
Fool, of thyself speak well. Fool, do not flatter.
My conscience hath a thousand several tongues,
And every tongue brings in a several tale,
And every tale condemns me for a villain.
Perjury, perjury in the highest degree.
Murder, stern murder, in the direst degree,
All several sins, all used in each degree,
Throng to the bar, crying all 'Guilty!', 'Guilty!'
I shall despair. There is no creature loves me;
And if I die, no soul will pity me.
Nay, wherefore should they, since that I myself
Find in myself no pity to myself?
Methoughts the souls of all that I had murdered
Came to my tent, and every one did threat
Tomorrow's vengeance on the head of Richard.

Shakespeare celebrates imagination

Every line in Shakespeare is an invitation to imaginative inference. Just as actors and audience enter into an imaginative conspiracy in the theatre, so too do students and teachers in the Shakespeare classroom. Students respond positively to activities which invite them to exercise their imaginations in some kind of dramatic enactment. In *Macbeth*, the witches' 'Round about the cauldron go' is an obvious example, but every scene has rich imaginative potential because of Shakespeare's dramatic sense and evocative imagery.

The imaginative intensity of certain scenes is obvious: the sleepwalking Lady Macbeth, Hermione's statue coming to life, Romeo and Juliet in the Capulet tomb, the entry of the Ghost in *Hamlet* and so on. But every scene in every play offers opportunities for imaginative enactment, and will repay closely focused active work. Because they are written to be enacted on stage, even the shortest scenes and most minor characters are charged with imaginative potential.

Exploring imagery

Shakespeare's script invites imaginative inhabitation in ways other than preparing a staged performance. Students can explore the imagery of Horatio's description of the dead King Hamlet:

> So frowned he once, when in an angry parle
> He smote the sledded Polacks on the ice.

A traditional textual approach explains that Polacks (or pollax) might mean Polish soldiers or a poleaxe. Such information lies inertly on the page. A script approach that celebrates imagination (both Shakespeare's and the students') invites groups of students to create two tableaux (frozen pictures) of the lines.

Did King Hamlet in a fierce argument strike the ice with his battle-axe? Or did he defeat a Polish army as it travelled on sledges over the frozen river? The physical enactment of the imagery is an effective spur to student discussion, as they weigh alternatives and appreciate that both are possible.

Using stage directions

Shakespeare's stage directions are obvious invitations to imaginative acting out; like musical scores, they invite performance. *The Tempest* is filled with such invitations, beginning with the shipwreck that opens the play, which includes the intriguing *Enter Mariners, wet,* and calling for a miraculously appearing and disappearing banquet, strange shapes, a harpy, spirits and hunting dogs (see pages 141–2).

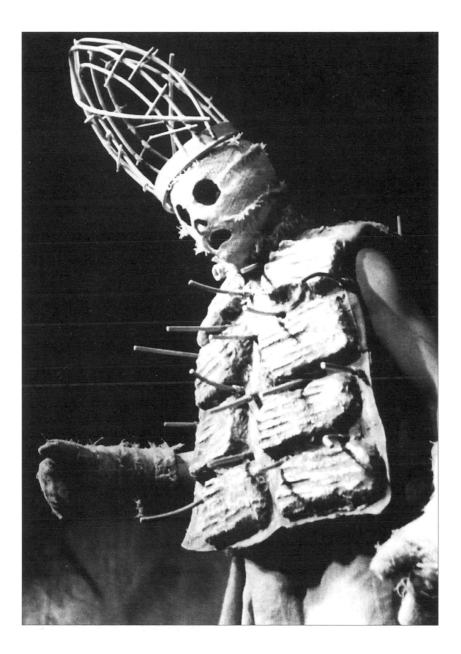

Imaginative invitation: *Enter several strange shapes ...*
How might your students present the 'strange shapes' of *The Tempest?*

Shakespeare is physical

'Suit the action to the word, the word to the action' advised Hamlet. His advice to the Players who visited Elsinore is one of the keys to successful school Shakespeare. Throughout each play Shakespeare's language provides actors with in-built cues for physical action. As an introduction, it is sometimes helpful for a teacher to demonstrate by speaking short sections of the script with an accompanying gesture or bodily movement. The whole class can then repeat the words and the action (see pages 175–7).

Macbeth's vision of the dagger he sees in the moments before he sets off to murder Duncan is an excellent opportunity for students to perform an action as they speak each line:

> Is this a dagger which I see before me,
> The handle towards my hand? Come, let me clutch thee:
> I have thee not, and yet I see thee still.
> Art thou not, fatal vision, sensible
> To feeling as to sight? Or art thou but
> A dagger of the mind, a false creation,
> Proceeding from the heat-oppressèd brain?
> I see thee yet, in form as palpable
> As this which now I draw...

The physicality of the language gives vivid life to action that is usually only described on stage. Ophelia's description of Hamlet's behaviour is an invitation to students to enact in detail just what he did:

> He took me by the wrist, and held me hard;
> Then goes he to the length of all his arm,
> And with his other hand thus o'er his brow
> He falls to such perusal of my face
> As he would draw it. Long stayed he so;
> At last, a little shaking of mine arm,
> And thrice his head thus waving up and down,
> He raised a sigh so piteous and profound
> As it did seem to shatter all his bulk,
> And end his being. That done, he lets me go,
> And with his head over his shoulder turned,

> He seemed to find his way without his eyes,
> For out-a-doors he went without their helps
> And to the last bended their light on me.

Although the Russian film of *Hamlet* actually portrays the episode described by Ophelia, certain passages, eminently suited to active classroom work, are never acted out on stage. For example, Juliet's declaration of all the things she would do rather than marry Paris is an excellent opportunity for students to fit actions to Shakespeare's intensely physical language:

> O bid me leap, rather than marry Paris,
> From off the battlements of any tower,
> Or walk in thievish ways, or bid me lurk
> Where serpents are; chain me with roaring bears,
> Or hide me nightly in a charnel house,
> O'ercovered quite with dead men's rattling bones,
> With reeky shanks, and yellow chapless skulls;
> Or bid me go into a new-made grave,
> And hide me with a dead man in his shroud...

Make Shakespeare exploratory

Students of all ages and abilities respond with intelligence and imagination to free-wheeling, active explorations of Shakespeare. One such exploratory activity can be undertaken very shortly after students' first encounter with *Romeo and Juliet*. Teachers can invite groups of students to speculate about, then prepare and show the actual incident, long ago, that set the Montagues and Capulets at each others' throats. Shakespeare does not tell how the feud began, he hints only that it was 'bred of an airy word'.

As students present their different versions of the origin of the feud, teachers will be reminded not only of the richness of students' imagination, but also that Shakespeare really does deal in universals. Most groups will present incidents relevant to, and drawn from, their modern world but they will all demonstrate humankind's enduring preoccupation with sex, money, power, territory, possessions, and honour (or, in its contemporary form, respect).

The paradigm case of exploratory possibilities is in *The Tempest* in Prospero's description of Sycorax:

> This damned witch Sycorax,
> For mischiefs manifold, and sorceries terrible
> To enter human hearing, from Algiers
> Thou knowest was banished. For one thing she did
> They would not take her life...

In the theatre, the lines often pass quickly, little noticed. In the classroom, they are rich in dramatic and imaginative possibilities. Just what were the 'mischiefs manifold' and 'sorceries terrible to enter human hearing' that Sycorax performed, and which so offended the citizens of Algiers?

Much more importantly, what was the 'one thing she did' for which she was spared from execution? The openness of that question is richly productive. Students (in groups) can be invited to discuss, prepare and enact the 'one thing' that pardoned Sycorax from death. They will have a host of ideas, and some presentations will be electric in their imaginative charge.

Critics who object that such speculation has nothing to do with the play, merely display the myopia that rigidly textual approaches can induce. Students' responses will illuminate this most imaginative of Shakespeare's plays. Sycorax is a brooding absent force on the island, and her imagined history enriches the mysterious quality that pervades *The Tempest*.

Every Shakespeare play has many such invitations to imaginative exploration: absent characters, missing scenes, silences, gaps, and so on. All are opportunities for students to infer and speculate.

The question 'How many children had Lady Macbeth?' was once used to ridicule an approach that assumes each character has a life previous to and beyond the play. The ridicule is misplaced. In school and college Shakespeare classrooms such exploratory imagining is a legitimate and productive method. The relevance to students of such imaginative inference, the 'What if...?' method of thoughtful speculation, is one of the many ways in which school and college Shakespeare is healthily different from an academic study of Shakespeare in universities.

Address the distinctive qualities of the play

Every Shakespeare play has its own distinctiveness (or quiddity or essence). Each play has its own particular story, its unique characters, its own distinguishing language and themes which express its preoccupations or interests (what Hamlet calls 'some necessary question of the play'). For example, the themes of *The Tempest* include nature and nurture, usurpation, imprisonment and freedom, reconciliation and forgiveness.

However, the core concerns of any play are redefined or given different emphasis at different times. Today, it would be difficult to teach *The Tempest* without addressing the theme of colonialism: to whom does the island belong? That theme was barely considered, or even acknowledged, in Victorian times or in the first half of the twentieth century. Similarly, it would be unusual today to teach *The Merchant of Venice* or *Othello* without serious attention to anti-semitism or racism. Our knowledge of the Holocaust, and the continuing anti-racist struggles give imperative urgency to features which in the past were often overlooked or ignored in school and college Shakespeare.

To recognise that each play has its peculiar distinctiveness is to acknowledge another guiding principle of successful Shakespeare teaching. However exploratory the approach, however imaginatively free-wheeling, each Shakespeare lesson should in some way enable students to experience something of that distinctive quality. This is not to impose a straightjacket on teachers or students, or inhibit experiment and exploration. Rather, by recognising uniqueness, it grounds personal response in the script, which has to justify that response, and brings possible interpretations into focus.

At the simplest level, students need to be clear about who a character is, and what his or her relationships to others are (daughter, brother, servant and so on). But how characters might be played, how their relationships are expressed, how their lines are spoken, are all open to a wide range of interpretation. Iago and Edmond *are* morally bad characters (that is their distinctiveness), but the script does not dictate how they should be played. That choice is open to students to argue and explore in different enactments.

In *Macbeth*, the theme of false appearance recurs throughout the play. Outward show does not match inward reality. That mismatch between appearance and reality is expressed in a variety of forms.

1   Entire scenes: in Act 1 Scene 6, Duncan and Banquo comment on the benign appearance of Macbeth's castle (where Duncan will be murdered), and are greeted with fair words by Lady Macbeth (who intends Duncan's murder).

2   Particular moments of dramatic construction: in Act 1 Scene 4 Duncan comments on the thane of Cawdor 'He was a gentleman on whom I built an absolute trust', followed by the stage direction *Enter Macbeth* (who, in the previous scene has had thoughts of murdering Duncan).

3   Lines that memorably express deceit:

> Look like th'innocent flower,
> But be the serpent under't

> Fair is foul and foul is fair

> Nothing is, but what is not

> False face must hide what the false heart doth know

Active teaching strategies help students gain insight into the theme. They explore how different stagings can intensify dramatic irony through the use of sound, gesture, facial expression and so on. For example, students as Lady Macbeth's alter ego can speak her inner thoughts to accompany her ceremonious and courteous, but utterly insincere, greeting of Duncan. Or, students can construct tableaux of the lines that express false appearance.

Language is part of the distinctiveness of any play (see pages 45–92). Repeated words help build up particular atmospheres or emotional climates: 'blood' in *Macbeth*, 'honourable' in *Julius Caesar*. Characters have their own styles of speaking: Lear's commands, questions and assertions; Tybalt's angry aggression. A play's themes have corresponding linguistic expression.

Romeo and Juliet is a play much concerned with oppositions and conflicts. Montagues *versus* Capulets; love *versus* hate; life *versus* death; light *versus* dark and so on. Shakespeare reflects these oppositions in the language of the play, most obviously in his use of oxymoron: two incongruous or opposing words brought together to make a potent expression. In 'parting is such sweet sorrow', 'sweet' and 'sorrow' feelingly oppose each other.

Romeo, on his first entrance, looks around him at the evidence of the brawl and speaks a long series of oxymorons:

> Here's much to do with hate, but more with love:
> Why then, O brawling love, O loving hate,
> O anything of nothing first create!
> O heavy lightness, serious vanity,
> Misshapen chaos of well-seeming forms,
> Feather of lead, bright smoke, cold fire, sick health,
> Still-waking sleep, that is not what it is!

There is a similar list of oxymorons in Juliet's 'O serpent heart...' Students can work in groups and choose one oxymoron to present as a tableau without words. As each group presents its tableau, the other students have to guess which oxymoron is shown (see pages 79–80).

Students respond readily and imaginatively to such an activity. With follow-up work, they soon grasp not only what an oxymoron is, but how they can invent their own, and how the form of the language is expressively appropriate to the many oppositions of *Romeo and Juliet*.

Measure for Measure is much concerned with the 'weighings' of justice. Shakespeare builds the balancing process into the language of the play by frequent use of antithesis (setting the word against the word in a phrase or line). On every page of the script, a character weighs or compares one thing or person with another, culminating memorably in the even balancing of:

> An Angelo for Claudio, death for death;
> Haste still pays haste, and leisure answers leisure;
> Like doth quit like, and measure still for measure.

This linguistic embodiment of the 'justice' theme can be physically enacted by students using their hands as a pair of scales to 'weigh' their way through this and other speeches. It also suggests a variety of design activities, as exemplified on the cover of the Cambridge School Shakespeare *Measure for Measure* (see page 22). Students can make their own judgements on the distinctiveness of whichever play they are studying and try to embody that distinctiveness in a cover design or theatre programme, or a poster advertising a production of the play.

The cover of the Cambridge School Shakespeare *Measure for Measure*
embodies aspects of the distinctive qualities and preoccupations of the play.

Choice and variety

A script approach to Shakespeare necessarily implies choice and variety in responses, resources and activities. It assumes that there is no 'one right way' to perform, teach, or experience the plays. Each teacher decides what constitutes appropriate choice and variety, taking into account his or her view of 'Shakespeare', the characteristics of the students, and the school context: time and space available, aims of the English or drama course, examinations and so on.

Students should have opportunities to express their response to Shakespeare in a wide variety of ways: performance, dramatic and physical exploration, discussion, design, all types of writing. All such responses can be active, informed and personal, rather than uncritical regurgitation of the views of others.

Teachers can draw on a range of resources to construct a course that is suitable for their own students. The range includes theatre visits, various editions of the play, videos and films, posters, reviews, traditional criticism, residential courses, visits by Theatre in Education groups and other visiting professionals providing productions and workshops of all types (see Chapter 9). Crucial resources are the teacher's own attitudes, knowledge and capacities, and the particular circumstances of the school or college: rooms, time-tabling, colleague co-operation and so on. But the prime resource is the students themselves: their imaginations combine with other resources to lift Shakespeare off the page and into dramatic life.

An unrelieved diet of any one single activity or teaching method is self-defeating. A Shakespeare course that comprises only watching videos is unbalanced, as is one in which students never get out of their seats, or one in which students never sit down to discuss and reflect on their activity. 'Appropriate methods and tasks' are those which are appropriate to students' abilities, and which always seek to extend and deepen those abilities.

Shakespeare celebrates plurality

A misconception that has weighed heavily on teaching Shakespeare in schools and colleges is the view that there exists an indisputable right answer in interpretation or staging. This narrow belief results in a readiness to condemn versions or interpretations that do not conform with that singular view. 'It's not Shakespeare' is all too frequently a depressing assertion that betrays an impoverished perception. Its lack of generosity is antithetical to Shakespeare's own expression of a host of competing viewpoints in every play.

It cannot be too often or too firmly stated that there is no 'one right way' to read, interpret or perform Shakespeare. Forget 'Shakespeare', and think of 'Shakespeares' is salutary advice. The plays are capable of and invite diverse interpretations. They resist the notion of definitive performance. Multiple interpretations are possible, necessary and desirable, because the plays (like drama, education and students themselves) are of infinite variety.

Students can be invited to stage or to interpret a scene from different points of view. The 'letter home from a servant at Macbeth's banquet' has long been a staple of school Shakespeare. Such alternative viewpoints can be expressed in diaries, reports, witness-statements, interviews, hot-seating activities and so on.

Recent theoretical writing extends the range of 'point of view' activities, and are further reminders of Shakespeare's multiplicity (see Chapter 3). Students can be invited to stage a particular scene guided by one of the newer interpretative perspectives (feminist, cultural materialist, psychoanalytic, and so on). All such theoretical standpoints can be translated into classroom activities in language suitable to the age of the students.

Alternative endings

An 'alternative endings' approach exemplifies the principle of plurality. In such an approach, groups of students take the final few lines of a play and prepare a performance of two stagings that represent radically different interpretations of how the play ends. For example, in *Romeo and Juliet*, one version might show that the feud between the Montagues and Capulets has really ended; the alternative version shows that the deaths of the young lovers has been in vain, the two families are still bitterly at war, and the final apparently reconciliatory words are a cover for unchanged hatreds. In *Macbeth*, alternative presentations might portray the promise of future harmony in Scotland under Malcolm, or the prediction of future strife.

Negative capability

'Negative capability' sounds dangerously like jargon, but it is the phrase that the poet John Keats used for what he saw 'Shakespeare possessed so enormously...that is when a man is capable of being in uncertainties, mysteries, doubts, without any irritable reaching after fact and reason' (letter to his brothers, 22 December 1817).

Keats felt this quality was essential for poets. It is no less vital for teachers and for students studying Shakespeare. It provides the very necessary assurance that you don't have to know it all, and is a warning against over-analysis.

Some unfortunate students are still told, as they embark on *Macbeth*, or *Antony and Cleopatra*: 'You must know it all – and all the notes.' The principle of negative capability prevents teachers from issuing such a dire, unintelligent injunction. It advises treating Shakespeare as a script, and accepts that the heart of Shakespeare's mystery can never be finally plucked out. Negative capability invites and encourages imaginative exploration and creative dissent in the knowledge that interpretations can never be fully complete, never the final word.

Shakespeare is about enjoyment

Whatever other motives Shakespeare had for play writing, he wanted his plays to entertain and to be enjoyed. In every age, people go to the theatre because they hope it will be a pleasurable activity. The fact that Shakespeare has attracted and entertained audiences for over 400 years is testimony to the enjoyment the plays provide.

The task for Shakespeare teachers is to make 'studying Shakespeare' equate with 'enjoying Shakespeare'. Treating the plays as scripts for active, imaginative and co-operative inhabitation is the key to successful school and college Shakespeare in which enjoyment goes hand in hand with insight and understanding.

Perspectives

'Look here upon this picture, and on this'

This chapter is concerned with theoretical approaches to Shakespeare. It identifies the major perspectives which currently inform the study of Shakespeare in universities. The significance of each perspective in relation to the principles of successful school Shakespeare (outlined in Chapter 2) is discussed to help school and college teachers judge how such perspectives might be suitable for their own students. Teachers will find that many of the new theories and assumptions are already present in some way in school and college classrooms.

In the last two decades of the twentieth century, the study of Shakespeare in universities has undergone radical transformation. Shakespeare has become a key battleground for critical theory. Traditional approaches have been challenged by a number of competing perspectives which hotly contest the interpretation and significance of Shakespeare.

This review of perspectives is not clogged with references. There is a kind of pseudo-scholarship that bedevils Shakespeare study at all levels, in which name-dropping is thought to carry great weight. It has no place in this book. A modest book list is provided at the end of this chapter to help those readers who wish to deepen their knowledge of recent approaches to Shakespeare.

A growing number of critics argue that traditional criticism has refused to face up to the real world within which Shakespeare is produced and received. The modern critics argue that instead of focusing on the historical and social realities which determine production and reception, traditional critics have focused on matters which evade those realities: the words on the page, the particularities of story, language and character; eternal truths, individual response. This, the argument goes, makes traditional criticism elitist, sexist, unpolitical and individualist. To divorce literary and aesthetic matters from their social context is to misperceive them.

The new perspectives are very different from, and often hostile to, each other, but they share one common characteristic: rejection of traditional literary studies, which they see as naive and untheoretical. The assumptions of traditional studies can perhaps be summarised in a short list.

1   There exists an undeniable canon of great literary works which has Shakespeare at its centre.

2   Literary works are the products of men (and occasionally women) of undeniable genius.

3   Discovering the intentions of canonical authors is a central task of literary studies.

4   Canonical authors somehow transcend the local limitations of their times (or any other time) to provide universal, eternal truths about the human condition.

5   The meanings of such works are 'transparent' or 'self-evident', and can be understood by a straightforward, commonsense reading of the literature, uncluttered by theory or ideology. Such straightforward readings are both possible and desirable. (Traditional criticism is deeply suspicious of theory.)

6   A canonical work has an 'organic unity': all parts relate to each other and create an integrated, harmonious whole.

7   A canonical work has certain essential attributes which are present in the text, irrespective of whoever reads it.

8   Literature and drama should be studied for aesthetic reasons rather than for social or ideological purposes.

Critical theorists (those who advocate the new approaches to studying Shakespeare) cast severely sceptical eyes over these claims of traditional literary studies, which they often call 'liberal humanism'. A thumbnail sketch of how critical theorists regard literature and Shakespeare shows why these new approaches often arouse passionate opposition.

1   There is no such thing as 'literature', or 'a canon' or even 'Shakespeare'. All these have been constructed by particular groups at particular times to serve particular interests.

2   'Great works' like the plays of Shakespeare do not convey universal truths about the human condition. Rather, they are used to express, sustain and reproduce the ideology of dominant groups in order to maintain the material well-being of those groups. Particular viewpoints (those of the traditionalists) on 'Shakespeare' are thus falsely claimed to be universal truths.

3   Shakespeare is often put in literal or implicit quotation marks ('Shakespeare'), in order to emphasise the social construction of the plays, the man, and the iconic significance.

4   There is no such thing as a straightforward, objective or disinterested reading. All interpretations are the products of particular ideologies. 'Commonsense' is misleading because it is a particular social viewpoint.

5   'Theory' provides more valid readings of Shakespeare: interpretations should draw upon the writings of major social or psychological theorists.

6   Shakespeare is not timeless. Ben Jonson's claim that Shakespeare was 'not for an age, but for all time' is wrong. Shakespeare does not transcend time, or place, or human understanding. He is to be understood in the context of the social, political and ideological production, and reception of his work. Far from transcending the social context, his work is deeply involved in the ideological and material practices and social relationships of his world, and our own. For most of the new perspectives, therefore, the study of Shakespeare is a political enterprise.

7   A text is not produced by an author, but by readers, who themselves are 'produced' by social and political forces.

8   The harmonies, coherences and unities that traditional approaches have found in the plays are fictions. They should

yield to subversive readings which emphasise contradiction, disjunction, fragmentation. Such readings challenge the affirmatory, reconciliatory interpretations of traditional criticism.

9 Any discussion of aesthetics is heavily influenced by social factors, because aesthetics is a social construct.

10 Literature is socially constructed and received. The new perspectives are deeply suspicious of claims of intuition, imagination, insight or empathy, and personal response.

The difference between traditional approaches and the new perspectives can be summed up in one word: 'theory'. New perspectives frequently attempt to establish their authority by specialised vocabularies and extensive appeal to theory. It is easy to gain the impression that Shakespeare is subordinate to the theory being employed. In much of this modern Shakespearian criticism, Shakespeare's plays disappear for long periods, and there is little interest in active, performance methods of teaching. However, each theoretical approach can be adapted in some way to add to students' Shakespeare experience.

For all their abstract language and difficult concepts, many central ideas and assumptions of these new perspectives are often familiar and easy to understand. Indeed, many are practised already in some form in schools and colleges. Encountering them for the first time, some teachers may experience that surprised delight felt by M. Jourdain in *Le Bourgeois Gentilhomme*, who was overcome with joy to discover, when the difference between prose and verse was explained to him: 'I've been speaking prose all my life, and never realised it until now!'

The existence of such widely differing perspectives is further evidence of Shakespeare's infinite variety. They show once again that there is no one way to study Shakespeare, no one master view. A Shakespeare script is like a mirror. It reflects back the preoccupations of the reader. Whatever you are interested in – history, psychology, politics, sexuality, class, culture – you will find it in Shakespeare.

Any summary is in danger of oversimplifying the rich variety that characterises each perspective. For example, there is no such thing as *the* feminist approach to Shakespeare. Feminism, like every perspective, speaks with a host of competing voices. Nonetheless, it is possible to identify the main assumptions, methods and intentions of each perspective, and to provide one or two examples of how each engages with Shakespeare.

Feminism

Feminist criticism is the fastest-growing and most widespread of all recent approaches to Shakespeare. It is also the new perspective most obviously present in schools and colleges. For many of today's students, it is a familiar viewpoint. In contrast, many teachers are able to recall that in their own school or university experience of Shakespeare, feminist issues were rarely, if ever, raised. The woman's point of view, questions of how meaning relates to gender, of the 'maleness' of traditional Shakespeare criticism, were (it now seems) conspicuously absent from many courses.

Feminist approaches to Shakespeare are best understood in the context of feminism itself: the drive to achieve rights and equality for women in social, political and economic life. Feminism is not necessarily anti-men, but is against sexism: the beliefs and practices which structure and maintain the subordination and oppression of women. Feminism reveals and challenges the cultural shaping of gender roles in all social institutions: the family, work, politics, religion, and, of course, in literature and drama.

Literature and drama have always played an important role in defining gender: Aristophanes' *Lysistrata* is an obvious example. Feminist criticism examines how female experience is portrayed in literature. It exposes how, in plays, in novels and other writing, patriarchal ideology often stereotypes, distorts, ignores or represses that experience, misrepresenting how women feel, think and act. Feminists are concerned to contest and resist such portrayals.

Feminist approaches to Shakespeare reveal how women's freedom to choose is strictly limited in the plays. But feminism also celebrates how women contest male power. The plays are filled with resourceful, self-confident women who create their own space and achieve or represent a spirited independence. They are very different personalities who assert themselves in very different ways: Cleopatra, Lady Macbeth, Gonerill and Regan, Viola, Portia, Beatrice, Katherina, Rosalind.

The very large number of books and articles on Shakespeare written from a feminist perspective testify to his crucial cultural significance. But although every feminist subscribes to the general aim of feminism, there is immense variation in their judgements on Shakespeare. Some feminists interpret the plays as sympathetic to feminism, genuinely alert to female experience, and actively subversive of male dominance. Other feminist readings are exactly the opposite. They see Shakespeare as supportive of patriarchy, and argue that his plays are a key instrument in sustaining male domination. Between these extremes are critics who see the plays as expressing the realities of the limited power and lower status of women in Elizabethan–Jacobean England, but also expressing the potential for female emancipation: the possibility of free and equal choice of lifestyle. Faced with such competing evaluations, each teacher and student will make up his or her own mind on whether Shakespeare attacks, defends or merely describes patriarchy.

Feminism is already well represented in school and college Shakespeare, albeit in a different form and level of expression from that practised in universities. Feminist literary criticism frequently roots patriarchy, misogyny and female stereotyping in the actual practices of Renaissance society. Students in schools and colleges actively explore such processes through direct experience of the language, taking parts as Juliet or Cordelia, Hermia or Desdemona or other daughters who have to endure their fathers' wrath. In role-play or in writing they report how it feels to be bartered as a bride, and used as a token in exchanges of wealth or power.

School and college students have no difficulty in sharing feminism's recognition that Shakespeare's female characters merit equal attention with male characters. In their commitment to imaginative habitation of the plays, they often go further and extend that recognition to minor roles. Students imagine themselves as Lady Macbeth's Gentlewoman, or Lady Montague; or as absent female characters: Rosaline in *Romeo and Juliet* or Sycorax in *The Tempest*. They have little hesitation in making Lords into Ladies, or servants and messengers into female roles for imaginative activities: how will a female servant report the events at Macbeth's banquet? What do Mrs Bottom or Mrs Quince make of their husbands' theatrical aspirations?

Was Shakespeare sexist?

No-one can really know for sure. Obviously, like any other writer, he reflected in his plays the beliefs and assumptions of his time, which was much more patriarchal than society today (for example, in *The Merchant of Venice*, Portia gives all her wealth and freedom to Bassanio).

Shakespeare put language into the mouths of many of his characters that today appears sexist in its uncomplimentary references to women. Cleopatra is variously described as a 'dish', a 'morsel', 'like a cow in June', a 'fragment', a 'boggler', 'this ribraud nag of Egypt'. In *The Comedy of Errors*, Dromio describes Nell with crude and insulting comparisons. In *The Taming of the Shrew*, Petruchio speaks of his wife, Kate:

> She is my goods, my chattels; she is my house,
> My household-stuff, my field, my barn,
> My horse, my ox, my ass, my anything.

Students can balance such evidence against Shakespeare's female characters, many of whom are clearly more intelligent and resourceful than their male counterparts. They can explore different ways of speaking Petruchio's lines. How serious is he? Is it all just a joke? And they can argue for and against the sexism and chauvinism of Dromio's language, taking roles as those wishing to include it and those wishing to exclude it from a stage performance.

Psychoanalysis

Psychoanalysis has thoroughly pervaded twentieth-century consciousness in Western societies. A brief outline of its central features will show why Shakespeare's plays, so rich in complex characters living at extremes, hold great attraction for psychoanalytic critics.

Freud, the founding father of psychoanalysis, lays great stress on the unconscious and the irrational. He argues that actions and motives do not spring simply from conscious, rational sources. This acknowledgement of the centrality of unconscious desires is accompanied by certain assumptions: the importance of repressed memories and wishes (repression), of sexuality, of fantasy, and of the role of anxiety and conflict in personality formation.

Freud's study of dreams, which claims that dreams attempt to fulfil the desires of the unconscious, often provides an illuminating analogy for Freudian critics of Shakespeare. Just as in the analysis of dreams the analyst distinguishes between manifest (the obvious story) and latent (hidden, forbidden) content, so the psychoanalytic Shakespearian scholar makes a distinction between the explicit and implicit meanings of a script. This might seem unexceptionable. After all, traditional scholars look for the subtext, the deeper levels of meaning in a character's language or actions. But Freudianism, with its particular assumptions about human development and behaviour, produces some surprising readings, as the following few examples (from the writing of different psychoanalytic critics) show:

- in *Othello*, the mainspring of the action is 'Othello's desire for Cassio'
- the phallus is 'a floating signifier' in *Macbeth*; the Ghost in *Hamlet* is seen as the phallus
- in *The Tempest*, Ferdinand's sword-dropping and log-carrying are interpreted as 'metaphorical castrations'
- in *The Merchant of Venice*, Portia's father had incestuous desires for her
- one study of *Coriolanus* totally ignores politics and social class, and refers only to Coriolanus' relationship with his mother.

Teachers may well feel that such interpretations arise from dogmatic adherence to Freudian theory and a desire to impose it on the script. The concentration solely on psychological factors, to the neglect of other elements in the play, hardly seems balanced.

The shortcomings of Freudian psychoanalysis are well known. It is sexist, determinist, middle-class fixated, neglectful of historical and cultural factors, and similarly neglectful of the conscious, rational aspects of human behaviour. It is neither provable nor disprovable. But in appropriate form, the psychoanalytic perspective does have relevance to school Shakespeare. Both psychoanalysis and the plays share a preoccupation with love and hate, with dreams, fantasy and confusion. Both can be seen as presenting characters as 'cases'; and in both the importance of the emotions is crucial.

Any form of character study which explores a character's feelings and personal relationships owes some kind of debt to psychoanalysis. That is probably especially true where the relationships concern family members: fathers and daughters, mothers and sons. Just what does motivate the many Shakespearian fathers who rage at their daughters? Does Hamlet have an Oedipus complex? Without the prompt of Olivier's film, older students spontaneously discuss whether Hamlet has highly ambivalent feelings towards his mother.

Psychoanalytic practice has proved a fruitful model for school and college Shakespeare. Many teachers set their students some form of 'on the psychiatrist's couch' activity. This can be hot-seating, in which a student steps into role and is questioned about their actions, feelings, thoughts and motivations. Such classroom questioning often concerns a character's 'experience' outside the play. Students as Hamlet or Cordelia might recall their childhood with memories of Yorick or what it was like to be King Lear's most loved daughter. The Kenneth Branagh film of *Hamlet* even shows Hamlet as a child with Yorick.

Structuralism

Structuralism derives from a particular view of language, located in the theories of the linguist Ferdinand de Saussure. A structuralist approach to Shakespeare assumes that certain structures or systems govern or explain each play. That sounds rather abstract, so here are some practical examples to illustrate structuralist approaches.

1   If you talk of tragedy, comedy, or history, you are using structural categories, because these literary and dramatic concepts strongly influence how a particular play is written, what its topic will be, how it will end, and how it is likely to be performed.

2   If you say 'the patriarchal society of Verona caused the death of Romeo and Juliet', you are using a social and political structure (patriarchy) to explain the play. That social structure implies that individuals are little more than puppets, dancing to society's tune.

3   If you argue that 'ambition is the mainspring of *Macbeth*', you

are using a psychological structure to explain both Macbeth the man and *Macbeth* the play. You might argue for emotional structures such as jealousy in *Othello* or pride in *Coriolanus* being the most powerful forces at work in the particular play.

4   If you say '*Macbeth* is a study in evil', that too is a structural statement. It claims that the most significant feature of *Macbeth* is 'evil', and that that metaphysical concept is the most powerful structure for understanding, because it pervades every aspect of the play.

5   If you claim that *The Two Gentlemen of Verona* is heavily influenced by the Romance tradition, you are making a structuralist statement. The Romance tradition was a complex literary tradition of stories of love and chivalry from which Shakespeare took many of the ingredients for his play (for example, journeys, adventures and misfortunes, infidelity, disguise, chivalrous knights). Structural explanations of the play are offered in terms of that tradition.

These examples demonstrate both the strength and weakness of structural explanation. Structural approaches are helpful in that they claim to identify a major feature of the play (against which it is valuable to argue if you don't agree). Structural explanations are familiar, because they correspond to everyday types of explanation: 'He behaves like that because he's in love' claims that being 'in love' explains everything about someone's behaviour.

These advantages are outweighed by some obvious disadvantages.

1   A Shakespeare play is too complex to be explained by a single dominant structure.

2   The list of structural categories is endless: anything can be claimed to be the most important structure.

3   A structuralist approach ignores the uniqueness and particularity of individuals and of dramatic works. *Macbeth* and *King Lear* are both tragedies, but their major interest surely lies in their particularities of character, story, language, and so on.

4   All action, in life and in drama, is the outcome of many

structures: psychological, social, economic, cultural, historical, ideological, genetic and so on. To explain a Shakespeare play in terms of only one structure is to under-value the richness and diversity of Shakespeare.

5   Structuralism is far too neat and tidy an approach. Human action cannot be explained in such determinist ways. Human beings are not puppets on strings; they resist structural forces, because they have the power of thought. Shakespeare's major characters are substantial, often many-sided figures who are believable as human beings – their actions in the plays are also too complex for such an approach.

Structural explanations do play an important part in school and college Shakespeare, just as they do in everyday life. To talk of themes is to take a structuralist approach to a play, for example, arguing that *King Lear* is about 'nature', or *Romeo and Juliet* about 'love and hate' and so on. These arguments are valid, but they are by no means the whole story. Shakespeare should be taught, experienced and understood in a wide variety of ways and at different levels. No single structure of any kind can sufficiently encompass a Shakespeare play.

Deconstruction

Deconstructive approaches to Shakespeare derive from one of structuralism's assumptions about language: that 'language is a system with no positive terms'. This asserts that no word or thing has meaning in itself, but derives meaning from the relationships it has within the structure of language. Deconstructive critics have seized upon this assertion to reject the possibility of objectivity or stability in language, character, or story. This position goes far beyond traditional criticism's stress on ambiguity: that a word or speech can have more than one meaning. It questions the possibility of meaning itself. And deconstruction has an even more radical challenge. It attacks the stability of human identity. This is quite contrary to the tradition of personal response which acknowledges individual subjectivity, and puts it at the centre of Shakespeare study in schools and colleges.

Deconstructionists claim that meaning is always deferred, never final. This inexhaustibility of meaning enables deconstructionists to read a text for its opacities, contradictions and paradoxes. The deconstructive perspective seizes on seemingly insignificant items, and by remorseless extension shows how these marginal, peripheral elements (the *aporia* or impasses of meaning) get the text into trouble, making it contradict itself, come unstuck, embarrass its own logic. Meanings constantly undermine each other, understanding is never reached, sense is always threatened by other meanings.

How does this apply to Shakespeare? It implies that no script is unified, whole, harmonious, or organic (to use the vocabulary and assumptions of traditional criticism). Rather, it is a fragmented, contradictory, conflicting construction without a stable essence. The silences and absences and marginal elements of a play are important to the deconstructive critic. Characters are merely a function of language, and language is assumed to be never stable, never objective, never capable of yielding certain or constant meaning.

Such radical assumptions about language makes deconstruction seem an unhelpful contributor to students' experience. After all, if meaning really is impossible, what's the point of education? (Or of writing books on deconstruction?) Most students and teachers accept that language refers to actual persons, actual states of mind and feeling, actual societies, events, things. In classrooms, as in everyday life, meaning is not endlessly deferred, or impossible. The central notion of deconstruction, that words refer only to words, is not entertained in school classrooms.

Commonsense rejects deconstruction's most radical aspects, but certain of its features are already present in Shakespeare study at all levels, particularly in the active methods that make for successful lessons in colleges and schools. Here, Shakespeare studies embody deconstruction's free-ranging playfulness, *jouissance*, uncertainty, and lack of closure. To parody a scene, or have a number of students sharing and speaking one character's lines, to bring absent characters into active life in the play (Sycorax and Claribel in *The Tempest*, Old Fortinbras or Lamord in *Hamlet*), or to import into a play lines or characters from other plays or from the Sonnets – all these express the spirit of carnival, the principle of dispersion that deconstruction espouses.

To deconstruct a text is to show how it came into being, how it works. That practice is familiar to many students as they seek to discover how Shakespeare's language achieves its dramatic effects (see Chapter 8). Each instance of Shakespearian ambiguity, punning, *double-entendre*, could also be seen as deconstructive in spirit. Such examples of wordplay acknowledge the labile nature of language: shifting, unstable, changing as context changes, never finally resolvable into a single meaning. But to recognise such complexity is not to assert the impossibility of meaning. When Hamlet speaks his final, dying words 'the rest is silence' his language can be interpreted literally or symbolically in different ways, at different levels, but each interpretation is determinate and meaningful.

Political perspectives

Political readings of Shakespeare reject traditional approaches which take little or no account of the social, political, economic and ideological circumstances of Shakespeare's time or our own. Political perspectives assert that every aspect of human life is rooted in politics and power. They insist that Shakespeare studies be taken out of the realms of aesthetics and personal response, into the political. Such perspectives hold that all judgement, all interpretation and evaluation, arises from social, rather than from individual factors. For example, a political reading of *As You Like It* sees the aristocrats in the play using nature to justify their freedom from work and to subordinate other social classes. *The Merchant of Venice* is read as a challenge to the triumph of merchant capitalism. Shylock is a mirror-image of his Christian persecutors. His values represent the actual values of Venice, a society premised upon barbarity: money is more important than human values; property has more significance than men and women; racial and sexual oppression disfigure relationships.

The focus on the plays is a social one: characters' behaviour is determined by material (economic) pressures. Political interpretation rejects a celebratory bardolatry, in which the Sweet Swan of Avon's transcending genius reveals optimistic truths about the beneficial qualities of human nature and society. In its place are readings which stress the injustice, inequality, and oppression that arise in societies in which power and wealth enable a ruling class to dominate subordinate groups.

Political criticism aims to strip away illusions of permanence and transcendence. Its object is to challenge and displace traditional interpretations which stress harmony and integration. It argues that Shakespeare criticism has been appropriated by conservatives who make him speak for the Right. In contrast, political critics read Shakespeare for his subversive potential.

Such perspectives derive from a Marxist reading of literature. The central tenet of Marxism holds that 'base determines superstructure'. That is, material or economic factors (base) dictate the form and content of all institutions of society (superstructure), for example law, religion, government, education, religion, literature and drama. The belief that all aspects of human life are utterly dependent upon economic relationships, has long been acknowledged as too crudely determinist. It has given way to less rigid, more complex formulations of the relationship between economic base and institutional superstructure: less deterministic, but still highly influential. In Shakespeare scholarship two major, closely related approaches assert the intimate relationship of culture (Shakespeare) and material factors (economics). These are new historicism, which is largely American, and cultural materialism, which is largely British.

New historicism

New historicism, situated in Renaissance studies, mainly concerns itself with the conditions of Shakespeare's own time: late sixteenth-century England. It sees the plays and the theatre of that time as strongly influenced by, and reflecting, contemporary political, economic and ideological conditions.

The key terms of new historicism are 'subversion' and 'containment'. Elements in the plays resist, contradict and undermine official ideology. Such subversion is nonetheless contained, somehow made complicit in the political processes of domination. Thus drama and theatre become part of the prevailing system of social control. Subversion and containment are symbiotically connected. The Elizabethan theatre subverted authority, yet at the same time expressed state power even as it questioned its ideology.

New historicist critics tend to use particular events or contemporary documents as their method of interpretative entry to a play. For example, *A Midsummer Night's Dream* has been interpreted as reflecting the 1595–6 riots in London and Oxfordshire: Bottom and his fellow Mechanicals remind the audience of the rioters. This political reading both exposes the subversive potential (an uncomfortable reminder to aristocrats of rebellious workers) and contains it through comedy.

Other new historicist readings use contemporary accounts of transvestism in sixteenth and seventeenth-century France as a way into *Twelfth Night*. A 1588 treatise on the colony of Virginia is the springboard for a study of *King Henry IV Part 1*, in which the rebels and Falstaff are adjudged far more favourably than Prince Hal or the 'law and order' characters. The same emphasis on subversive characters judges Jack Cade and Caliban much more sympathetically than the 'authority' characters in the *King Henry VI Part 2* and *The Tempest*.

New historicism's claim that Shakespeare's plays are 'centrally and repeatedly concerned with the production and containment of disorder' is hardly novel. All drama is based on conflict, a disruption of the status quo, usually followed by its containment or resolution. *Macbeth*, *King Lear*, or any of Shakespeare's tragedies, are very obvious examples. The comedies illustrate a similar process of disruption and containment. Such understanding has been part of a traditional approach to the plays, both in schools and universities, reading them as variations on the theme of order and disorder (see page 132). The power of theatre in Shakespeare's time has also long been recognised. Perhaps the best known example is the performance of *King Richard II* (showing the deposition of a king) given at the time of the Essex rebellion. Generations of school and college students have quoted Queen Elizabeth's 'I am Richard, know ye not that?'

The difference is that new historicism makes subversion and containment the prime focus of attention. It analyses Tudor and Jacobean documents to claim that subversion and containment typified the Renaissance period. The contrast with a 'Merrie England' view of the Elizabethan period is evident. That older, socially cohesive 'Elizabethan world picture' (of E. M. W. Tillyard) is now acknowledged as false. It portrayed Elizabethan society and beliefs as characterised by harmony, stability and unity. The new political critics argue that this picture itself should be recognised as an ideology. The vision of order, patriotism, kingship, and the 'great chain of being' simply masked the fractures, dissents, struggles and contradictions of Shakespeare's world. Political critics read the plays as exposing and criticising these contradictions and paradoxes.

But how valid are such interpretations? The writings of modern political critics contain the same flaws as those of Tillyard. He selected particular speeches to claim they represented both Shakespeare's own view, and the beliefs of the time. New historists are just as selective in their evidence to support the 'Shakespeare as subversive' thesis. Counter evidence is ignored. The conclusion must be that Shakespeare's own views cannot be deduced from the plays: the plays can be quoted selectively to support *any* political viewpoint.

Cultural materialism

Cultural materialism argues that culture (in all its forms) and materialism (economic factors) are always related. Shakespeare cannot be understood without reference to the economic and political system of his age, and that of our own. Studying Shakespeare is a political activity, because Shakespeare is not separate from other social practices, but is shaped by politics, ideology and economics.

Cultural materialists declare their own political commitment to the transformation of any society that exploits people on grounds of class, race or gender. They thus seek to find in Shakespeare subversive questioning of social inequalities and the privileges of dominant groups. Several strands of such lines of inquiry can be detected: scholarship, education, and Shakespeare as icon.

Textual and critical scholarship
Cultural materialist approaches make much of the long history of textual and critical scholarship. They show how Shakespeare texts have been constructed over the centuries. Because every edition is a different edition, no script has the coherence and stability it appears to claim.

Cultural materialism is also highly sceptical about criticism which claims to be disinterested, to provide interpretations free from bias and distortion. The sceptics argue that such criticism favours the interests of a dominant class because that particular social group stifles dissent and conflict by asserting the universality and naturalness of its own values, interpretations and practices. Cultural materialist critics claim that all interpretations are to some extent shaped by ideology. They focus on the social class of the critics and the particular circumstances of the time at which they wrote. Traditional literary criticism, argue the cultural materialists, constructs Shakespeare as a cultural symbol, the keystone of literature, the guarantee of quality. Such readings, the argument goes, are conservative interpretations.

Education

Cultural materialism argues that in education, Shakespeare acts as a mechanism of social selection and exclusion. It sees 'the two fundamental mystifications of bourgeois ideology' at work in school Shakespeare.

1   The interests, values and assumptions of one dominant social class group are claimed as universal and natural.

2   An individual is assumed to be fully independent, unaffected by history or society.

These two mystifications are claimed to underlie the teaching of Shakespeare, and can be seen in examinations set for school students. For example, questions like 'Discuss Shakespeare's presentation of goodness in *Macbeth*' are claimed to prevent students from realising that 'mystified concepts' like goodness or evil have been socially produced in the activity of literary criticism. Such concepts deflect attention from real social factors: Macbeth's tyranny has everything to do with the oppressive feudal social structure of Scotland, and nothing to do with supernatural forces of witchcraft.

Cultural materialism, like all political criticism, is similarly sceptical of the notion of personal response, which it sees as yet another bourgeois mystification. Individuals are not autonomous, but shaped by history and ideology. The plays themselves are similarly determined: written, read, performed and interpreted subject to the conditions of particular times.

Shakespeare as icon

Cultural materialism makes much of how Shakespeare has been constructed as a national and international icon: the Great National Poet, who speaks universal truths. It charts the rise of bardolatry over the centuries. Recurring themes in such accounts are the Garrick Shakespeare Jubilee of 1769, the rise of Romanticism, the decline of religion, and the growth of literary studies in education.

Cultural materialists also emphasise the appropriation and use of Shakespeare in all aspects of media and commercial life. The man or his works figure in cartoons, magazine and newspaper headlines ('The dogs of war'), everyday language ('he's a Romeo'), advertisements ('a cigar called Hamlet'), and numerous commercial products from beer mats to credit cards. The heritage industry frequently figures in such accounts, with Shakespeare and Stratford-upon-Avon seen as key parts of the marketing of England as a tourist destination.

The 'Shakespeare as icon' approach also highlights the reaction to Shakespeare that such pervasive, familiar representations evoke. These range from awe to contempt; from religious-like worship of the gold seal of all that is valuable, to the boredom, indifference or hostility experienced by those who see Shakespeare as exclusive and elitist.

Reception theory

Active Shakespeare clearly shares many of the assumptions of reception (reader response) theory. This perspective sees reading as a creative, constructive process. It emphasises the reader's active role in 'making' any text or script, and therefore epitomises those teaching practices which stress personal response. Readers are not passive, but actively make sense out of what they read, and so may be said to be creators of the text.

The notion of informed personal response that is central to contemporary teaching of English and drama, has its roots in reception theory. A response is 'informed' because it relates both to the text and to the culture and community to which the reader belongs. It is 'personal' in that it is the reader's own unique interpretation. However, as a response it will have many things in common with other responses, for example, there will be commonalities between the responses of a school class because all members of the class belong to a particular community. The response is nonetheless distinctive, because it stems from the reader's own experience and point of view.

Using perspectives

Teachers in schools and colleges will make up their own minds as to how much recent theoretical perspectives will influence their Shakespeare lessons, but here are some questions to consider.

1   How much of the theory outlined in this chapter do my students need?

2   Do I give special lessons on theory, or do I bring it in as I see appropriate at particular points in the play we are studying?

3   What critics, if any, do I want students to read?

4   What emphasis shall I give to 'political Shakespeare'?

5   How much time and emphasis shall I put on Shakespeare as socially and historically constructed?

6   How far do I see concepts like resistance, contradiction, and appropriation as relevant to my students' Shakespeare experience?

7   Will 'Shakespeare as an icon' be part of my course? For example, shall I encourage students to compile a wall display of 'Shakespeare' examples from the media or elsewhere?

Further reading

Deborah E Barker and Ivo Kamps (editors), *Shakespeare and Gender: a history*, Verso, 1995

Graham Bradshaw, *Misrepresentations: Shakespeare and the Materialists*, Cornell University Press, 1993

Michael D Bristol, *Big-Time Shakespeare*, Routledge, 1996

James C Bulman (editor), *Shakespeare, Theory and Performance*, Routledge, 1996

Jonathan Dollimore and Alan Sinfield (editors), *Political Shakespeare: New Essays in Cultural Materialism*, 2nd edition, Manchester University Press, 1994

Terence Hawkes (editor), *Alternative Shakespeares*, volume 2, Routledge, 1996 (volume 1 edited by John Drakakis, Methuen, 1990)

Gary Taylor, *Reinventing Shakespeare*, Hogarth Press, 1990

Brian Vickers, *Appropriating Shakespeare: Contemporary Critical Quarrels*, Yale University Press, 1993

Shakespeare's language

*'Speak the speech I pray you as I pronounced it to you,
trippingly on the tongue'*

Introduction

Round about 1590, Shakespeare began his career as a dramatist. It was a time particularly opportune for a writer of his genius. At that period, the English language was exceptionally fluid and malleable and that lack of fixity offered endless dramatic possibilities. Rules of grammar, spelling, pronunciation and punctuation were relatively relaxed. A person's name could be spelled in different ways (as the various spellings of Shakespeare show). There was no dictionary of English (the first would be published in 1604) to tie down words, to confine their meanings, to give precision to language by restricting fluidity.

Elizabethan England was a society intensely self-conscious about language. The human voice was held in high esteem. People went 'to hear' a play rather than, as today, 'to see' it. Sermons and proclamations were a regular feature of daily life. The vigour of language, its sound and evocative power, mattered as much as its logic. Rhetoric, the techniques of speaking persuasively, was taught in schools. Reading and writing poetry were part of a nobleman's education, and were also practised by others much further down the social scale.

It was a time that encouraged exploration and playfulness with language. Poets and playwrights experimented endlessly with words, phrases, imagery. They felt free to make up words, to adapt old ones, and to change old meanings to new. If a word did not exist, Shakespeare remoulded an old one or made up a new word to fit his imaginative and dramatic needs (see page 87). His was a synthesising imagination, reworking all he read or experienced into poetic drama. The times encouraged creativity in language, and Shakespeare seized that invitation, responding in a joyous overflow of dramatic and linguistic invention. He gave his language dramatic power by his use of certain devices, most notably imagery (in metaphor, simile and personification), antithesis, repetition, lists and verse.

No-one really knows what Shakespeare's personal beliefs and politics were. His characters express all kinds of views, but Shakespeare's own are unknown. Only one thing is certain about his intentions: he wanted his plays to be performed on stage. Shakespeare was essentially a man of the theatre. He was a playwright, a theatrical entrepreneur, an actor and a poet, whose genius was for dramatic language. He wrote scripts: words to be spoken by actors on stage, accompanied with gestures, action, movement, and with all the resources of theatre of his day.

His very practical concern was that his language would seize an audience's interest and attention, and retain it throughout the play. His success can be seen in *Hamlet* from the opening challenge 'Who's there?' to the final command 'Go bid the soldiers shoot.' Every play displays Shakespeare's consuming fascination with dramatic language: the power of words to fire the imagination, to persuade the intellect, to move the emotions. His plays explore the widest range of human experience: love and hate, peace and war, longing and fulfilment. He gives his characters the language best suited to express their thoughts and feelings at any given moment.

Because Shakespeare wrote scripts, students studying his language are not confined to the question 'What does it mean?' Other necessary questions arise from the possibilities of enactment, most obviously 'How might it be spoken and performed on stage?' Answers to such questions are never final, never definitive, and they are accompanied by explorations of widely differing interpretations.

Shakespeare's schooling

Shakespeare is an outstanding example of how schooling can foster talent. His education at Stratford-upon-Avon Grammar School gave him a thorough grounding in the use of language and classical authors. Although his schooling might seem narrow and severe today (schoolboys learned by heart over 100 figures of rhetoric), it proved an excellent resource for the future playwright. Everything Shakespeare learned in school he used in some way in his plays. At first, he applied his knowledge of the rules of language as he had acquired it at school. Some of his early plays seem to have a very obvious pattern and regular rhythm, almost mechanical and like clockwork. But having mastered the rules, he was able to break and transform them; to move from *Titus Andronicus* and *The Two Gentlemen of Verona* to *Hamlet* and *The Tempest*. On this evidence, Shakespeare's education has been seen as an argument for the value of learning by rote, of constant practice, of strict rule-following. Or, to put it another way, 'discovery favours the well-prepared mind'.

Even the early plays show the same *quality* of writing that characterises his greatest plays. Shakespeare turned his school knowledge into striking dramatic action and vividly realised characters. His dramatic imagination was fuelled by what would now be seen as sterile exercises in memorisation and constant practice. What was mechanical became fluid, dramatic language that produced thrilling theatre.

Dramatic language

All drama depends on the acceptance of a number of conventions. In every age, audiences and actors enter into an imaginative conspiracy of some sort. Today, much theatre and most television drama is realist and naturalistic. It seems like an imitation of everyday life, easy to recognise and to identify with in its use of familiar language, characters and situations.

The spectacular realism that film can imitate, and that television and modern stages can successfully attempt, was denied to Shakespeare. His theatre was non-realist, non-naturalistic, relying on conventions shared by actors and audiences, a few props, elaborate costumes, but above all on language and the human voice. In Shakespeare's time, theatre audiences expected most plays to be about kings, queens and aristocrats. They accepted the stage convention of heightened rather than everyday language, often in verse. Such style was felt to be appropriate to the stage, even though no-one spoke in verse outside the theatre.

Those first Elizabethans had no problem with stage magic, and could accept the illusions of gods and goddesses on stage, of identical twins, of characters who could assume a disguise and be completely unrecognised, even by those who knew them well. They accepted conventions that are less used in drama today: long speeches, soliloquies, the aside to the audience, patterned dialogue, prologues and epilogues, complex imagery, rhyme, nobles who speak in verse, lower-status characters who use prose.

Today, stage and film performances are assisted by a far richer range of resources than was available when the plays were first staged. Shakespeare's theatre did not possess the complex stage machinery found in modern theatres to create elaborate sets, lighting, and sound effects. Shakespeare was acutely conscious that he must create atmosphere and setting through language. His scene painting was done in words, his lighting effects achieved through language.

Shakespeare's dramatic language is intensely active and physical, pulsating with verbal energy. The physicality of the language is palpable:

> I could a tale unfold whose lightest word
> Would harrow up thy soul, freeze thy young blood,
> Make thy two eyes like stars start from their spheres,
> Thy knotted and combinèd locks to part
> And each particular hair to stand on end
> Like quills upon the fretful porpentine

Following Hamlet's advice to 'suit the action to the word, the word to the action' the language contains inbuilt stage directions for action:

> Avaunt and quit my sight!

> Turn thee, Benvolio, look upon thy death

> By this sword, he that makes the first thrust,
> I'll kill him, by this sword I will.

> My lord, most humbly on my knee I beg

> Give me thy torch, boy. Hence, and stand aloof

For the first Elizabethan audiences, the fullest experience of any play was created through words. Language evoked tempests and sheepshearings, graveyards and battlefields, feelings of fear and joy. Language created a sense of place:

Upon this blasted heath you stop our way

Unto Southampton do we shift our scene

In fair Verona where we lay our scene

It conjured up darkness in vivid images:

> Light thickens,
> And the crow makes wing to th'rooky wood

> 'Tis now the very witching time of night
> When churchyards yawn, and hell itself breathes out
> Contagion to this world

Language created a shipwreck at sea or a raging storm:

> 'Mercy on us!' –
> 'We split, we split!' – 'Farewell my wife and children!' –
> 'Farewell, brother' – 'We split, we split, we split!'

> Blow, winds, and crack your cheeks! Rage, blow,
> You cataracts and hurricanoes spout....

It embodied the unearthly, mysterious world of the supernatural:

> Double, double toil and trouble;
> Fire burn, and cauldron bubble

Language created and intensified the emotional mood of a character, whether of tortured conscience:

> Nought's had, all's spent
> Where our desire is got without content

or grief and loss:

> Death lies on her like an untimely frost
> Upon the sweetest flower of all the field

or fear:

> Shall I not then be stifled in the vault,
> To whose foul mouth no healthsome air breathes in

or the tender generosity of unqualified measureless love:

> My bounty is as boundless as the sea,
> My love as deep; the more I give to thee
> The more I have, for both are infinite

The remainder of this chapter identifies linguistic devices which Shakespeare used to intensify dramatic effect in his plays. Each teacher will decide how and when to introduce his or her students to these language uses, but any sustained study of Shakespeare's language will include the major elements: imagery, personification, antithesis, repetition, rhyme, lists, verse and prose.

A technical vocabulary?

Every teacher will exercise his or her professional judgement as to which technical terms need to be part of their students' classroom vocabulary. That judgement will be informed by the needs and interests of the students, external examinations and so on. The terms used in this book represent a basic vocabulary which will help almost all students. Most are in familiar, everyday language. Words like 'lists' or 'repetition' are preferred to older Latinate terms, and do the job of description more effectively.

A few terms are less familiar, even though the activity or skill they describe is already part of students' language practice. For example, students don't need to know the technical term 'deixis' to enjoy an activity in which they point to the characters mentioned as you, he, they, and so on (see page 84). Each teacher will judge whether the term is a suitable one for their students to acquire. Similarly, whether a teacher says 'enjambement' or 'run on' (see page 68) is a matter of professional judgement.

However, it is sensible to use the appropriate terms as the opportunity arises. Students enjoy acquiring the vocabulary through active, meaningful use. Commonsense is the best guide. No student needs to be told what 'a line' is, and yet it is a fundamental element of Shakespeare's craft. You are not denying your students access to Shakespeare if they never hear the word anadiplosis (not to be found again in this book). But if you decide to make a study of Shakespeare's verse central to your course, the term 'iambic pentameter' becomes necessary. For younger students, experiencing a play for the first time, other matters have greater priority.

Imagery

Imagery is the use of emotionally charged words and phrases which conjure up vivid mental pictures in the imagination. King Lear, waking from his madness, and seeing his daughter Cordelia, expresses his suffering in powerful imagery:

> You do me wrong to take me out o'th'grave.
> Thou art a soul in bliss, but I am bound
> Upon a wheel of fire, that mine own tears
> Do scald like molten lead.

Such images play a key part in every Shakespeare play. They are a kind of verbal scene painting which appeals to the emotions. They deepen and intensify imaginative and dramatic impact, giving insight into characters' feelings and thoughts, from the humour in *Much Ado About Nothing*:

> Why what's the matter,
> That you have such a February face,
> So full of frost, of storm, and cloudiness

to the anguish of Macbeth's:

> O, full of scorpions is my mind, dear wife!

Clusters of repeated images in each play build up a sense of the themes of the play. Examples are the images of violence and disorder in *Macbeth* 'pour the sweet milk of concord into hell'; of light and darkness in *Romeo and Juliet*; of torture, fracture and suffering in *King Lear*. In *King Richard II*, England is pictured as a neglected garden, and the king as the sun.

In every play, Shakespeare uses imagery from nature: sun, moon and stars; the seasons; the sea; animals and birds and so on. His imagination also drew on the bustling daily life of Elizabethan England: farming, sports and hunting; jewels; banking; religion; education, medicine, shipping and the law. The bear-baiting he saw near the Globe Theatre on Bankside gave him a key image for Macbeth, surrounded by his enemies, and facing death:

> They have tied me to a stake; I cannot fly,
> But bear-like I must fight the course

Shakespeare's own profession in the theatre provided him with many images. In *As You Like It*, Jacques sees the world as a stage, with men playing out parts as they grow older (see page 137). Macbeth expresses the same image more bleakly:

> Life's but a walking shadow, a poor player
> That struts and frets his hour upon the stage
> And then is heard no more.

All Shakespeare's imagery uses metaphor or simile. Both are comparisons. A simile compares one thing to another using 'like' or 'as':

> The whining schoolboy...creeping like snail unwillingly to school

> Humanity must perforce prey on itself
> Like monsters of the deep

> They'll take suggestion as a cat laps milk

> The quality of mercy is not strained
> It droppeth as the gentle rain from heaven

A metaphor is a comparison which suggests that two dissimilar things are actually the same, as when Antony grieves over the dead body of Julius Caesar, slain by Brutus and his fellow conspirators:

> O, pardon me thou bleeding piece of earth
> That I am meek and gentle with these butchers!

In *Macbeth*, Donaldbain's vivid expression 'There's daggers in men's smiles' shows how the economy of metaphor intensifies imaginative power. Expressed as a simile, it would be the incomparably weaker 'men's smiles are like daggers'.

Personification

Shakespeare often uses personification: a special kind of imagery that turns all kinds of things (death, time, war, love, life, England and so on) into persons, giving them human feelings and attributes.

King John is especially rich in personifications. The city of Angiers is given many human attributes: eyes, cheeks, ears, waist, flinty rib, bosom. It is described as winking, sleeping, peevish, and is threatened with shaking fever.

Personification adds to dramatic effect because it endows objects or abstractions with life, enabling them to act, feel and respond like a living person. It brings a particularly active quality to the language, as feelings or things spring to life:

> Grief fills the room up of my absent child
> Lies in his bed, walks up and down with me.

> I think our country sinks beneath the yoke;
> It weeps, it bleeds, and each new day a gash
> Is added to her wounds.

Shakespeare endows death with many human qualities, and presents it in many guises:

> This fell sergeant Death is strict in his arrest

> O now doth Death line his dead chaps with steel,
> The swords of soldiers are his teeth, his fangs,
> And now he feasts, mousing the flesh of men

In *King Richard II*, Richard broods on the vulnerability of kings: within the hollow crown

> That rounds the mortal temples of a king
> Keeps Death his court...

Shakespeare's imagery can employ metaphor, simile and personification in the space of a few lines:

> She never told her love,
> But let concealment like a worm i'th'bud
> Feed on her damask cheek. She pined in thought,
> And with a green and yellow melancholy
> She sat like Patience on a monument
> Smiling at grief.

Students' identification of metaphors, similes and personification in such passages can be the prelude to more active work of enactment or illustration or creating similar comparisons.

Imagery in film and video

Film and video provide examples of illustrating the imagery of the speech with appropriate pictures. In the Zeffirelli film of *Hamlet*, as Hamlet speaks the 'To be or not to be' soliloquy, the camera slowly pans around a burial vault, showing skulls and bones and so on. In Polanski's film of *Macbeth*, a bear-baiting post is used at several points in the play to emphasise the bear-baiting image.

Students can prepare a camera 'shooting script' to suggest how the imagery in particular passages might be illustrated in a film production.

Antithesis

Antithesis is the opposition of words or phrases against each other. In 'To be or not to be…' 'To be' is the thesis, 'not to be' is the antithesis.

Shakespeare uses antithesis frequently in every play. As a playwright, he thought antithetically. He knew that the essence of drama is conflict, and his plays depict conflict at every level. In the history plays there are bloody struggles for the throne. In the comedies, lovers are beset by all kinds of mishaps, mistakes and quarrels. In the tragedies, good and evil oppose each other. Shakespeare's language embodies conflict in its use of antithesis. Just as character is set against character (Hamlet *versus* Claudius, Iago *versus* Othello), so Shakespeare sets the word against the word:

> For night-owls shriek where mounting larks should sing
>
> The more I love, the more he hateth me
>
> To sue to live, I find I seek to die
>
> With mirth in funeral and with dirge in marriage
>
> My grave is like to be my wedding bed

Coriolanus uses antithesis to express his contempt for the Plebians:

> What would you have, you curs,
> That like not peace nor war? The one affrights you,

The other makes you proud. He that trusts to you,
Where he should find you lions, finds you hares,
Where foxes, geese. You are no surer, no,
Than is the coal of fire upon the ice,
Or hailstone in the sun. Your virtue is
To make him worthy whose offence subdues him,
And curse that justice did it. Who deserves greatness
Deserves your hate.

Through physical activity, students can discover the see-sawing, conflicting movement of the language. Individually, they can weigh out each antithesis as if their hands were a pair of scales. Working with a partner, students can link hands and gently arm-wrestle back and forth as they speak the lines to each other to discover how the antitheses give the language a physical, to and fro, opposing movement.

Repetition

Shakespeare's use of repetition gives his language great dramatic force: 'Put out the light, and then put out the light'. Repeated words, phrases, rhythms and sounds (rhyme, alliteration, assonance) add to the emotional intensity of a moment or scene, heightening serious or comic effect. *Hamlet* contains much repetition that quietly contributes to its dramatic force ('To be or not to be', 'this too too solid flesh' and so on).

Early in his play writing career Shakespeare made much use of repetition in fairly obvious ways. *King Richard III* is full of examples of highly patterned repetition:

Was ever woman in this humour wooed?
Was ever woman in this humour won?

and:

Where is thy husband now? Where be thy brothers?
Where be thy two sons? Wherein dost thou joy?
Who sues, and kneels and says 'God save the Queen'?
Where be the bending peers that flattered thee?
Where be the thronging troops that followed thee?

Shakespeare knew that repeating a single word can deepen irony. In *Julius Caesar*, Antony constantly repeats 'honourable' in his Forum speech when his meaning is quite the opposite. Repetition can also heighten comedy, as when Petruchio teases Katherina in *The Taming of the Shrew*:

PETRUCHIO Good morrow Kate, for that's your name I hear.
KATHERINA Well have you heard, but something hard of hearing –
       They call me Katherine that do talk of me.
PETRUCHIO You lie, in faith, for you are called plain Kate,
       And bonny Kate, and sometimes Kate the curst.
       But Kate, the prettiest Kate in Christendom,
       Kate of Kate-Hall, my super-dainty Kate –
       For dainties are all Kates – and therefore, Kate,
       Take this of me, Kate of my consolation....

Shakespeare also knew that a single repeated word can be deeply moving. At the end of *King Lear*, Lear grieves over the dead body of his cruelly murdered daughter Cordelia:

       Thou'lt come no more,
       Never, never, never, never, never

Repetition also contributes to dramatic effect. In *Measure for Measure*, Isabella calls for justice against the corrupt Angelo who has used his power to sexually blackmail her:

       Justice, justice, justice, justice!

But the effect can be very different in the repetitions of the Ghost in *Hamlet*:

       Oh horrible, oh horrible, most horrible!

Students can turn at random to two or three pages of the play they are currently studying and identify all the ways in which Shakespeare uses repetition on those pages. They can try out different ways of speaking the lines to discover how emphasising or playing down the repetitions contributes to dramatic effect.

Repetition can have ritual effect as in Queen Margaret's command in *King Richard III*:

       Go thou to Richmond and good fortune guide thee!
       Go thou to Richard and good angels tend thee!
       Go thou to sanctuary and good thoughts possess thee!

In *King Richard II*, Richard resigns all the symbols and powers of kingship to his cousin Henry Bullingbrook. Shakespeare ensures that the deep seriousness of the ritual of abdication is built into the repeated rhythms of the language:

> With mine own tears I wash away my balm;
> With mine own hands I give away my crown:
> With mine own tongue deny my sacred state;
> With mine own breath release all duteous bonds...

Students can invent a ceremony with repetitive actions to accompany the language. Or they can write a parody of Richard's language to be spoken on the day they cease to be a school or college student.

In *The Winter's Tale*, Shakespeare uses different kinds of repetition to intensify the emotional impact of Leontes' fevered and obsessional jealousy. Leontes believes (wrongly) that his wife is having an affair with his best friend Polixenes:

> Is whispering nothing?
> Is leaning cheek to cheek? Is meeting noses?
> Kissing with inside lip? Stopping the career
> Of laughter with a sigh? – a note infallible
> Of breaking honesty. Horsing foot on foot?
> Skulking in corners? Wishing clocks more swift?
> Hours, minutes? Noon, midnight? And all eyes
> Blind with the pin and web but theirs, theirs only,
> That would unseen be wicked? Is this nothing?
> Why, then the world and all that's in't is nothing;
> The covering sky is nothing, Bohemia nothing,
> My wife is nothing, nor nothing have these nothings,
> If this be nothing.

Students can experiment with ways of delivering the lines to convey the deranged state of Leontes' mind.

Shakespeare parodies the use of repetition in *A Midsummer Night's Dream* as Bottom begins the play within the play that he will perform with his fellow Mechanicals:

> O grim-looked night, O night with hue so black,
> O night which ever art when day is not!
> O night, O night, alack alack, alack,

> I fear my Thisbe's promise is forgot!
> And thou, O wall, O sweet, O lovely wall.
> That stand'st between her father's ground and mine
> Thou wall, O wall, O sweet and lovely wall,
> Show me thy chink, to blink through with mine eyne.

Students can speak Bottom's lines emphasising all the repetitions of words, sounds, phrases and so on. They can then write and perform their own parody of one of Shakespeare's scenes or characters, using as much repetition as they can in the style of Bottom's speech.

Alliteration, assonance and onomatopoeia

Alliteration is the repetition of consonants, usually at the beginning of words:

> *M*ore *m*atter for a *M*ay *m*orning!

Assonance is the repetition of vowel sounds. In *King John*, Shakespeare gives Lewis the Dauphin a tongue-twister, full of assonance as it squeezes seven repetitions of the same sound into one line:

> What lusty trumpet thus doth summon us?

Shakespeare knew that a pattern of repeated sounds offers opportunities to actors to intensify emotional impact. In *Macbeth*, the witches combine assonance with alliteration to hypnotic effect:

> Thrice to thine, and thrice to mine,
> And thrice again, to make up nine

Onomatopoeia is the use of words whose sound mimic what they describe. In *King Lear*, Edgar conjures up the sounds of the sea-shore:

> The murmuring surge,
> That on th'unnumbered idle pebble chafes

Shakespeare was never afraid to poke fun at language. In *A Midsummer Night's Dream* he puts words into the mouth of Quince to mock poet-playwrights who took alliteration too seriously:

> Whereat with blade, with bloody, blameful blade,
> He bravely broached his bloody boiling breast.

Identifying alliteration, assonance and onomatopoeia can be an arid task for many students. It is vital to encourage them to play with and create their own examples, and to discover how these language devices contribute to dramatic impact by exploring ways of speaking.

Students can invent their own headlines for reviews of Shakespeare plays ('Denmark's Dangerous Dane Delays Delightfully'), or write short poems or other pieces using as much alliteration, assonance and onomatopoeia of their own as possible.

Rhyme

In *Much Ado About Nothing*, Benedick regrets (in prose) his inability to find rhymes:

> I can find no rhyme to lady but baby, an innocent rhyme: for scorn horn, a hard rhyme: for school fool, a babbling rhyme: very ominous endings. No, I was not born under a rhyming planet....

Rhyme in verse involves matching sounds at the end of each line. It gives an audible pattern to language and makes it easier to learn:

> If we shadows have offended,
> Think but this, and all is mended.

Shakespeare uses rhyme in songs, prologues and epilogues, masques and plays within plays, and for the supernatural, for example, the witches in *Macbeth* or the fairies in *A Midsummer Night's Dream*. Should the rhymes be stressed on stage? In each case, it is appropriate for students to explore possible ways of speaking to discover their own answer to that question.

Long speeches in blank verse (unrhymed) often end with a rhyming couplet, as do many scenes or acts. The Elizabethan stage had no lights or curtains to signal the end of a scene. So Shakespeare often provides his characters with a strong rhyming couplet to accompany their exit (and perhaps act as a cue for other actors to enter). As Macbeth leaves to murder Duncan he hears the bell:

> Hear it not Duncan, for it is a knell,
> That summons thee to heaven or to hell

Such rhyming couplets often express foreboding, or operate as a prophecy, or farewell epitaph or blessing:

> God's benison go with you, and with those
> That would make good of bad, and friends of foes

Rhyme and parody

Shakespeare uses the Mechanicals' play in *A Midsummer Night's Dream* to mock the conventions of rhyming poetry. Thisbe (played by Flute) laments over the dead Pyramus (played by Bottom):

> Asleep, my love?
> What, dead, my dove?
> O Pyramus, arise.
> Speak, speak! Quite dumb?
> Dead, dead? A tomb
> Must cover thy sweet eyes.
> These lily lips,
> This cherry nose,
> These yellow cowslip cheeks
> Are gone, are gone.
> Lovers, make moan;
> His eyes were green as leeks.
> O sisters three,
> Come, come to me
> With hands as pale as milk;
> Lay them in gore,
> Since you have shore
> With shears his thread of silk.
> Tongue, not a word!
> Come, trusty sword,
> Come blade, my breast imbrue *(Stabs herself.)*
> And farewell, friends.
> Thus Thisbe ends –
> Adieu, adieu, adieu! *(Dies.)*

Students can step into role as Thisbe and do their thing! They can also try their hands at writing a similar rhyming speech to parody a well known Shakespeare play (for example, Juliet lamenting over Romeo).

Sometimes the rhymes occur in shared speech to express shared emotion:

JULIET O now be gone, more light and light it grows
ROMEO More light and light, more dark and dark our woes!

As Shakespeare grew older, he tended to use rhyme less frequently. *Love's Labour's Lost* has well over 1000 rhymes; *A Midsummer Night's Dream* almost 800; *Romeo and Juliet* and *King Richard II* about 500 each. In contrast, the Roman plays, *Antony and Cleopatra*, *Julius Caesar* and *Coriolanus* each have under 40 rhymes.

Lists

One of Shakespeare's favourite methods with language is to accumulate words or phrases rather like a list. He knew that such piling up of language increased dramatic effect by intensifying description, atmosphere or argument. Perhaps the best known list (and most frequently acted out by students) is that of the ingredients of the revolting stew prepared by the witches in *Macbeth*:

FIRST WITCH Thrice the brindled cat hath mewed.
SECOND WITCH Thrice and once the hedge-pig whined.
THIRD WITCH Harpier cries, ''Tis time, 'tis time.'
FIRST WITCH Round about the cauldron go;
        In the poisoned entrails throw.
        Toad, that under cold stone
        Days and nights has thirty-one
        Sweltered venom sleeping got,
        Boil thou first i'th'charmèd pot.
ALL Double, double toil and trouble;
        Fire burn, and cauldron bubble.
SECOND WITCH Fillet of a fenny snake,
        In the cauldron boil and bake:
        Eye of newt, and toe of frog,
        Wool of bat, and tongue of dog,
        Adder's fork, and blind-worm's sting,
        Lizard's leg, and howlet's wing,

> For a charm of powerful trouble,
> Like a hell-broth, boil and bubble.
> ALL Double, double toil and trouble;
> Fire burn, and cauldron bubble.

There are a host of very different kinds of lists. Richard III's mother describes her son:

> Techy and wayward was thy infancy;
> Thy schooldays frightful, desperate, wild and furious;
> Thy prime of manhood daring, bold and venturous
> Thy age confirmed, proud, subtle, sly and bloody.

Shylock in *The Merchant of Venice* insists on his humanity, and his list adds compelling force to his argument:

> Hath not a Jew eyes? Hath not a Jew hands, organs, dimensions, senses, affections, passions? Fed with the same food, hurt with the same weapons, subject to same diseases, healed by the same means, warmed and cooled by the same summer and winter as a Christian is?

In *King Henry V*, the catalogue of names of the French nobility killed at the Battle of Agincourt, creates an impression of a medieval world of chivalry:

> Charles Delabret, High Constable of France;
> Jacques of Châtillon, Admiral of France;
> The master of the Crossbow, Lord Rambures;
> John, Duke of Alençon; Antony, Duke of Brabant
> The brother to the Duke of Burgundy;
> And Edward, Duke of Bar...

In *King Richard II*, John of Gaunt paints a picture of England:

> This royal throne of kings, this sceptred isle,
> This earth of majesty, this seat of Mars,
> This other Eden, demi-paradise,
> This fortress built by Nature for herself
> Against infection and the hand of war,
> This happy breed of men, this little world,
> This precious stone set in the silver sea,

Which serves it in the office of a wall,
Or as a moat defensive to a house
Against the envy of less happier lands,
This blessèd plot, this earth, this realm, this England,
This nurse, this teeming womb of royal kings....

Gaunt's description vividly contrasts with that of the city of Ephesus in *The Comedy of Errors*:

They say this town is full of cozenage,
As nimble jugglers that deceive the eye,
Dark-working sorcerers that change the mind,
Soul-killing witches that deform the body,
Disguisèd cheaters, prating mountebanks
And many suchlike liberties of sin.

The vast range of Shakespeare's use of accumulating language includes every type of emotional effect, many intensely moving. For example, Ophelia's description of Hamlet ('Oh what a noble mind is here o'erthrown...'); her distribution of flowers in her madness ('There's rosemary, that's for remembrance...'); or Cordelia's description of the appearance of her father King Lear:

As mad as the vexed sea, singing aloud,
Crowned with rank furmitor and furrow-weeds,
With burdocks, hemlock, nettles, cuckoo-flowers,
Darnel, and all the idle weeds that grow
In our sustaining corn.

Shakespeare was never afraid to repeat a particular kind of listing that he had used in an earlier play. In *Romeo and Juliet*, Juliet lists all the things she would rather do than marry Paris (see page 17). In *Much Ado About Nothing* Benedick similarly catalogues all the things he would rather do than meet Beatrice:

Will your grace command me any service to the world's end? I will go on the slightest errand now to the Antipodes that you can devise to send me on. I will fetch you a tooth-picker now from the furthest inch of Asia; bring you the length of Prester John's foot; fetch you a hair off the great Cham's beard; do you any embassage to the Pygmies, rather than hold three words conference with this Harpy.

63

Both Juliet's and Benedick's lists are intensely physical. Students can act them out or compile a list of all the things they would rather do than meet or marry someone not of their own choice. Similar acting out or writing activities can be undertaken on all the lists on pages 61–3.

Shakespeare mocks the compiling of lists through Dogberry, the comic constable in *Much Ado About Nothing*, who lists his complaints against the men he has arrested. Don Pedro replies in the same fashion:

DON PEDRO Officers, what offence have these men done?

DOGBERRY Marry, sir, they have committed false report, moreover they have spoken untruths, secondarily, they are slanders, sixth and lastly, they have belied a lady, thirdly they have verified unjust things, and to conclude, they are lying knaves.

DON PEDRO First I ask thee what they have done, thirdly I ask thee what's their offence, sixth and lastly why they are committed, and to conclude, what you lay to their charge?

Students can make up some lists of their own based on Dogberry's style, for example, 'Why I like (or dislike) Shakespeare.'

In a performance of a play, most lists are only spoken. The actor tries to find an appropriate pace, rhythm and emotional tone for each list. But the lists are full of active possibilities for the classroom.

Malcolm's description of Macbeth can be enacted to show a brief dramatisation of each of his qualities. There are at least seven characteristics to enact – or fourteen if students act out the seven deadly sins:

> I grant him bloody,
> Luxurious, avaricious, false, deceitful,
> Sudden, malicious, smacking of every sin
> That has a name.

Students can identify as many lists as possible in the play they are studying (each play contains dozens), and select several to speak and act out. Each list has its own distinctive qualities. Students can experiment with ways of speaking to find a suitable style, and to give each item different expression to make it unique and memorable.

A *Macbeth* miscellany

Students can experiment with changing the order of words in some of Shakespeare's lists. The discussion generated will involve questioning why Shakespeare decided that the order he chose was the most powerful. Students do not always agree with his judgement! Offering the reasons for their disagreement takes students to the heart of the nature of dramatic language. Here are a number of lists from *Macbeth* that are suitable for this activity.

Sons, kinsmen, thanes

The innocent sleep;
Sleep that knits up the ravelled sleep of care,
The death of each days's life, sore labour's bath,
Balm of hurt minds, great nature's second course,
Chief nourisher in life's feast

King, Cawdor, Glamis, all

Hounds, and greyhounds, mongrels, spaniels, curs,
Shoughs, water-rugs, and demi-wolves

the swift, the slow, the subtle, the housekeeper, the hunter

cabined, cribbed, confined, bound in

Approach thou like the rugged Russian bear,
The armed rhinoceros, or th'Hyrcan tiger

Maggot-pies, and choughs, and rooks

Though you untie the winds and let them fight
Against the churches, though the yeasty waves
Confound and swallow navigation up,
Though bladed corn be lodged and trees blown down,
Though castles topple on their warders' heads
Though palaces and pyramids do slope
Their heads to their foundations, though the treasure
Of nature's germens tumble altogether
Even till destruction sicken

the net, nor lime, the pitfall, nor the gin

> each new morn
> New widows howl, new orphans cry, new sorrows
> Strike heaven on the face

> Justice, verity, temp'rance, stableness,
> Bounty, perseverance, mercy, lowliness,
> Devotion, patience, courage, fortitude

> honour, love, obedience, troops of friends

Verse

Today, audiences expect films and television plays to use language which is everyday and familiar. But in Shakespeare's time, audiences expected actors, especially in histories and tragedies, to speak in verse. The poetic style of verse was felt to be particularly suitable for kings, great affairs of war and state, tragic themes and moments of high dramatic or emotional intensity.

Four of Shakespeare's plays are entirely in verse (*King Richard II*, *King John*, *King Henry VI Parts 1 and 3*). Most plays contain far more verse than prose. Only five plays have more prose than verse (*The Merry Wives of Windsor*, *Much Ado About Nothing*, *As You Like It*, *Twelfth Night* and *King Henry IV Part 2*).

Shakespeare's verse is written in iambic pentameter. The technical term may be daunting to some students, but through practical activities they quickly grasp that it simply means that each line has five stresses ('penta' is from the Greek for five). Typically, five stressed (/) syllables alternate with five unstressed (x) syllables, giving a ten-syllable line.

> x / x / x / x / x /
> But soft, what light through yonder window breaks?

The dangers when verse is analysed in this way are that it looks like algebra, and seems to suggest a mechanical, repetitive rhythm:

> de *dum*, de *dum*, de *dum*, de *dum*, de *dum*

The stress pattern in iambic pentameter is not like the beat in electronic music where the sound is unvaried and unvarying. The 'weight' of each stress can vary, and the spaces or pauses in a line can be of different length. Just as the human heartbeat is not exactly regular, but has tiny, unnoticed variations, so iambic pentameter is a human, not a mechanical measure. Some people say it reflects the natural rhythm of human speech.

The human heartbeat, the rhythm of the iamb

Get students to listen to each other's heartbeat to hear the basic rhythm of weak and strong stresses: de-*dum*, de-*dum*, de-*dum*...

Poetry that is exactly regular becomes doggerel, so within the framework of iambic pentameter Shakespeare varies the rhythmic pattern. He sometimes writes lines of more or fewer than ten syllables, he often varies the position of the caesura (mid-line pause). He ensures that the rhythm of the verse is appropriate to the meaning and mood of a speech: reflective, or fearful and apprehensive, or anguished confusion and so on.

Actors always try to ensure that verse, rhymed or unrhymed (blank verse) does not sound boring and repetitive on stage. They use the clues and contexts that Shakespeare provides to match the rhythm to the thoughts and feelings of the characters. For example, when Henry V urges his soldiers to attack Harfleur yet again, he can put seven or even eight stresses into his first line:

> /   /   x x x   /   /   /   /   /
> Once more into the breach, dear friends, once more

In Shakespeare's early plays, the rhythm of the verse tends to be very regular. The lines are often 'end-stopped', each line making sense on its own, with a pause at the end of the line. In *Titus Andronicus* (a very early play) Titus speaks in measured, formal style, even at the most melodramatic moments, as when he threatens the two men he intends to kill and bake in a pie:

> Hark, villains, I will grind your bones to dust,
> And with your blood and it I'll make a paste,
> And of the paste a coffin I will rear,
> And make two pasties of your shameful heads.

As Shakespeare's play writing developed, he used fewer end-stopped lines and made much greater use of enjambement (running on), where one line flows on into the next, seemingly without pause. *Macbeth*, for example, contains a great deal of enjambement:

> I have lived long enough. My way of life
> Is fall'n into the sere, the yellow leaf

To experience the rhythm of iambic pentameter, students can speak the lines aloud, and emphasise the five stresses physically. They can clap hands, or tap their desk, or walk five paces to accompany each line, or work out a fivefold movement with a partner and so on. Such physical activity is crucial help for most students in acquiring a feel for the rhythm.

To begin, students usually speak verse lines very regularly, with five strong stresses in each line, and a marked pause at the end of each line. But teachers and students experiencing such emphatic stressing of the rhythm quickly become aware of the limitations of such regularity. It is a useful and necessary first step for many, if not most, students into appreciating verse rhythm, but excessive stress on form (iambic pentameter) can overwhelm feeling (dramatic effect, emotion). Later, knowledge of the caesura can be helpful. It is one of Shakespeare's ways of giving actors an indication of where they might pause. He often shapes a line into two sections divided by a caesura:

> So shaken as we are, so wan with care

Students can explore using the caesura to find more dramatic and effective ways of speaking to bring out a character's thoughts and feelings. They can work through any speech a line at a time, suggesting where pauses are appropriate.

Nearly all the students' out-of-school experience of verse is in some other metrical form, usually tetrameter (see page 69), from 'Jack and Jill went up the hill' to pop songs. Experience shows that to write Shakespearian 'five-beat' verse, many students require direct help like the activities above which will assist with the following exercise.

Invite students to make up eight to ten lines of their own in iambic pentameter, using simple examples:

- I think I'd like a plate of ham and eggs.
- My birthday is the twenty-first of May.

Tetrameter

> Full fathom five thy father lies,
> Of his bones are coral made.

A verse line with four stresses is called tetrameter ('tetra' is from the Greek for four). It is the common rhythm of nursery rhymes. Shakespeare uses it for songs, the witches' chants in *Macbeth*, Orlando's doggerel verses in *As You Like It*, and the Duke's soliloquy in *Measure for Measure*. In *A Midsummer Night's Dream*, Puck and the fairies often speak in tetrameter rhythm. One of Shakespeare's Sonnets (number 145) is written in tetrameter.

Unpunctuated lines

Many students enjoy the challenge of restoring an unpunctuated passage back to iambic pentameter verse lines. It is usually appropriate to begin with examples that are fairly regular, so that students experience early success. Prepare an extract in which Shakespeare's blank verse is printed as prose, with all punctuation removed and with no capital letters:

> but soft what light through yonder window breaks it is the east
> and juliet is the sun arise fair sun and kill the envious moon
> who is already sick and pale with grief that thou her maid art
> far more fair than she

The extract can be given to students with the reminder that there are usually five stressed syllables in each iambic pentameter line, but because Shakespeare used verse so flexibly, many lines do not have a perfectly regular rhythm. It is best to speak the words aloud, accompanied with a physical movement, to find the rhythm.

Examples that have been successfully used are: from *Romeo and Juliet*, the Prologue and Juliet's 'How if when I am laid into the tomb'; from *Twelfth Night*, 'If music be the food of love'; from *Hamlet*, 'Oh what a noble mind is here o'erthrown'.

Shared lines

Lines can be 'loosened' by dividing them between one or more characters. There are many such lines in *Antony and Cleopatra* in which Shakespeare frequently runs on meaning and rhythm from one line to the next, often sharing lines between two speakers. In this example, Cleopatra and Eros help Antony put on his armour:

ANTONY If fortune be not ours today, it is
        Because we brave her. Come.
CLEOPATRA   Nay I'll help too
        What's this for?
ANTONY   Ah, let be, let be! Thou art
        The armourer of my heart. False, false, this, this.
CLEOPATRA Sooth, la, I'll help. Thus it must be.
ANTONY   Well, Well,
        We shall thrive now. Seest thou, my good fellow
        Go, put on thy defences.
EROS   Briefly, Sir
CLEOPATRA Is not this buckled well?
ANTONY   Rarely, rarely.

It is a stage convention that shared lines are spoken with little or no pause between speakers. According to this custom, the half line acts as a cue for the other actor, rather than a pause. But is that tradition always dramatically effective? Students can take parts and experiment with the lines above from *Antony and Cleopatra*, and with the single line below from *King John* in which John orders Hubert to murder Arthur. Students can speak the lines in a number of different ways, without and with pauses:

JOHN Death.
HUBERT   My Lord.
JOHN   A grave.
HUBERT   He shall not live.
JOHN   Enough.

Prose

How did Shakespeare decide whether his characters should speak in verse or prose? A rough answer is that he followed the stage conventions of his time. It was conventional for prose to be used in a particular range of situations as detailed on the next page.

1 In proclamations, written challenges or accusations, and letters (for example, Macbeth's letter to Lady Macbeth telling of his meeting with the witches).

2 For lines spoken by low-status characters such as servants, clowns, or drunks. The low-status villains, Iago (*Othello*) and Edmond (*King Lear*) speak many prose lines.

3 To express madness. King Lear, Hamlet, Edgar as Poor Tom, and Lady Macbeth (all high-status characters) express their madness (or assumed madness) in prose.

4 For comedy. Falstaff and Sir Toby Belch, both knights (high-status characters) use prose. Among Shakespeare's comedies, almost 90 percent of *The Merry Wives of Windsor* is prose, and, as noted on page 66, over half of *Twelfth Night*, *As You Like It*, and *Much Ado About Nothing*.

But Shakespeare never followed any rule slavishly, and exceptions can always be found. Low-status characters sometimes speak in verse, for example, Juliet's Nurse and Caliban, while high-status characters sometimes switch to prose, for example King Henry V. After the assassination of Julius Caesar, Brutus uses prose for his speech to the citizens of Rome, but Antony uses verse.

The context of a speech sometimes explains why prose or verse is spoken. For example Macbeth speaks some prose when talking to the low-status murderers. The villainous Iago typically speaks prose, but switches to verse when he is with Othello. Students can check through the play they are currently studying to discover who uses verse and who uses prose, and suggest reasons for the difference.

Prose is sometimes said to be less interesting than verse because verse, with its repetitions and strong sense of rhythmical pattern, is like music in setting the feet tapping and the body moving. But prose, too, has its patterns and rhythms, and sometimes they are very apparent. Shakespeare's prose often has strong symmetry (particularly in the plays he wrote early in his career). In *The Comedy of Errors*, Dromio of Ephesus complains about his treatment by his master:

> When I am cold, he heats me with beating; when I am warm, he cools me with beating; I am waked with it when I sleep, raised with it when I sit, driven out of doors with it when I go home, welcomed home with it when I return; nay, I bear it on my

shoulders, as a beggar wont her brat, and I think when he hath lamed me I shall beg with it from door to door.

Dromio's prose can be set out to show its structures and rhythms:

When I am cold	he heats me with beating
When I am warm	he cools me with beating
I am waked with it	when I sleep
raised with it	when I sit
driven out of doors with it	when I go from home
welcomed home with it	when I return
nay I bear it on my shoulders	as a beggar wont her brat
And I think	when he hath lamed me
I shall beg with it	from door to door

Hamlet tells of the effect that his melancholy has on him:
I have of late, but wherefore I know not, lost all my mirth, forgone all custom of exercises; and indeed it goes so heavily with my disposition that this goodly frame, the earth, seems to me a sterile promontory; this most excellent canopy the air, look you, this brave o'erhanging firmament, this majestical roof fretted with golden fire – why, it appeareth no other thing to me but a foul and pestilent congregation of vapours. What a piece of work is a man! How noble in reason, how infinite in faculties, in form and moving how express and admirable, in action how like an angel, in apprehension how like a god! The beauty of the world, the paragon of animals – and yet to me, what is this quintessence of dust? Man delights not me – no, nor woman neither, though by your smiling you seem to say so.

Hamlet's prose has often been claimed to have the qualities of poetry. Invite students to speak the lines, then to discuss whether they could think of them equally as both prose and poetry. Students might also try writing out the lines as verse, to see if they can create a version that looks like poetry.

Students can use the above method of setting out prose to reveal the pattern of balanced contrasts used in the following speech by Macbeth's Porter to describe the effects of drink:

Lechery, sir, it provokes, and unprovokes; it provokes the desire, but it takes away the performance. Therefore much drink may be said to be an equivocator with lechery: it makes him, and it mars him; it sets him on, and it takes him off; it persuades him and it disheartens him, makes him stand to and not stand to. In conclusion, equivocates him in a sleep, and giving him the lie, leaves him.

Rhetoric

Today, 'rhetoric' is often used to describe language that is insincere and artificial, not to be trusted. The modern politician's soundbite is rhetoric. It is vivid and memorable, but empty, the triumph of sound over meaning. But in Shakespeare's time, rhetoric enjoyed high status and was taught in schools. As a schoolboy, Shakespeare would have learned by heart more than 100 figures of rhetoric, and he used most of them in his plays (for example, *epizeuxis*: immediately repeating a word to give it greater impact, as in King Lear's 'Howl, howl, howl, howl!').

For Shakespeare and his contemporaries, rhetoric was the art of persuasion. It involved all the ways of using language that make it more eloquent and convincing. It was the use of particular linguistic techniques to gain the confidence of listeners, and appeal to their reason, their emotions, and their imagination.

Language is power. In every play, powerfully persuasive voices are heard as characters try to convince others (or themselves) or move someone to action. Antony, in his carefully constructed speech, uses rhetoric to move the citizens of Rome to revolt against Julius Caesar's assassins. Iago knows his very words can destroy Othello. The witches' prophecies set Macbeth off on his long murderous road.

Henry V uses language to motivate his soldiers to risk their lives in assaulting Harfleur once again: 'Once more into the breach, dear friends, once more'. Lady Macbeth persuades Macbeth to murder Duncan, appealing to Macbeth's courage, soldierliness and ambition, and attacking his male self-esteem: 'When you durst do it, then you were a man'.

Students can explore different ways of speaking such episodes. A rhetorical speech can often be shared, spoken by students in pairs or threes as if it were an argument developed by two or more persons. As students work on speeches that try to persuade others, they can use the five fold framework below. It is a simple version of the more complex classical framework Shakespeare would have used in his own school work.

1   Is the speech a logical argument? How does it begin, handle evidence and counter objections, conclude?

2   How does it appeal to the emotions and the imagination? (Here, students should identify the rhythm of the speech, its imagery, repetitions, lists, antitheses and other language techniques described in this chapter.)

3   Does it give the speaker an air of authority, and gain the confidence of the listeners?

Rhetorical figures

Shakespeare, like most other Elizabethan grammar school boys, would have memorised a very large number of figures of rhetoric. Here are a few of the most common.

Anaphora – the same words begins successive sentences.

> That never words were music to thine ear
> That never object pleasing to thy eye...

Parison – repeating an entire sentence or clause almost exactly.

'In such a night' is repeated eight times in the first twenty lines of Act 5 Scene 1 of *The Merchant of Venice*.

Ploce – repeating words in a line or clause.

> For she that scorned at me, now scorned of me

Epizeuxis – repeating words in immediate succession.

> O, horror, horror, horror

Antanaclasis – punning on a repeated word to obtain different meanings.

> Put out the light, and then put out the light

> Light, seeking light, doth light of light beguile

---

4 Is it effective? Will the speech achieve the speaker's intentions, and persuade the listeners?

5 How should the speech be spoken to be most persuasive?

Shakespeare used his training in rhetoric to great effect, but he often took verbal ornateness as a target for ridicule. When Polonius engages in rhetorical pedantry, Gertrude snaps at him 'More matter with less art'. Hamlet parodies the affected courtier Osric, Falstaff mocks 'King Cambyses vein', and Pistol's language shows just what can happen as rhetoric becomes merely boastful over-the-top windbaggery.

Self-persuasion

Macbeth struggles with his conscience. Should he kill King Duncan? Students can share the speech as a tortured conversation between two persons who set out their reasons against the murder. They can catch the see-sawing effect of Macbeth's thoughts by joining hands and gently pushing or pulling as they speak, expressing the rhythms of each phrase, line or sentence:

> If it were done when 'tis done, then 'twere well
> It were done quickly. If th'assassination
> Could trammel up the consequence and catch
> With his surcease, success, that but this blow
> Might be the be-all and the end-all – here,
> But here, upon this bank and shoal of time,
> We'd jump the life to come. But in these cases.
> We still have judgement here that we but teach
> Bloody instructions, which being taught, return
> To plague th'inventor. This even-handed justice
> Commends th'ingredience of our poisoned chalice
> To our own lips. He's here in double trust:
> First, as I am his kinsman and his subject,
> Strong both against the deed; then, as his host,
> Who should against his murderer shut the door,
> Not bear the knife myself. Besides, this Duncan
> Hath born his faculties so meek, hath been
> So clear in his great office, that his virtues
> Will plead like angels, trumpet-tongued against

> The deep damnation of his taking-off.
> And pity, like a naked newborn babe
> Striding the blast, or heaven's cherubin horsed
> Upon the sightless couriers of the air,
> Shall blow the horrid deed in every eye,
> That tears shall drown the wind. I have no spur
> To prick the sides of my intent, but only
> Vaulting ambition which o'erleaps itself
> And falls on th'other –

Macbeth's soliloquy richly displays the major linguistic devices of rhetoric: vivid imagery, all kinds of repetitions and lists, powerful antitheses and compulsive rhythms. All contribute to its dramatic potential, and students can use their exploratory activities to prepare a staging of the lines.

Bombast

The first mention of Shakespeare as a playwright parodies one of his lines (italicised) from *Henry VI Part 3* as an example of bombast:

> There is an upstart crow, beautified with our feathers, that with his *Tiger's heart wrapped in a player's hide*, supposes he is as well able to bombast out a blank verse as the best of you.

Bombast is boastful or ranting language. In *King Henry IV Part 1*, Owen Glendower claims that when he was born 'The heavens were all on fire, the earth did tremble'. In *A Midsummer Night's Dream*, Bottom throws out his chest and declaims bombastically:

> The raging rocks
> And shivering shocks
> Shall break the locks
> Of prison gates.

Hamlet uses similarly inflated language when he challenges Laertes and leaps into Ophelia's grave. His bombast offer students the opportunity to find a style of speaking appropriate to his words:

HAMLET I loved Ophelia; forty thousand brothers
           Could not with all their quantity of love

> Make up my sum. What wilt thou do for her?
>
> CLAUDIUS Oh he is mad Laertes.
>
> GERTRUDE For love of God forbear him.
>
> HAMLET 'Swounds, show me what thou't do.
> Woo't weep, woo't fight, woo't fast, woo't tear thyself?
> Woo't drink up eisel, eat a crocodile?
> I'll do't. Dost thou come here to whine,
> To outface me with leaping in her grave?
> Be buried quick with her, and so will I.
> And if thou prate of mountains, let them throw
> Millions of acres on us, till our ground,
> Singeing his pate against the burning zone.
> Make Ossa like a wart. Nay, and thou'lt mouth,
> I'll rant as well as thou.

Hyperbole

Hyperbole is extravagant and obvious exaggeration, as when someone today says 'I'm dying for a drink.' It is the root of the modern expression 'hype', the hyperbole of advertisers who make grandiose claims for their products. Prince Hal describes Falstaff as a 'Huge hill of flesh.' Othello, tortured by the knowledge that he has wrongly killed Desdemona, exclaims:

> Blow me about in winds! Roast me in sulphur!
> Wash me in steep-down gulfs of liquid fire!

Right at the start of *Antony and Cleopatra*, a play full of hyperbolic language that matches its world-ranging theme, Antony expresses his rejection of Rome:

> Let Rome in Tiber melt and the wide arch
> Of the ranged empire fall!

In Shakespeare's time, many poets and dramatists 'went over the top', using elaborate and fanciful words, images, and styles. In *Love's Labour's Lost*, Shakespeare mocks the use of hyperbole in Biron's 'three-piled hyperboles', but made use of it himself in the same play: 'A lover's eyes will gaze an eagle blind.' Bassanio's description of Portia's portrait in *The Merchant of Venice* is an example of where rhetorical excess becomes hyperbole: 'What demi-god hath come so near creation?' Such elaborate and fanciful language presents students with the challenge of how it might be spoken in each context: seriously, mockingly or in some other way.

Students can collect examples of hyperbole in the play they are studying, and make a presentation which compares them with examples from advertisements in newspapers and magazines. Students can also make up a few lines of hyperbole of their own, for example to describe William Shakespeare, or one of his plays.

Irony

Shakespeare frequently uses two types of irony: verbal and dramatic. In both, the audience knows something that a character on stage does not.

Verbal irony is saying one thing but meaning another. For example in *Julius Caesar*, Mark Antony repeatedly calls Brutus 'an honourable man' when he means quite the opposite. Macbeth says to Banquo, 'Fail not our feast', knowing that Banquo will never arrive, because he will be murdered by Macbeth's hired killers. When the young Duke of York asks for his dagger, Richard III, full of murderous intentions, ironically replies, 'My dagger, little cousin? With all my heart.'

Dramatic irony is structural: one scene, event or line contrasts sharply with another. For example King Duncan's line 'He was a gentleman on whom I built an absolute trust', is immediately followed by the stage direction *Enter Macbeth*. The audience has only moments ago seen Macbeth thinking of murdering Duncan. A little later, the scene in which Macbeth plans to murder King Duncan is immediately followed by the unsuspecting Duncan praising the appearance of Macbeth's castle: 'This castle hath a pleasant seat'.

> Irony comes from Eiron (dissembler), a clever underdog character in Greek comedy who always manages to come out on top by pretending to be stupid.

When a character uses irony intentionally, its purpose is usually to mock, to dissemble, or to mislead. Shakespeare's fondness for disguise (women pretending to be men, or characters hiding their real motives or identity) is a rich source of many shades of irony. The disguised Viola in *Twelfth Night* and the villainous Iago in *Othello* both say 'I am not what I am'. Viola's irony has comic effect, Iago's is chilling.

Dramatic and verbal irony intertwine. In *The Tempest*, Miranda sees a group of people which includes would-be murderers, and she exclaims:

> O wonder!
> How many goodly creatures are there here!
> How beauteous mankind is! O brave new world
> That has such people in't!

Miranda's remark is an example of dramatic irony, her innocent joy contrasts with the evident villainy of the men she sees. Prospero (who is aware of the villains as Miranda is not) replies, ''Tis new to thee' – a remark that the actor can, if he chooses, speak in a heavily ironic tone.

Irony is often conveyed by tone of voice or facial expression or gesture. An actor can make even seemingly neutral lines sound ironic. Students can experiment by speaking lines with and without irony. For example, in *Julius Caesar*, Casca gives a long ironic description of what happened when Caesar was offered the crown to become supreme ruler of Rome. Students can try speaking Casca's lines as ironically as possible, and then delivering them 'straight', as if Casca is giving a plain, objective account.

Oxymoron

'Parting is such sweet sorrow' says Juliet, bidding farewell to Romeo. 'Sweet sorrow' is an oxymoron: two incongruous or clashing words brought together to make a striking expression. The term oxymoron comes from two Greek words meaning 'sharp' and 'dull or foolish'. In Shakespeare's time it was fashionable to use oxymorons in love poetry, and he often employs the technique in his plays.

Much of *Romeo and Juliet* is about the clash of opposites (Montagues against Capulets, youth against age, fate against free will and so on). Those oppositions are mirrored in the play's oxymorons:

ROMEO Here's much to do with hate, but more with love:
       Why then, O brawling love, O loving hate,
       O any thing of nothing first create!
       O heavy lightness, serious vanity,
       Misshapen chaos of well-seeming forms,
       Feather of lead, bright smoke, cold fire, sick health,
       Still-waking sleep, that is not what it is!

Teachers can show students a different way of setting out Romeo's language to reveal some of the oxymorons:

- loving *versus* hate
- heavy *versus* lightness
- serious *versus* vanity
- misshapen chaos *versus* well-seeming forms
- feather *versus* lead
- bright *versus* smoke
- cold *versus* fire
- sick *versus* health
- still-waking *versus* sleep.

Students can then make up oxymorons of their own. It is often helpful to provide a few 'starters' for students to fill in the blanks:

- slow *versus* —
- cowardly *versus* —.

A physical activity that gives students insight into the structure of the oxymoron is the tableau. Students work with a partner or in small groups. They portray a still photograph or tableau of one oxymoron from Romeo's lines above or Juliet's below. The class guesses which oxymoron has been chosen.

JULIET O serpent heart, hid with a flow'ring face!
       Did ever dragon keep so fair a cave?
       Beautiful tyrant, fiend angelical!
       Dove-feathered raven, wolvish-ravening lamb!
       Despisèd substance of divinest show!
       Just opposite to what thou justly seem'st,
       A damnèd saint, an honourable villain!

Puns

The Elizabethans loved wordplay of all kinds, and puns were especially popular. When a word has two or more different meanings, the ambiguity can be used for comic effect as in *Love's Labour's Lost*:

ARMARDO By the North Pole, I do challenge thee.
COSTARD I will not fight with a pole, like a Northern man

Hamlet, acutely alert to language mocks Polonius:

POLONIUS I did enact Julius Caesar. I was killed i'th'Capitol. Brutus
 killed me.
HAMLET It was a brute part to kill so capital a calf there

Puns can be put to more serious use. In *Romeo and Juliet*, Mercutio, close to death, cannot resist making a pun:

Ask for me tomorrow, and you shall find me a grave man.

Even Lady Macbeth puns on the near sounds of gild/guilt as she speaks of the dead Duncan:

If he do bleed
I'll gild the faces of the grooms withal,
For it must seem their guilt.

Dr Johnson, the eighteenth-century scholar and critic disliked Shakespeare's fondness for wordplay, thinking it reduced the seriousness of the plays. For Johnson, a pun was 'quibble'. He wrote that for Shakespeare, 'A quibble was the fatal Cleopatra for which he lost the world and was content to lose it.'

Certainly, in Sonnet 135 Shakespeare puns relentlessly on his own name, exploiting no fewer than eight meanings of 'Will'. He puns on 'nothing' throughout *Much Ado About Nothing* and often in other plays, again taking advantage of the word's sexual connotations in Elizabethan ears. Other of his favourite punning words include 'light', 'dear', 'lie', 'kind' and the similar sounding heart/hart, sun/son, cousin/cozen (to cheat).

The pun has lost none of its power to amuse some and irritate others. Most students find puns appealing, and much contemporary humour is based on a word's capacity for communicating different meanings.

But it is all too easy in the classroom to produce laboured explanations of Shakespeare's puns. The wordplay needs handling with a light touch as it occurs. Students become alert to double meanings when they meet them in scenes they are enacting and face the challenge of how the puns might be spoken or shown. Student-invented dialogue in which mistakes arise from puns has also been found a popular and helpful activity.

Malapropism

Shakespeare suffered fools very gladly indeed. He created characters who mangle the English language with happy abandon. Some of them delight in malapropisms: inappropriate, muddled or mistaken use of words. Hostess Quickly in *King Henry IV Part 2* is a notable example, and in *Much Ado about Nothing*, Dogberry's language is filled with malapropisms:

> Comparisons are odorous
>
> Is our whole dissembly appeared?
>
> Dost thou not suspect my place? Dost thou not suspect my years?

In *Measure for Measure*, Elbow, (another comic constable) speaks in the same style: 'My wife, sir, whom I detest before heaven and your honour'.

Malapropisms present students with interesting questions of staging and response. What kind of laughter would they would wish to evoke from an audience? As ever with such problems, the most appropriate activity for students is to prepare and present their own versions!

Malapropisms are named after Mrs Malaprop who muddled up similar sounding words in Sheridan's play *The Rivals* (1775). In Shakespeare's time, a confused jumble of words and ideas was called catachresis.

Monosyllables

Shakespeare knew that simple, short words can carry a high emotional and dramatic charge. He frequently used monosyllables to create memorable phrases of compelling intensity: 'To be or not to be', 'I am not what I am', 'False face must hide what the false heart doth know'. Some highly dramatic passages are written almost entirely in monosyllables. For example, when King Lear awakes from his madness, his speech starts: 'You do me wrong to take me out of the grave…', and 64 of the 69 words are monosyllables. In *Twelfth Night*, the disguised Viola conceals her true identity from Olivia in an exchange of 68 words of which 65 are monosyllables (Act 3 Scene 1 lines 122–9).

Pronouns

You and thee

Shakespeare's use of 'thee', 'thou', 'thy' and 'thine' can initially worry students. Those concerns are eased when, through active use, students appreciate that although these old-fashioned pronouns have now dropped out of use in English, they were common in Shakespeare's time alongside 'you' and 'your'. Elizabethans were very sensitive to the different implications of using 'you' or 'thee', which sent clear social signals. Speakers would switch from one to the other depending on the social context (as is still the practice in other European languages).

In the plays, 'thou' can imply either closeness or contempt. It can signal friendship towards an equal or superiority over someone considered a social inferior. Used to address someone of higher social rank, it can be aggressive and insulting. In *Twelfth Night*, Sir Toby Belch advises Sir Andrew Aguecheek to use 'thou' as an insult.

'You' is a more formal and distant form of address suggesting respect for a superior or courtesy to a social equal. But Shakespeare never stuck rigidly to any rule, and there are always exceptions. What is important is to recognise that when a character switches from one style to the other, it suggests a change of mood or attitude towards the other character.

Students can research the use of pronouns in the play they are studying to suggest reasons why a particular form is used. The research is best done actively, by speaking lines and emphasising the pronouns. For example, in *The Two Gentlemen of Verona*, Silvia rejects the advances of the deceitful Proteus, switching from 'you' to 'thou'. Students can speak her lines emphasising 'thou' to express her contempt:

SILVIA What's your will?
PROTEUS   That I may compass yours.
SILVIA You have your wish; my will is even this,
        That presently you hie you home to bed.
        Thou subtle, perjured, false, disloyal man,
        Think'st thou I am so shallow, so conceitless,
        To be seducèd by thy flattery,
        That hast deceived so many with thy vows?
        Return, return, and make thy love amends.
        For me – by this pale queen of night I swear –
        I am so far from granting thy request
        That I despise thee for thy wrongful suit
        And by and by intend to chide myself
        Even for this time I spend in talking to thee.

Deixis: who's who

Deixis (usually pronounced dake-sis) is Greek for 'pointing'. This technical expression simply refers to those elements of speech or writing (words such as I, you, he, myself, them, there, then, and so on) whose meaning depends on knowledge of who the speaker is, and when and where he or she speaks. Deixis offers excellent opportunities for active work that enjoyably increases students' understanding of who's who in the play. Many passages in Shakespeare's plays are thickly studded with pronouns and references to others. The teacher can identify several such passages and set the following activity.

Students can work in groups, each taking the role of a character who is mentioned in some way. As one student slowly reads, everyone points emphatically to whoever is referred to. For example, in *The Tempest*, Ferdinand says:

                    Sir, she is mortal,
        But by immortal providence, she's mine.
        I chose her when I could not ask my father
        For his advice...

Students can take parts as Prospero, Miranda, Ferdinand and Alonso. Ferdinand speaks, and everyone points:

Sir *point to Prospero*

she *point to Miranda*

is mortal, But by immortal Providence *point upwards!*

She's *point to Miranda*

mine *point to Ferdinand*

I *point to Ferdinand*

chose her *point to Miranda*

when I *point to Ferdinand*

could not ask my *point to Ferdinand*

father *point to Alonso*

For his advice *point to Alonso*.

In *Romeo and Juliet*, Friar Lawrence's story from 'Romeo, there dead, was husband to that Juliet' to 'But as it seems, did violence on herself' recapitulates much of the action of the play.

Eight students can take parts (Friar Lawrence, Romeo, Juliet, Tybalt, Paris, Friar John, the Nurse, Capulet). As the Friar slowly reads, everyone points to whoever is named or implied. There are at least 100 deixis-type references in the speech (not only characters, but locations: Verona, the tomb, Friar Lawrence's cell, 'there dead' and so on).

Changing language

Some words that Shakespeare used have changed their meaning since his time. In the following list, the meaning that Shakespeare probably had in mind is given in brackets:

- silly (simple, homely, innocent)
- still (always)
- habit (dress, garment, clothes)
- naughty (wicked, worthless)
- marry (indeed)
- neat (ox, cow)
- luxurious (lustful)
- tell (count)
- owe (own)
- fond (foolish)
- sudden (violent)
- let (hinder)

- humour (temperament)
- presently (immediately)
- several (separate)
- shrewd (unpleasant)
- quick (alive, living).

Other words that Shakespeare used have dropped out of use altogether:

- haply (perhaps)
- hight (called)
- inch-meal (inch by inch)
- clepe (call)
- leman (sweetheart)
- dole (sorrow)
- wight (person)
- yare (ready, nimble)
- eke (also)
- perdy (by God)
- mocks and mows (insulting gestures and faces)
- hardiment (valour)
- tristful (sad)
- hie (hasten).

The meanings of unfamiliar words can often be understood from their context, but not always. In *The Tempest*, Caliban promises to collect 'young scamels from the rock'. 'Scamels' might be seagulls or clams, or might have meant something quite different in Shakespeare's time. Today, no-one really knows, but it is that very lack of certainty that legitimises students' imaginative speculations and enactments.

Question: How can I help my students turn Shakespeare's language from a strange enemy into a familiar friend?

Answer: By helping them to enact the language and to speak it aloud. Such enactment in the classroom employs the many active methods whereby students experience the dramatic power of the language through direct and personal response. Enactment gives students 'ownership' of the language, enabling them to use it purposefully and successfully. 'Owning' even a single line can be a motivating experience.

Exploring unfamiliar meanings can be a fascinating activity for many students. It involves searching in a good dictionary for the origins of the words and how they have changed over the years.

Students can take one scene and write down all the words that are unfamiliar. They can then find out the meanings and decide, with reasons, whether there are any they would change in performance.

Inventing language

Shakespeare wrote at a time when the English language was extremely fluid. Poets and playwrights felt free to make up words, to adapt old words, and to change old meanings to new. If a word did not exist, Shakespeare used his dramatic imagination to remould an old one or make up a new one. He played with language to invent active, lively words to suit his dramatic purposes, as the following selection shows.

1   He invented mock-Russian in *All's Well that Ends Well* for the ambush of Parolles:

    LORD DUMAINE Throca movousus, cargo, cargo, cargo.
    SOLDIERS Cargo, cargo, cargo, villianda par corbo, cargo

2   He made up nonsense words that seem to have meaning in context (skimble-skamble, hugger-mugger, hurly-burly, kickie wickie, miching mallecho).

3   He made verbs out of adjectives (happies, bolds, gentle, pale) and nouns (he childed as I fathered).

4   He added prefixes such as un- (unkinged, unsex, uncaught, unhair, undeaf, unfathered, unpeople); be- (behowl, bespeak, bemock, bemoan, bemask, bedim); en- (endanger, enthrall, engoal, enskied, entomb, entame, enwheel, encircle, enlist); and dis- (discandy – meaning to dissolve or melt, disbench, disburden), because he knew that such prefixes increased the active and dramatic potential of words.

Students can follow Shakespeare's practice and make up their own nonsense words or add prefixes to existing words. But teachers should encourage their students to give the new words a context by writing a short scene with characters who use such language (like that of Cleopatra who angrily threatens the messenger 'I'll unhair thy head').

   Shakespeare frequently uses the hyphen to create compound words that conjure up vivid images (tell-tale, love-sick, grim-looked, lack-brain). Such twofold words present exciting challenges to students' imagination, as for example in *The Tempest*:

- wide-chopped
- o'er-prized
- sea-swallowed
- up-staring
- pinch-spotted
- side-stitches
- hag-seed
- sea-nymphs
- over-topping
- sea-sorrow
- sight-outrunning
- still-vexed
- hag-born
- brine-pits
- sea-change
- fresh-brook.

Few of these hyphenated words can be pinned down to a single, exact meaning. Shakespeare may have used them because their lack of stability expresses the sense of wonder and ever-changing reality in the play. Students can create their own compound words with the hyphen and use the words to describe characters, events and actions in a short play or story of their own.

Everyday language

If you say that something smells to heaven, or that you see something in your mind's eye, or that something is a foregone conclusion, or that the course of true love never did run smooth, then you are speaking Shakespeare. These, and hundreds of other Shakespearian expressions have become part of our everyday language.

Students can listen out for such expressions in everyday speech and writing, and make a collection of those they recognise from the play they are studying. Here are just a few expressions from *Romeo and Juliet* that you can hear today:

- star-crossed lovers
- last embrace
- light of heart
- in a fool's paradise
- what must be shall be
- parting is such sweet sorrow
- above compare
- past hope
- what's in a name?
- I will not budge

- I know what
- leave to go
- let me alone
- where have you been gadding?
- if love be blind
- last farewell
- as gentle as a lamb
- on a wild goose chase
- stiff and stark
- the weakest go to the wall
- my only love
- where the devil?
- in one short minute
- I thought all for the best
- fortune's fool
- a rose by any other word would smell as sweet
- as true as steel
- cock a hoop
- past help
- we were born to die
- on pain of death
- go like lightning
- a plague on both your houses.

Many of Shakespeare's expressions have been used as headlines for articles and stories in newspapers and magazines: 'All's well that ends well', 'Much ado about nothing' and so on. Students can take on the roles of sub-editors on a newspaper whose job it is to write headlines for stories and articles. They can create a front page in which every item has a Shakespearian phrase as a headline.

Two types of language

Shakespeare suits his language to character and situation. Soldiers, lawyers, courtiers, lovers, politicians, clowns speak in their own distinctive language registers. But Shakespeare also knew how effective switching from one style to another could be, from abstract to concrete, poetic to prosaic. Macbeth's shift from complex to simple language as he gazes at his bloodstained hands is probably the best known example of Shakespeare's use of words derived from Latin or Anglo-Saxon:

> Will all great Neptune's ocean wash this blood
> Clean from my hand? No: this my hand will rather
> The multitudinous seas incarnadine
> Making the green one red

In *As You Like It*, Touchstone translates his 'courtly' language into 'common' language as he orders William to give up Audrey:

> Therefore, you clown, abandon – which is in the vulgar 'leave' – the society – which in the boorish is 'company' – of this female – which in the common is 'woman'; which together is 'abandon the society of this female', or clown, thou perishest, or, to thy better understanding, diest; or, to wit, I will kill thee, make thee away, translate thy life into death, thy liberty into bondage. I will deal in poison with thee, or in bastinado, or in steel; I will bandy with thee in faction; I will o'er-run thee with policy; I will kill thee a hundred and fifty ways.

The development of Shakespeare's language

For all his evident passion for words, Shakespeare is personally silent on language. A number of his contemporaries (Ben Jonson, Thomas Nashe, Philip Sidney, Thomas Campion) published their views of the nature and purposes of language. Shakespeare would certainly have known and read Campion's *Observations in the Art of English Poesie*, and Sidney's *A Defence of Poetry*, but he himself, for reasons no-one knows, did not set down his own views on his plays and poetry.

Shakespeare's play writing career seems to have lasted for a little over twenty years (from about the early 1590s to somewhere around 1611). No-one can know for certain the precise date of the composition of any play. Heated arguments still take place over when he might have written particular plays, but there is general agreement about the order in which he wrote them.

Every generalisation about Shakespeare must be treated with great caution. However, the list below suggests some ways in which Shakespeare's skill as a writer developed from an early play such as *Titus Andronicus*, to what was probably the final play he wrote on his own, *The Tempest*.

1   A decreasing use of rhyme, and an increasing use of blank verse.

2   An increasing preference for metaphor over simile.

3 Less obviously patterned language: verse becomes less regular, less end-stopped, and makes greater use of the caesura (mid-line pause).

4 A move away from 'sticking to the rules' (the conventions of Elizabethan poetry and drama) to much freer, more flexible use of such conventions. For example, decreasing use of alliteration and the rhetorical devices he had learned by heart in his Stratford schoolroom.

5 Imagery becomes more organic to the play, less decorative, more condensed. The early plays give an impression of the imagery being 'stuck on' as a display of ingenuity. In later plays, imagery is an integral part of Shakespeare's dramatic purpose and design, as in the highly controlled use of telescoped and complex imagery in *Macbeth*.

6 Decreasing lyrical use of language.

7 A move away from wordplay for its own sake, as in the rich conceits of *Love's Labours Lost*.

8 A greater use of prose. Shakespeare's use of prose peaks in the middle of his career with, for example, *Much Ado About Nothing* and *The Merry Wives of Windsor*.

9 Decreasing use of classical allusions.

10 Fewer instances of bombastic and 'heroic' language.

Shakespeare increasingly selected, cut, and restrained his early impulse to display, overtly and at length, his knowledge of how language worked. In contradiction of Ben Jonson's criticism, Shakespeare learned how to 'blot' his lines. He became less inclined to put all his goods in the shop window, and more willing to leave gaps for the audience's imagination to fill. For example, in early plays, characters announce their deaths explicitly – 'O I am slain.' In *Antony and Cleopatra* Charmain's dying words are 'Ah, soldier!' None of which is to diminish the dramatic or poetic quality of the early plays; they still make wonderful theatre.

The Sonnets

Shakespeare's Sonnets give teachers an opportunity to create a finely focused language course. They are not, of course, dramatic in the way that *Hamlet* and *Macbeth* are dramatic. There is no action or dialogue. Nonetheless, the Sonnets are intensely dramatic in subject, theme and imagery. The cast list is small (a poet, a young man, a woman, a rival poet), but its members are like characters in a play, caught up in the conflicts of divided emotions. Other 'characters' play their parts: death, love, and poetry itself. As personifications, they enact their own drama.

The Sonnets display all the characteristics of Shakespeare's dramatic language: antithesis, imagery, repetition, lists, verse, irony, and rhetoric. As Shakespeare reflects on the perplexities of love, his language expresses the same dynamic qualities as the language of the plays. In what seem like soliloquies or monologues, the Sonnets attempt to persuade: they plead, warn, reason, chide, argue, and assert.

The Cambridge School Shakespeare series includes *The Sonnets*, an edition specially prepared for school and college students.

Replaying the action

There are no action replays in a theatre performance. The play unfolds in a linear sequence, building atmosphere, developing character, moving to its conclusion. If you miss a word or an action, the opportunity is gone. Only after the play can the line be re-visited, thought over, discussed, enacted in a variety of different ways.

Knowledge about Shakespeare's language is best acquired actively. When the language is spoken, enacted, explored, performed and used in ways which recognise and celebrate its dramatic qualities, response to the language is enlivened.

In the classroom, there is opportunity to pause over a particular word or line or speech. It can be explored in all kinds of different ways to see how it contributes to dramatic effect. A video obviously greatly extends possibilities of re-viewing, and can be a fruitful resource for close study of language, complemented by students' own activity.

Story

'I could a tale unfold whose lightest word
Would harrow up thy soul, freeze thy young blood'

The story of the play

Stories fascinate people of all ages and cultures. One reason for Shakespeare's enduring appeal is that he is a master storyteller. Each play has its own unique story, its plot, together with many other stories within the play. All provide excellent opportunities for different kinds of active work.

There are many ways to act out *Romeo and Juliet*, and no limit to the number of ways you can tell the story of the play. You could tell it in a single sentence:

> A boy and a girl, from families that hate each other bitterly, fall in love, but everything goes wrong for them and they kill themselves rather than be parted.

Or you might tell it briefly, but put in more detail:

> The Montagues and Capulets are the two chief families of Verona. For years they have been enemies in a bitter feud. Their teenage children, Romeo, a Montague, and Juliet, a Capulet, meet by accident at a grand party and fall instantly in love. They marry in secret, but cannot escape the consequences of their families' savage quarrel. Romeo's best friend Mercutio is killed by Tybalt of the Capulets. In revenge, Romeo kills Tybalt and is banished from Verona. Friar Lawrence devises dangerous plans to help Romeo and Juliet live together in happiness, but his schemes go terribly wrong. Romeo, believing Juliet is dead, kills himself to join her in death. Juliet, finding Romeo dead, kills herself, not wishing to live without him. Their deaths end the quarrels of the Montagues and Capulets.

Or you could tell a much, much longer story, beginning:

> Long ago in the Italian city of Verona lived two young people, Romeo and Juliet. They were the children of the city's two leading families, the Montagues and the Capulets...

Getting to know the story

1 How much do students already know before they begin their study of the play? Use the first lesson for the whole class to brainstorm what they already know, or what they guess the play is about from its title (it sometimes proves helpful to provide students with the names and descriptions of a few of the major characters). List all the suggestions. Students can then work in groups to write, narrate or to act out their own short speculative version of the story.

2 When students have had some acquaintance with the play (which might be as brief as watching a 30-minute *Animated Tales* video version) they can write the story as:
   • a mini-saga (in exactly 50 words)
   • a fairy tale for young children
   • a modern novel set in today's times.

3 Write the story of the play:
   • in a single sentence
   • in a paragraph (3–4 sentences)
   • as a long story (write the opening two paragraphs).

4 Collect re-tellings of the story from theatre programmes or from books of Shakespeare stories. Compare and evaluate two versions for content (what's been left out?), style, target readership, your own response and so on.

5 The story of the play can be grasped by reading through the summary at the top of each left-hand page of the Cambridge School Shakespeare edition.

The story you tell depends on many things. Here are just a few:

• the audience for your re-telling (young children? examiners?)
• whether or not your audience has seen a production of the play (what do they already know?)

- the reasons why you tell it (to inform? to entertain? to teach a moral?)
- the style in which you tell it (factual? nursery tale? melodrama?)
- how much detail you wish to include (Rosaline? the musicians?)
- how much you use your imagination (to add extra scenes? characters' secret thoughts?).

There is no one single right story of a play, as the numerous published versions of 'stories from Shakespeare' testify. Every story is a re-telling, a different way of recounting what happens. In *Romeo and Juliet*, Shakespeare himself was re-telling a story that had been around for hundreds of years. He used his imagination to create his own dramatic version of the story he had read. For example, Mercutio is almost entirely Shakespeare's invention, and Paris does not die in other versions.

Enacting the story

Storytelling is an excellent way into Shakespeare (see pages 227–31). Students welcome a sense of knowing the whole story. But Shakespeare was a playwright, and his stories were intended for acting out. Students need early experience of fitting actions to Shakespeare's words. The following introductory lesson gives students active experience of the whole story using Shakespeare's language. The activity works best in a hall or drama studio or other empty space, but some teachers have ingeniously adapted it to the classroom without students leaving their seats.

The teacher selects ten lines which give an outline of the play and writes the ten quotations in large lettering on a large sheet of paper. The lines should be pinned up where everyone can see them, but covered so that in the lesson they can be revealed line by line. Alternatively, the lines can be prepared on a transparency for the overhead projector and kept covered, so that one line at a time can be revealed.

1   Down with the Capulets! Down with the Montagues!

2   But soft, what light through yonder window breaks?

3   O Romeo, Romeo, wherefore art thou Romeo?

4 They have made worms' meat of me. I have it.

5 And fire-eyed fury be my conduct now! (*They fight, Tybalt falls*)

6 Hang thee, young baggage, disobedient wretch!

7 Romeo, Romeo, Romeo! Here's drink – I drink to thee. (*She falls upon her bed, within the curtains*)

8 Here's to my love! (*Drinks*) Thus with a kiss I die. (*Dies*)

9 O happy dagger! This is thy sheath; (*Stabs herself*)
   There rust and let me die. (*Falls on Romeo's body and dies*)

10 For never was a story of more woe,
   Than this of Juliet and her Romeo.

The teacher narrates the story, introducing and revealing each line with suitable narrative (and sometimes adding actions). Students, working in pairs, can speak the language with accompanying actions. After the first run-through, students speak and practise the ten events in all kinds of different ways (for example, in slow motion, running). After some practice with all the lines clearly visible, the teacher covers up the lines, and the students enact ten scenes – having learned the words by heart through active practice.

Every teacher will adapt the activity to his or her own style and students, but here's how one teacher ran the first part of the lesson with a class of fifteen-year-olds:

Teacher We'll do something easy together – the whole of *Romeo and Juliet*! I'll tell the story of the play, you will speak the language and perform the actions.

Long ago, in the city of Verona, lived two families, the Montagues and Capulets, who were always at each other's throats… (*Reveals line 1*)

Students (*Adding suitable actions*) Down with the Capulets! Down with the Montagues!

Teacher But one night, at a party, young Romeo Montague fell head over heels in love with Juliet – a Capulet. After the party, he found himself in the orchard of Capulet's house. Looking up – what did he see and hear? (*Reveals line 2*)

Students (*With actions*) But soft, what light through yonder window breaks?

Teacher Yes – Juliet! And she was longing for Romeo – the son of her family's deadly enemy! (*Reveals line 3*)

Students (*With actions*) O Romeo, Romeo, wherefore art thou Romeo?

Teacher But the course of true love never runs smooth. Although Romeo and Juliet married in secret, the hatred between their families exacted its terrible toll. Romeo's best friend Mercutio challenged the fiery Tybalt, a Capulet, to a sword fight. They fought. Mercutio was killed – food for worms! (*Reveals line 4*)

Students (*With actions*) They have made worms' meat of me. I have it.

Teacher (*Speeding up the action*) Romeo was enraged! He fought with Tybalt and killed him. (*Reveals line 5*)

Students (*With actions*) And fire-eyed fury be my conduct now! (*They fight, Tybalt falls*)

Teacher (*Urgently*) Romeo was banished to Mantua, and Juliet, left behind in Verona, was about to be married to Paris – her father's choice! She refused, and what was her father's reaction? (*Reveals line 6*)

Students (*With actions*) Hang thee, young baggage, disobedient wretch!

Teacher What could she do? She loved Romeo – was married to him! But her father was forcing her to marry Paris! She went to Friar Lawrence who concocted a plan: drink this potion, it will make you seem dead. You will be put in the Capulet tomb, but you won't really be dead – just sleeping! Romeo will come from Mantua to take you away to live happily together.

So – here she is, all alone – can she trust the Friar – will the poison work? What can she do? (*Reveals line 7*)

Students (*With actions*) Romeo, Romeo, Romeo! Here's drink – I drink to thee.

Teacher But there's a terrible mix up. News reaches Romeo that Juliet really *is* dead! He rides furiously to Verona, breaks into the tomb, and resolves to kill himself with poison. He cannot bear to live without Juliet. (*Reveals line 8*)

Students (*With actions*) Here's to my love! (*Drinks*) Thus with a kiss I die. (*Dies*)

Teacher But Juliet isn't dead! She wakes, finds her beloved Romeo dead beside her – She cannot bear to live without him. What does she say and do? (*Reveals line 9*)

Students (*With actions*) O happy dagger! (*Takes Romeo's dagger*) This is thy sheath; (*Stabs herself*) There rust and let me die. (*Falls on Romeo's body and dies*)

Teacher The deaths of the lovers brought the feuding families to their senses. They grieved as the Prince of Verona pronounced the tragedy of Romeo and Juliet's story. (*Reveals line 10*)

Students (*With actions that ensure a quiet end to the sequence*) For never was a story of more woe Than this of Juliet and her Romeo.

The two aims of the lesson are to give students an active grasp of the outline of the story and to help them learn by heart some of Shakespeare's language. To achieve those aims, after the first run-through, teachers can guide students' practice of the lines and actions in some or all of the ways listed below.

1   Do one or two more run-throughs of the story with the teacher still narrating as above. Have lines 1–10 fully on view.

2   Promenade: do another practice, but this time the students run 10 paces to perform each line in a different place. This gives added urgency and enjoyment.

3   Give students five or ten minutes to practice on their own, to work on accompanying movements and gestures to the language.

4   Set students to perform a 'fast-forward' version. All the language must be spoken, all the actions performed in as short a time as possible.

5   Students perform the play backwards: lines 10-1!

6   Set a tableau activity. Each pair chooses just one line that they like. They freeze into a still picture of that moment. The other students' task is to guess which line is being portrayed.

An effective way of doing the tableau activity that saves both time and embarrassment, is to divide the class into two groups. As one group looks away, each pair in the other group freezes into position. The result is a 'sculpture park'. When the first group of students turn round, they see various statues depicting moments from the play set out before their eyes. Their task is to identify as many of the sculptures as possible (see pages 192–5).

Teachers and students can of course invent many other activities of their own. But what the teacher should have in mind is that the lesson is leading up to a 'check your learning' activity. After repeated variations of practising the sequence, the lines can be covered up and the students given a challenge: now try it from memory – all the language, all the actions, all the story!

If the students have had sufficiently varied practice, their recall of the sequence and the language is impressive. In an enjoyable way, they have acquired a firm grasp of the outline of the play, and some imaginatively charged lines.

This introductory lesson can be used with classes of all ages and abilities. Teachers can vary the tasks and the pace of working to suit the students (most students respond well to the pressure of pace). It is important not to embark on the 'without the lines' activity until after a number of varied practices, to ensure the students can successfully recall the lines and perform the story.

For most classes this very active lesson, using ten short extracts, is complete in itself. It makes a lively scene-setting, appetite-whetting introduction to the play. If there is time, some teachers end the lesson with student discussion. Such discussion can take different forms:

• students re-tell the story to each other
• students speculate about the characters (just who was Tybalt?)
• students compile a list of questions about gaps or puzzles in the story.

This first outline necessarily leaves out much, but it begins to give students a feeling for the shape of the play. And most importantly, the physical activity imprints some language firmly in their minds.

The 10-line technique can be used for any play. The teacher simply selects nine or ten moments that he or she thinks are particularly significant, which have powerful language, and which provide a brief outline of the story. Teachers will be all too aware of the gaps, but there will always be gaps in any story of the play.

Teachers should select their own key moments and lines, rather than simply using the examples given above and below. Many teachers have adapted the *Romeo and Juliet* outline above, substituting for line 4 a version of Mercutio's final words: 'A plague on both your houses!'

Make up your own linking commentary to accompany this short version of *Macbeth*.

1 All hail, Macbeth, that shalt be king hereafter!

2 Look like th'innocent flower, but be the serpent under't.

3 Is this a dagger which I see before me?

4 O horror horror horror!
 Ring the alarum bell! Murder and treason!

5 O, full of scorpions is my mind dear wife!

6 O treachery! Fly, good Fleance, fly, fly, fly.
 Thou mayst revenge.

7 (*Sees the ghost*) Avaunt and quit my sight!
 Let the earth hide thee!

8 Double, double toil and trouble;
 Fire burn, and cauldron bubble.

9 What you egg! Young fry of treachery! (*He stabs him*)
 He has killed me, mother!

10 Out damned spot! Out I say!
 Here's the smell of the blood still.

11 Lay on, Macduff,
 And damned be him that first cries, 'Hold, enough!' (*Exeunt fighting*)

Teachers can adapt such outlines as appropriate for particular classes. For example, for some students, moments 4, 6, 9, 10, and 11 can be reduced to single lines.

Stories in the play

Every Shakespeare play contains all kinds of stories. Each of these stories within a play can be acted out by students. For example, in the first Act of *Romeo and Juliet*, the Prologue outlines the whole story of the play in a fourteen-line sonnet. Benvolio recounts the story of the fight between the Montagues and Capulets. Montague then tells of Romeo's strange behaviour. The Nurse relates her long story of Juliet's childhood. Mercutio spins out his fanciful tale of Queen Mab, and in a few lines Capulet and his cousin hint at their long ago 'dancing days'.

Such stories have many functions, helping to create character, atmosphere and context. They fill gaps and move the play's action along. Some stories tell of events that happened before the play opens, as, for example, early in *Hamlet*, when Horatio explains why Denmark is arming for war. Other stories relate events that happen off-stage, or recapitulate the events of the play, or give glimpses of characters who never appear but whose actions and personalities help to create the imaginative world of the play, notably for example, Sycorax, the mother of Caliban in *The Tempest*.

On stage, most of these stories within the play are usually only spoken, not acted out. But they offer exciting opportunities for groups of students to enact each event as one or more persons narrate. In *Macbeth*, King Duncan is told the story of the execution of the Thane of Cawdor for treason:

> ...very frankly he confessed his treasons,
> Implored your highness' pardon, and set forth
> A deep repentance. Nothing in his life
> Became him like the leaving it. He died
> As one that had been studied in his death,
> To throw away the dearest thing he owed
> As 'twere a careless trifle.

Cawdor's story is packed with action that gives a vivid insight into character (he confessed, implored pardon from King Duncan, and repented). Shakespeare invites the audience to speculate imaginatively on just what Cawdor did, behaving with impressive dignity in the face of death.

Roman Polanski's film of *Macbeth* includes a sequence portraying

Cawdor throwing away his life ('the dearest thing he owed') with studied indifference. Students preparing a showing of his death pay close attention to the detail of the language as they seek a suitable style, tone and mood for an imaginative dramatisation of the story.

Recapitulating the story

Shakespeare often gives a character a speech that in some way recapitulates the story of the play. Such recapitulations provide students with illuminating opportunities to enact the story as seen by one of the characters. For example, near the end of *Romeo and Juliet*, Friar Lawrence's recapitulation has well over two dozen actions for students to perform. The stories that immediately follow Friar Lawrence's, told by Balthasar, Paris' page and the Prince, add more than a dozen further events for enactment.

In *Hamlet*, Horatio gives a highly condensed summary of the story he will tell. It lists seven elements of Hamlet's story:

> So you shall hear
> Of carnal, bloody, and unnatural acts.
> Of accidental judgements, casual slaughters,
> Of deaths put on by cunning and forced cause,
> And in this upshot, purposes mistook
> Fallen on th'inventors' heads.

Students can identify each element and prepare a short drama that acts out each: carnal (acts), bloody (acts) and so on. The teacher usually stipulates how related to the play the enactments should be. For students who are not yet familiar with *Hamlet*, a completely free response to each of the seven elements could be appropriate.

If students have studied *Hamlet*, they can select quotations or events from the play that illustrate each element of the story. For example, unnatural acts might be illustrated with the Ghost's 'Revenge his foul and most unnatural murder' and a tableau of that moment in the play. Students who undertake this challenge can test the validity of Horatio's description of the story he proposes to tell.

Interestingly, *Titus Andronicus*, written long before *Hamlet*, contains a story summary in a style strikingly similar to Horatio's lines:

> 'Twill vex thy soul to hear what I shall speak,
> For I must talk of murders, rapes and massacres,
> Acts of black night, abominable deeds,
> Complots of mischief, treason, villainies,
> Ruthful to hear, yet piteously performed.

This example can also be used for an enactment activity. As written work, students can summarise, in similar style, the Shakespeare play they are currently studying.

Perhaps the best known story recapitulation is that by Lady Macbeth, who, while sleepwalking, recalls crucial events in the play. Students can choose to work on the whole scene, involving the Doctor and Gentlewoman who watch the sleepwalker, or they can concentrate solely on Lady Macbeth's language:

> Yet here's a spot.
> Out damned spot! Out, I say! One, two. Why then, 'tis time to do't. Hell is murky. Fie, my lord, fie, a soldier, and afeared? What need we fear? Who knows it, when none can call our power to account? Yet who would have thought the old man to have had so much blood in him?
>
> The Thane of Fife had a wife. Where is she now? What, will these hands ne'er be clean? No more o'that, my lord, no more o'that. You mar all with this starting.
>
> Here's the smell of the blood still; all the perfumes of Arabia will not sweeten this little hand. O, O, O.
>
> Wash your hands, put on your night-gown, look not so pale. I tell you yet again, Banquo's buried; he cannot come out on's grave.
> To bed, to bed; there's knocking at the gate. Come, come, come, come, give me your hand; what's done cannot be undone. To bed, to bed, to bed.

Groups of students can act the pictures she sees in her mind as she speaks, perhaps using lines and actual events from earlier moments in the play. One student group chose to act as the three witches, orchestrating Lady Macbeth's movements and miming actions to her words. The imaginative possibilities for students and actors alike have proved inexhaustible. Just what does she do as she says 'O, O, O'?

Point of view narratives

A Shakespeare play is not a story told from a single point of view, but through a series of voices. Unlike a novel, there is no omniscient narrator, no single storyteller. Shakespeare does not impose his viewpoint, but allows each character to express his or her own thoughts and feelings. The point of view shifts each time a different character speaks.

Each point of view is partial, because each character has only limited knowledge of what happens in the whole story. For example, Juliet would have a different story to tell from that of her Nurse. Hamlet's account of events in Denmark would not be the same as that told by Gertrude or by Rosencrantz.

Students can tell the story from the point of view of one of the characters in the play. How much does the character know, what have they seen or heard, what can they guess or infer? Marginal characters may have special stories to tell, for example the servant who brings to Macbeth news of the approaching English army, and is called a 'cream-faced loon' for his pains. What else might he have seen and heard as a member of Macbeth's household?

Ariel's story

The Tempest contains wonderful stories suitable for acting out: Prospero's usurpation, Ariel's story of the shipwreck, the story of Sycorax, Caliban's story. The following teacher-directed activity on Ariel's story of the shipwreck is valuable preparation for independent work. It needs a large empty space.

Students should stand in a large circle and note who is on either side of them. Each student should have a copy of the script open at the description of the shipwreck.

The teacher can now walk round the circle allocating a small piece of the script to each student and asking them to quietly repeat back the line(s) they have been given. Because each student has a copy of the script they can follow the lines as they are allocated.

In the example below, the lines below have been divided into 30 units, but teachers may wish to give students larger or smaller sections of the script. If this is the first time the students have undertaken such an activity, it is advisable to use very short units. The speeches can be cut or combined to make a coherent presentation suitable for the number of students and their aptitudes.

PROSPERO Come away, servant, come; I'm ready now.

Approach, my Ariel. Come!

ARIEL All hail, great master, grave sir, hail!

I come to answer thy best pleasure

Be it to fly

To swim

To dive into the fire

To ride on the curled clouds

To thy strong bidding task Ariel, and all his quality

PROSPERO Hast thou, spirit, performed to point the tempest That I bade thee?

ARIEL I boarded the King's ship

Now on the beak, now in the waist, the deck

In every cabin, I flamed amazement

Sometime I'd divide and burn in many places

On the topmast, the yards and bowsprit

Would I flame distinctly

Then meet and join

Jove's lightning, the precursors O'th' dreadful thunder-claps

More momentary and sight-out running were not

The fires and cracks of sulphurous roaring

The most mighty Neptune seemed to besiege

And make his bold waves tremble

Yea, his dread trident shake

Not a soul but felt a fever of the mad

And played some tricks desperation

All but mariners plunged in the foaming brine

And quit the vessel, then all a-fire with me

The King's son, Ferdinand, with hair up-staring

Then like reeds not hair

Was the first man that leaped

Cried 'Hell is empty, And all the devils are here'.

Teachers will know which students can probably cope with longer sections. It might be appropriate to have only one student speak as Prospero, but it is inadvisable to be seen 'selecting' particular lines for particular students. Better to start with the student to play Prospero and hand out the other lines to the other students as they stand.

The students should keep the circle intact and first speak all the lines, in order, around the circle, so that everyone hears the whole story. This is likely to be a very undramatic presentation, but it serves the purpose of reminding each student who speaks immediately before their own line.

Next, the students need to memorise their words, but with their scripts open until the teacher decides the time has come to rely on memory. Any of the following activities can be used to help memorisation. Students can be reminded that Ariel is 'an airy spirit'.

1   Move around the room greeting other students with your line.
2   Greet other students with your line as if it is the funniest joke in the world.
3   Greet other students with your line as if it were the saddest story ever told.
4   Shout your line three times at the ceiling.
5   Whisper your line 3 times to the floor.
6   You are a spy! Speak your line confidentially to several other students. No-one else must hear.

7   Close your eyes, stretch out your arms, walk slowly around the room, repeating your line aloud as you walk. Don't bump into anyone else!

8   Jump up and down in the spot, saying one word at each jump.

To help students' confidence, they can be asked to quickly reassemble into the circle (they will remember who was on each side of them) and then simply speak the words in order (without scripts) to hear the whole story. After due praise, the students might need to move individually around the room on a few further memorising exercises.

After a few minutes, the teacher can ask the class to freeze and tell the story with students standing just where they are. The successful result gives great pleasure to the students as the whole sequence is spoken, in order, from memory.

It is now time to work out a dramatic presentation. The students with Prospero's lines should stand in the centre of the room while the Ariels stand or crouch around the walls. Prospero calls Ariel to him:

> Come away, servant, come; I'm ready now.
> Approach, my Ariel. Come!

Each Ariel in turn then moves to join Prospero in the centre of the room, speaking their line and using gestures and moving in whatever way they think suitable to the language. Each Ariel should wait until the preceding Ariel has arrived at the centre. The Ariels will invent a wide range of movement and gestures. The activity can be re-run with Prospero in another part of the room, or perhaps walking slowly around the room.

Another variation is to run the sequence with the Ariels clustered as close to Prospero as they can get. However, some students find such close physical contact uncomfortable, so teachers should not insist on very tight packing if it is obviously unhelpful. The clustered students speak the whole story again, putting as much imagination and urgency into their language as possible. Whispering is effective, as is speaking fearfully or gleefully. So, too, is a dream-like, slowly spoken version. Everyone might repeat the final 'Hell is empty' lines.

Students' sense of achievement is palpable, with a shared sense of enjoyment at what the group has been able to achieve co-operatively. Every student has made their own unique contribution by voice, gesture and movement to a whole class presentation. The personal ownership of just a few words, and the shared sense of ownership of a group presentation is a motivating experience that increases confidence and self-esteem.

As is evident, this is a teacher-directed activity. The teacher directs and orchestrates the students. It can be a valuable step towards the students taking responsibility for their own presentation. It also shows that it is legitimate to share out the lines in all kinds of ways for dramatic presentation. One way of following-up is to use the same lines, but to divide the class into smaller groups of seven to ten students whose task is to work out their own presentation of the story in any way they wish. Student-directed presentation is the goal of such activities, with students choosing the lines and the mode of enactment.

Dramatic construction

Shakespeare took the plots for his plays from all kinds of sources: history books, romances, poems, folktales, and myths. He transformed the stories he found into enthralling dramatic action. Because he did not invent the stories for his plays, some critics have denied Shakespeare's ability as a storyteller, claiming that his genius lies entirely in language. But that is surely disproved by the international success of his plays, spoken in German, Japanese, and a host of other languages. Cassius' words in *Julius Caesar* are eerily prophetic: Shakespeare's plays are now performed 'in states unborn and accents yet unknown' to Elizabethan and Jacobean England. Such worldwide success is testament not only to Shakespeare's portrayal of character, but to his skill as a dramatic storyteller: his dramatic construction. In every play, Shakespeare juxtaposes speeches and scenes so that each comments upon and deepens the meaning of the other.

In *The Two Gentlemen of Verona* the servants ironically reflect the main love plot. In *Macbeth*, the Porter scene is much more than a comic interlude in its echoes of the themes of equivocation, deceit, ambition, and evil. Shakespeare's genius for dramatic construction is powerfully obvious in *King Henry IV Part 1* as he interweaves the comic and political plots to explore the theme of order and disorder. Scenes of court, rebels and tavern alternate, and Falstaff creates an ironic parallel and contrast to the main plot as he conducts his own 'rebellion' and questions the value of honour.

Character

'What is Pyramus? A lover or a tyrant?'

Introduction

Shakespeare's plays present an immense range of memorable characters who spring to life afresh in every performance, every active lesson. They offer students many opportunities to explore the rich variety of human experience: Hamlet, Macbeth, Malvolio, Falstaff and Hal, Romeo and Juliet, Nick Bottom and his fellow Mechanicals. Minor characters also possess their own fascinating possibilities for active work. In *The Comedy of Errors*, Dr Pinch has only a dozen lines, but his description makes him leap off the page, inviting portrayal in action or art or parody:

> A hungry, lean-faced villain,
> A mere anatomy, a mountebank,
> A threadbare juggler and a fortune-teller,
> A needy, hollow-eyed, sharp-looking wretch,
> A living dead man.

Nearly every character in Shakespeare is given his or her distinctive voice, enabling the actor to create a unique personality. For example, the Nurse in *Romeo and Juliet* enters with a style of speaking that is in striking contrast to all the audience has so far heard in the play:

> Now by my maidenhead at twelve year old,
> I bade her come. What, lamb! What, ladybird!
> God forbid, where's this girl? What, Juliet!

The titles of Shakespeare's plays might seem to predict that the major focus will be on particular named characters. Twenty-three titles are personal names: *Macbeth, Othello, Coriolanus, Romeo and Juliet, King Lear, King Henry V* and so on. But there is no strict rule: neither Julius Caesar nor Cymbeline appear to be the major characters of the plays bearing their names.

Part of the appeal of studying Shakespeare's characters is the mixed feelings they evoke. Hamlet and Prince Hal display both admirable and unpleasant qualities. Hamlet laughs at his own absurdities and yet shrugs off the arranged killing of old student friends. Prince Hal can be seen both as an ideal Christian prince and as a Machiavellian manipulator. It is this capacity for defying simplifying, single categorisation, that makes Shakespeare's characters so suitable for students' classroom explorations: they are perennially open to fresh portrayal and interpretation.

Interest in character is an abiding human preoccupation, its study a necessary part of any education. Character study is a potent source of learning. Students can recognise, understand, and identify with fictional characters, and can empathise with their emotional and moral predicaments.

In the plays, language *is* character, and students gain insight by imaginatively inhabiting the script, speaking the characters' lines, performing their actions, experiencing their feelings and thoughts, their relationships with others, the dilemmas in which they find themselves. These active approaches to character are not substitutes for intellectual analysis, but enrichingly complementary to it. Valuable in their own right, they resource students' discussion, written work, and design activities.

Perhaps the best known example of a character-based approach to Shakespeare's plays is that of A. C. Bradley, first published in 1904 in *Shakespearian Tragedy*. Certain critics frown on such inquiries which treat characters as if they were living human beings with emotional relationships with others, and an actual past before the play begins. They mock investigations that speculate about characters' backgrounds.

L. C. Knights' ironically titled essay 'How many children had Lady Macbeth?' is representative of those critics who wish to treat the plays as dramatic poems. Other critics pedantically point out the fictional nature of drama: neither the characters nor the situations are real ('How *can* you possibly believe in Hamlet as if he were a living person?'). Such a stance is misplaced intellectualism, a narrow and impoverished textuality. It is resolutely anti-dramatic in its neglect of the very evident appeal of character study. Shakespeare's characters are indeed fictions, and they can be played in very different ways (as the examples of Hamlet below illustrate), but they have an uncanny and delightful way of living in the mind and heart.

Phil Bowen, 1978.

Sarah Bernhardt, 1899.

Mark Rylance, 1988.

Master Betty, a thirteen-year-old actor who was a famously successful Hamlet in 1804–5.

Fundamental questions

Like an actor in rehearsal seeking his or her character, students can use a simple inquiry framework of four questions to guide their own investigations of character. In pairs or small groups they can take parts to speak aloud in a short scene or episode. After two readings, which give an initial impression of character, students should remain in role and, based on the evidence of the language they have spoken, explore answers to four questions.

1   *Who* am I?

2   *What* am I saying?

3   *Why* am I saying it?

4   *How* do I speak?

The answers to question 1 are usually factual, identifying the character and his or her relationships to other characters. For example 'Lady Macbeth, wife of Macbeth.' Many students also like to make suggestions about the character's appearance, costume, props and so on.

For question 2, a brief statement of meaning is typical: 'I'm telling Macbeth to stop worrying so much, and to take the daggers back.'

The exploration of motives needed to answer question 3 is usually the lengthiest response. It can involve a host of possible reasons, and students should be encouraged to speculate freely about motivations, feelings and thoughts. The following framework helps many students organise their responses:

• Because I want... (what the character wants to achieve)

• Because I think... (what the character thinks about the other characters and the situation they are in)

• Because I feel... (fears, hopes, love, hate, envy, contempt, and so on)

• Because this is what I'm like... (statements about the character's nature).

Answers to the last question are concerned with speech style, tone, emphases, speed, pauses, gestures, movements, facial expressions, and so on.

One student transformed this framework into her own '5 Ms': meaning, mind, mood, motivation and method.

Complexity of character

Few of Shakespeare's characters could be called 'flat' or 'two-dimensional', but it is obvious that some are far more complex than others. Hamlet clearly has many more facets to his personality than Laertes or the Gravedigger. Duncan and the Porter are much less complex characters than Macbeth.

In *Romeo and Juliet,* Tybalt and the Nurse are firmly established from their very first appearance. They are recognisably human, but they can also be seen to represent character types. Tybalt is the quarrelsome man, a contrast to the peaceful Benvolio and witty Mercutio. The Nurse provides an earthy contrast to Juliet's idealised view of love. Both show a narrower range of emotion, behaviour and thought than the two major characters, Romeo and Juliet.

A valuable technique for students is to take a less complex character and to follow him or her through the play. Because such characters have fairly few lines, it is an relatively easy process for students to speak all of a character's language to see how far, if at all, it changes.

For example, Tybalt in *Romeo and Juliet* speaks only 36 lines in total. But the language of ill-will that Shakespeare consistently puts into his mouth marks Tybalt out as an angry, violent man. When first he arrives to find the servants of the Montagues and Capulets fighting and Benvolio trying to stop them, Tybalt's words have unambiguous meaning and his motivation is evident:

> What, art thou drawn among these heartless hinds?
> Turn thee, Benvolio, look upon thy death.
> What, drawn and talk of peace? I hate the word,
> As I hate hell, all Montagues, and thee.
> Have at thee, coward.

His intentions towards Benvolio are quite clear – he certainly doesn't intend to join him in peace-keeping! But just how he speaks the lines is open to a range of possibilities, as are the actions that accompany his words.

The actor playing Tybalt (described in the script as 'fiery' and 'bloody') might portray him as a violent, brainless thug; or as a silky and sinister dandy; or as a dangerous psychopath, alternately laughing and snarling. He might even play him as someone who is really a coward at heart, but tries to put on a courageous face. In each case the words are the same but the speaking style is different.

A similar activity, in which students follow a major character through the play, quickly reveals a much greater range of action, thought and feeling. The complex characters behave differently with different characters and in different situations. They display many aspects of their personalities, and are by no means consistent. Their personality has different, even conflicting elements, a mixture of good and bad. This potential for many different but justified interpretations makes Shakespeare's characters eminently suitable for classroom work.

Such complex characters cannot be judged by first impressions. What he or she is like emerges as the play develops. For example, Hamlet has been variously described as a noble prince, a madman, an avenger, a philosopher, an unhappy adolescent, a man tortured by irreconcilable moral dilemmas, and in a host of other ways. He is at different times brave, depressed, disillusioned, harsh, hesitant, cruel, resentful, remorseless, mad, sarcastic and so on. His mood swings are obvious, shown in a small selection of his language:

> O that this too too solid flesh would melt

> Now could I drink hot blood

>   Bloody, bawdy, villain!
> Remorseless, treacherous, lecherous, kindless villain!
> Oh, vengeance! Why, what an ass am I!

> What a piece of work is a man! How noble in reason, how infinite in faculties, in form and moving how express and admirable...

> There's a divinity that shapes our ends,
> Rough-hew them how we will

> The rest is silence

Another way in which students can think about different characters is to ask whether they seem to be 'observed' (for example, Tybalt), or 'entered into' (for example, Hamlet). That is, how far a character seems to invite psychological involvement, how much of the inner experience of a character is shared with an audience. Hamlet constantly takes the audience into his innermost thoughts and feelings, but Tybalt does not. Even a major character like Coriolanus (who has no soliloquies) usually expresses his thoughts and feelings in action rather than inviting the audience to share them.

Language and character

Shakespeare's characters *are* the language they speak. King Lear's language is unmistakably his own. Its distinctive features (command, assertion, question, oath) are revealed only a few minutes after the play opens. His first words are imperious command to Gloucester:

> Attend the lords of France and Burgundy, Gloucester.

The order is followed by an emphatic assertion of his decision to divide his kingdom between his three daughters. He sets his daughters a love test. Whoever loves him most, will get the largest share:

> Meantime we shall express our darker purpose
> Give me the map there...
>
> ...Gonerill,
> Our eldest born, speak first.

Gonerill and Regan make flattering replies, but Cordelia, the youngest refuses to play Lear's game:

LEAR   What can you say to draw
              A third more opulent than your sisters? Speak.
CORDELIA Nothing, my lord
LEAR Nothing?
CORDELIA Nothing.
LEAR Nothing will come of nothing, speak again.

Cordelia's continued refusal to humour her father provokes another incredulous question, followed by a threatening oath:

LEAR So young, and so untender?
CORDELIA So young, my lord, and true.
LEAR Let it be so, thy truth then be thy dower.
              For by the sacred radiance of the sun,
              The mysteries of Hecate and the night,
              By all the operations of the orbs
              From whom we do exist and cease to be,

> Here I disclaim all my parental care,
> Propinquity and property of blood,
> And as a stranger to my heart and me
> Hold thee from this forever.

Lear's language style of command, assertion, question, oath, continues throughout the play, even though it moves into a softer register in the final scenes.

Introduction to activities

A range of activities all focused on exploring Shakespeare's characters follows. As always in this book, the stress is on active, student-centred learning. Shakespeare provides scripts, not texts, and scripts are completed by performance.

Cast the play

Students can cast the play from well known figures: politicians or pop stars, singers or sportsmen and women, television personalities and so on. Alternatively, the play could be cast from the teachers in your school or college - or from other students in the class.

Job interviews

Staging a job-application interview can be both insightful and funny. Lady Macbeth applies for a post as a nursery nurse, Mercutio interviews for the job of undertaker's assistant, Iago for the post of bank manager.

Students can work in twos or threes, and have about fifteen minutes to prepare their character for the interview, or to prepare as interviewers. There are many variations of the job-interview technique.

1   The names of the major characters in a play can be written on slips of paper and one slip given to each group of students (so that no group knows any other groups' characters). Each character is interviewed for the same job. The interviews are

conducted without the interviewee's name being mentioned. Watching students have to guess which character is applying.

2 Characters can apply for obviously incompatible posts. For example, Tybalt might apply for a social worker's job; Juliet for the post of prison warder; Richard III for a post as stress counsellor.

3 Characters can act as interviewers. Lady Macbeth might wish to employ a reliable servant, or King Duncan a bodyguard. Alternatively, a group of characters can form an interviewing panel: for example, Verona needs a police chief and an interview panel is formed from characters in *Romeo and Juliet* to interview candidates.

4 Students can step into role as a character and write a letter applying for a job, describing how they are particularly suited to the post. They might attach the character's curriculum vitae (CV) to the letter, detailing qualifications and experience.

Absent characters

Every Shakespeare play has fascinating absent characters who are mentioned, but never appear. Students can write or speak as those characters, giving their viewpoint on the play and other characters. In *Romeo and Juliet*, absent characters include Rosaline and everyone listed in Capulet's party invitation especially 'the lively Helena'; in *Macbeth*, Cawdor, the sea captain, King Edward, and Sweno; in *Hamlet*, Old Fortinbras, Yaughan, Yorick, Lamord, the King of England, and a Player.

This is your life

In the popular television programme *This is your life*, a presenter takes a well known person through the events and personalities involved in his or her life. As the presenter narrates, various friends and relatives appear to tell their part in the story.

Students can work in groups of around eight or more. Each group chooses a Shakespeare character as the subject of the programme. One person in each group takes the role of presenter, another takes the character (for example, Macbeth) whose life will be told. The other students take on appropriate roles (for example, the three witches, Banquo, the cream-faced loon, Lady Macbeth).

This activity usually works best over two lessons: one devoted to preparation, the second for each group to make its presentation.

Obituaries

Many of Shakespeare's characters die in the course of the play. Writing obituaries is a valuable way for students to explore both character and point of view. Different obituary writers will see a character quite differently. Malcolm's description and evaluation of Macbeth's life and achievements is unlikely to mirror an obituary written by Seyton, Macbeth's armour bearer.

Students should write two versions of a character's obituary; each is by a different character in the play. Another obituary might give the student's own views.

Point of view

As noted on page 104, a play is unlike a novel in that it is not told from the viewpoint of one character or an omniscient narrator. The point of view shifts as each character speaks.

In *The Tempest*, Caliban's experience offers vivid and dramatic ways of showing how much depends on point of view. Students can tell Caliban's story first from his own point of view, then from Prospero's. The story can be told as a narrative (spoken or written) or can be enacted by groups as series of tableaux, a mime, or a short play.

In students' presentations, Prospero invariably sees Caliban as savage and untrustworthy. But some students have presented very sympathetic portraits of Caliban. They depict his innocent child-like relationship with Miranda, in which a misunderstood friendly action condemns him into slavery and warps his nature.

Students can write, tell or perform different accounts of the same event as seen by different characters. For example, how was Macbeth's banquet experienced by Macbeth, Lady Macbeth, Ross, a servant? How was the play scene in *Hamlet* experienced by Hamlet, Claudius, Ophelia?

Hot-seating

A student can step into role as a character and be questioned about his or her motives, feelings and actions. A popular variant of this activity is 'Meeting the media'.

Meeting the media

Today, most major public figures have to face the media. They meet a group of newspaper, radio and television journalists, to make a prepared statement and to answer questions.

The class can be divided into small groups. Students in some groups take roles as two or three of a play's characters. In the other groups, students are reporters of different types (for example, the newspaper journalists are divided into 'popular' and 'serious' papers and so on). Each group has fifteen minutes to prepare.

Each 'character' group prepares a statement of their view of the story to deliver at a press conference. Each 'media' group prepares a list of questions they want answered.

It is all too easy for one enthusiastic and powerful reporter to hog all the time available (as happens in real life). The teacher will need to set simple rules by which the media conference will be run. For example, each media group could be restricted to four questions (with one follow-up question each). Characters must not give monosyllabic replies.

Public and private

Should a character's speech sound as if it is spoken to a large audience or to a single listener? This may seem a simple question to answer, because (apart from soliloquies, see page 125) it is usually clear to whom any speech is addressed. But the style of delivery is always open to experiment. After all, Queen Victoria once complained about her Prime Minister, Mr Gladstone, that in their private conversations, 'He addresses me like a public meeting!'

Students can be asked to speak some lines as a public utterance, then as a private confidence, accompanying the language with appropriate gestures. Public deliveries can be made standing on a platform or desk, with other students grouped around. Private deliveries can be seated, head to head.

Students can attempt the activity with any speech but three of Claudius' speeches in *Hamlet* are valuable examples.

1 'Though yet of Hamlet...'.

2 'O my offence is rank...'.

3 'O this is the poison of deep grief...'.

Students should be encouraged to explore a variety of styles for each mode. The private style might be intimate, or sorrowfully or fearfully whispered. The public style could be as a devious politician, a fundamentalist preacher or a television news announcer.

As a follow-up to this activity, students can discuss whether certain characters' speeches necessarily require a public or private style.

Props

The teacher provides a simple prop such as a chair, a mirror, or a spoon. Students can show how different characters in the play they are studying would use the prop in a stage performance. The actions should suggest something important about each character's personality.

Free-wheeling associations

Students can choose a character and decide what they think would be his or her favourite film, television programme, hobby, and holiday location. In school or college, what would be the character's favourite lesson? What job would he or she be doing today? Students should stay in role and show a typical gesture, action and facial expression for their character.

List of characters

Every edition of a Shakespeare play includes a list of characters. Every theatre programme gives a cast list showing which actor plays which character. Some lists are arranged in order of appearance, but many are in order of social status in Shakespeare's time: kings, princes and noblemen at the top, women at the bottom. Juliet, Lady Macbeth and Cleopatra finish up at the foot of such lists, after the male servants. Relationships are male-defined: Juliet is 'Capulet's daughter'. A modern alternative is to list characters in order of dramatic importance. Here, Juliet would head the list of the Capulet family, and Capulet himself be described as 'her father'.

Students beginning a play can often make very convincing groupings. Given a random or traditional list of characters, students can discuss why Juliet is placed where she is, or how characters might be grouped. They can then rewrite or re-design and illustrate the list to make it as helpful as possible to a modern theatre audience.

Ranking characters

Ordering characters by particular criteria provides many opportunities for active and written work. Some activities can be undertaken quite early on in a Shakespeare course. Others are better attempted after students have had some experience of the play.

Individual work

Students can rank characters according to personal preference. Each student can draw a line about twenty centimetres long, labelling one end 'Character I'd most like to play' and the other end 'Character I'd least like to play'. Each character can be placed somewhere on the line.

Variations on this activity can use different criteria for personal choice:

* character I like most ... like least
* character I identify with most ... identify with least
* character I learn from most ... learn from least
* character I feel involved with most ... involved with least.

Group work

When students have some familiarity with the play, the teacher can divide the class into groups of about twelve, and prepare about a dozen slips of paper with the name of a character on each. Each student in a group is given a slip, and takes the role of that character. The task is for the group to line up in order of age, social status or some other quality. There will be animated discussion as students argue about just which character stands next to which. Possible ranges are:

- oldest to youngest
- highest social status to lowest social status
- most moral (good) to least moral (bad)
- most dramatically important to least dramatically important
- most trustworthy (honest) to least trustworthy (dishonest).

Other qualities that are particular to the play can be used. For example, in *The Tempest*, characters can be ranked as 'most loved by Prospero' to 'most hated by Prospero'. In *Macbeth*, the ordering could be 'most false' (appearance does not match reality) to 'least deceitful' (appearance matches reality); or 'most ambitious' to 'least ambitious' and so on. Every play has its own distinctive preoccupations and these ranking of characters' qualities are helpful ways of developing students' insight into themes (see pages 128–37).

Journeys through the play

Many of Shakespeare's characters change over the course of their play. King Lear learns, through intense suffering, the folly of his self-centred authoritarianism. Hamlet's long journey reaches its fulfilment in stoic acceptance, recognising that 'the readiness is all'. Othello descends from the calm, almost musical confidence of:

> Keep up your bright swords, for the dew will rust them

to the tortured fractured language of mad jealousy:

> Pish! Noses, ears, and lips. Is't possible? — Confess? Handkerchief? O devil!

Malvolio's journey: This is how different productions have presented Malvolio at particular moments of *Twelfth Night*.

Students select a character and invent a succession of tableaux to show his or her emotional/physical progress through the play. Suitable quotations from the script can accompany each image.

Students can find ways of showing the 'emotional journey through the play' of one or two characters of their choice. Working individually, students might present a series of illustrations, short quotations, or an essay, identifying what each character has learned. Groups of students could show four to six moments, enacted as mimes or tableaux or brief playlets, together with some language for each moment shown. The journey is the character's emotional or spiritual progress expressed as events, feelings, thoughts, bodily postures, and so on (see page 123).

Two student groups both showed King Lear's journey as a six-stage progress. Each began in absolute authority, and moved through rage and madness to contrition, brief happiness and death. One presentation lasted about six minutes and was a series of 'mini-scenes' from the play which flowed one after the other from side to side of the classroom. The other group presented a six-person tableau, each student frozen into an appropriate posture, whilst a student narrator moved in sequence behind the tableau, pausing to speak a line or lines at each of the six expressions of Lear's journey.

Relationships

Every character is partly defined by his or her relationships with other characters. Actual relationships (son, brother, servant) are given in the list of characters for each play; the more interesting dramatic and emotional relationships can be explored by students in the classroom.

With other characters

Students can work in pairs, and prepare a series of tableaux to show one character's relationships with other characters. Relationships that could be explored include:

- Juliet's relationships with Romeo, Capulet, Nurse, Friar Lawrence, Lady Capulet
- Hamlet's relationships with Claudius, Polonius, Gertrude, Ophelia, Rosencrantz and Guildenstern
- Macbeth's relationships with Lady Macbeth, Duncan, Banquo, Seyton.

Complex characters have complex relationships. When students show

Hamlet's relationship with Gertrude, they may wish to present a number of tableaux, mimes or lines to show different aspects of the relationship of son and mother.

As seen by other characters

Students can work in pairs to show how one character perceives another. For example, Polonius as seen by Hamlet, Ophelia, or Claudius. The reverse perception is then shown: how does Polonius see Hamlet, Ophelia, or Claudius?

Physical and emotional distance

Students can take roles as characters in a play. One particular character (say, Juliet) tells the others where to position themselves around the room such that the physical distance expresses something of the emotional relationship of each character to Juliet. In practice, there is often intense discussion between students because a character being positioned claims a closer or more distant relationship than the positioning character decrees.

Group tableaux

The class can be divided in half, and each group asked to prepare a single tableau in which the major characters in the play appear, expressing something of their relationships to each other. Each group shows its tableau, staying frozen for one minute. The watching group's task is to identify each character portrayed.

Exploring character

1   Soliloquies and asides reveal a character's inner thoughts, what he or she is really thinking. Soliloquies offer actors and students a wide choice of delivery style: are they spoken direct to the audience, to oneself, to a prop, or...? The chosen method helps to create the character.

2   Are characters insincere or ambiguous? Characters may seek to deceive, to conceal truth behind false appearance, for very

different reasons. Obvious villains like Edmond, Iago and Richard III openly declare their intention to deceive, but even very honest characters use deliberately ambiguous language. Juliet gives misleading replies to her parents' questions, and Viola (in *Twelfth Night*) declares 'I am not what I am'.

3   The use of syntax and rhythm, the way a character constructs his or her sentences, smoothly or disjointedly, can give an indication of the character's mind and feelings. For example, as the minds of Lear, Leontes and Othello begin to break up, so does their control over language.

4   What does the imagery a character uses suggest about him or her?

Character types

How far is a character a 'type'? Prince Escales in *Romeo and Juliet* is clearly a symbol of authority. Grandpré in *Henry V* has only one speech, which vividly reports the condition of the English army before the battle of Agincourt. He seems less of a character than a function, brought in to perform a particular dramatic task (description) at a particular moment.

Although every actor who plays Escales or Grandpré will wish to make the characters as interesting and watchable as possible to the audience, they have far fewer opportunities to develop their character through the language Shakespeare provides than other characters with more appearances and lines. Even Romeo may be seen as a type (the lover), but on stage he springs to life as if he were a living person.

When students act out Shakespeare's characters, their preparation explicitly or implicitly questions how far each should be portrayed as believably human. Discussion of types will usually lead to stereotypes, especially when students encounter the comic constables in *Much Ado About Nothing* and *Measure for Measure*, or the Frenchman and Welshman in *The Merry Wives of Windsor*:

CAIUS   By gar, you are de coward, de jack dog, John ape.

EVANS   I will knog your urinal about your knave's cogscomb

Character names

The names of some of Shakespeare's characters can provide clues as to what they are like. In *Twelfth Night*, Sir Tony Belch suggests an earthy, crude character; Feste, someone festive and quick-witted (from the Latin *festinare*); Sir Andrew Aguecheek sounds like a sickly faced person; Malvolio hints at 'evil wishing' (from the Latin *male volente*); in *Romeo and Juliet*, Benvolio suggests someone who is well-intentioned.

In *The Two Gentlemen of Verona*, Shakespeare's audience would probably recognise the significance of the names of the two gentlemen. Proteus, the false character is a 'shapeshifter', named after the deceitful Greek sea god who could change shape. Valentine, the true, innocent lover, bears the name of St Valentine, the patron saint of lovers, whose name symbolises the ideal lover.

In *Romeo and Juliet*, Mercutio suggests a mercurial temperament, or Mercury messenger of the gods, a trickster renowned for eloquence, luck and magic, and a bringer of dreams.

Many students enjoy a research activity, tracing possible associations of characters' names. For example, Iago (a Spanish form of James) might have reminded Shakespeare's audiences watching *Othello* of St Iago de Compostella, known as 'El Matamoro' (the Moor killer).

A caution: this research activity obviously does not work for the historical characters in the history plays. But even in these plays, some characters are defined by their names, for example, Pistol, Doll Tearsheet, Shallow and Silence, Bullcalf and Feeble and others in *King Henry IV Part 2*.

Shakespeare creates characters in three major ways:

1 By what the character says: the language Shakespeare gives him or her to speak (Iago's own words reveals what he is really like).

2 By what others say about him or her (Lady Macbeth is called 'fiend-like'; Iago is often described 'honest' – but he's not!).

3 By what the character does: his or her actions (Macbeth murders Duncan, Juliet kills herself for love).

Themes

'Some necessary question of the play'

Introduction

The question 'What is *Romeo and Juliet* about?' has all kinds of answers. An answer might simply re-tell the story of the play, or it might include the notion that every Shakespeare play has its own particular themes, and *Romeo and Juliet* explores the opposing themes of love and hate, light and dark, life and death, youth and age, and so on. An answer might even give comparative examples from another play, saying that the themes of *Macbeth* include ambition, order and disorder, equivocation, appearance and reality, what it is to be a man.

Themes are the recurring issues or topics that define the preoccupations of the play. They are the subject matter that Shakespeare explores dramatically through the experience of his characters. The analogy of music is helpful in understanding the concept of theme. Like the repeated melodies that run through a symphony, themes are the underlying motifs that give shape, pattern and significance to a play.

As the story unfolds, so Shakespeare enfolds themes into the language. Sometimes individual words recur that express the theme: 'England' throughout the history plays; 'honest' in *Othello*; 'blood' in *Macbeth*; 'nothing' in *King Lear*, and so on.

Sometimes use of a particular language device embodies the theme: the many antitheses in *Measure for Measure* mirror the theme of justice (see page 21); the oxymorons in *Romeo and Juliet* reflect the oppositions of the play (see pages 79–80). *King Lear*, so much concerned with the nature of authority, is filled with imperious language: commands, assertions, exclamations and vehement curses.

Universal appeal

One reason why Shakespeare's plays have proved so popular for so long is that their themes have universal appeal across centuries and across cultures. The plays are very obviously about matters which interest and perplex people in all ages: love and hate, the relationships between the sexes, false appearance, war, politics, power and so on. Their themes can be human emotions (jealousy in *Othello*, pride in *Coriolanus*), and can express the widest range of human preoccupations: forgiveness, ambition, justice, time, revenge, madness, blindness, evil, violence and tyranny, guilt and conscience, witchcraft and magic, fate and free will, nature and nurture, theatre and acting, corruption, racism, self-deception, and so on.

Each theme has a modern application. Students are never slow at identifying and enacting the contemporary relevance of any Shakespearian theme.

Enduring appeal: Baz Luhrmann's dazzling film version of *Romeo and Juliet*.

Themes may also be expressed through recurring images. In the spectator's mind (often below the level of consciousness), such imagery builds up a sense of the deep preoccupations of the play: the many images of light and darkness in *Romeo and Juliet*; the imagery of torture, and of fractured, suffering bodies in *King Lear*. In *Macbeth*, the theme of false appearance is embodied in disquieting images: 'Look like th'innocent flower/But be the serpent under't'.

Each succeeding generation finds different themes in Shakespeare's plays, or re-defines or gives different emphasis to old ones. Feminism's objections to patriarchy has given much sharper social focus to the traditional fathers and daughters theme. Similarly, most performances and discussions of *The Tempest* now take colonisation to be a theme. Some modern productions and critics make it the central aspect of the play, showing Caliban as the victim of (European) exploitation. In the nineteenth century, such an interpretation was ignored. The question 'To whom does the island belong?' was simply not asked.

Four common themes

Certain themes seem to have interested Shakespeare all his life. He returned to them again and again in different ways in his plays. The four common themes found in every Shakespeare play are:

- conflict
- appearance and reality
- order and disorder
- change.

Conflict

Conflict is the essence of all drama. In Shakespeare's plays, conflict takes different forms. It can be the strife of rivals in love or war. It can be quarrels within families (parents *versus* children, brother *versus* brother), or between families (Montagues *versus* Capulets). In the history plays, the conflict expresses dynastic or international struggles (York *versus* Lancaster, England *versus* France and so on). In the comedies it is quickly obvious that love will be the source of conflict: 'The course of true love never did run smooth'.

Appearance and reality

In every play, things and people are not what they seem: 'All that glisters is not gold'. Women disguise themselves as men; evil intentions are hidden behind masks of friendship; characters pretend to be mad; identities are mistaken; illusions abound. The theme of appearance and reality finds incisive expression: 'I am not what I am', 'Fair is foul and foul is fair'.

Some plays have appearance and reality as a central theme. In *Othello*, Iago hides his real nature behind a mask of honesty. *Measure for Measure* is about 'seeming', as the outwardly incorruptible Angelo proves to be a deceitful would-be seducer. Macbeth hides his intention to murder Duncan behind a mask of welcome: 'False face must hide what the false heart doth know'.

'Smiling damnèd villain!' exclaims Hamlet, thinking of his treacherous uncle. Shakespeare's imagination seems to have been haunted by the image of the smiling villain, the wrong-doer who hides his wickedness behind a smiling face. He uses different forms of the image to express the theme of deceptive appearances:

> There's daggers in men's smiles

> Some that smile have in their hearts, I fear,
> Millions of mischief

> Why, I can smile, and murder whiles I smile

> I did but smile till now

> One may smile, and smile, and be a villain

The stage convention of disguise is intensely dramatic, and Shakespeare exploited it to the full to express the theme of appearance and reality. Villains disguise their evil intentions; some characters pretend to be mad; others disguise their true identity: King Henry V assumes the role of a soldier as he visits his troops before the battle of Agincourt; the Duke of Kent becomes a servant in *King Lear*.

A favourite variation that Shakespeare often played on this theme is that of the girl who disguises herself as boy:

- Julia in *The Two Gentlemen of Verona*
- Portia in *The Merchant of Venice*
- Rosalind in *As You Like It*

- Viola in *Twelfth Night*
- Imogen in *Cymbeline*.

In Shakespeare's time, the device had added theatrical and sexual resonances because women actors were not allowed on the stage; the part of the girl would be played by a young male actor.

Order and disorder

In every play, stability gives way to confusion. The disruptions occur in persons (Lear goes mad), in society (England is split by civil war), and in nature (storms and tempests echo the disorders in persons and societies). The disruptions have many causes, varying from play to play: love, hatred, jealousy, ambition, the lust for political power, self-centredness and so on. But the suffering that individuals experience often results in the learning of new understandings and greater humanity. Characters acquire a determination to endure.

Many critics have argued that Shakespeare always ensures that order is restored at the end of a play. Marriage, or the restoration of a rightful ruler, or the reconciliation of former enemies brings harmony after chaos. But this interpretation is strongly disputed by other critics (see pages 28–9), and many stage productions end suggesting that any 'return to order' will be short-lived, or that disorder still exists.

Perhaps the best known expression of the theme of order and disorder is the speech on degree by Ulysses in *Troilus and Cressida*. Ulysses argues that nature and society observe degree or hierarchical order. If that order is disturbed, chaos results. Just as disruption of the planets causes earthquakes and other catastrophes in nature, so the overthrow of hierarchy in society causes anarchy in every social institution:

> Degree being vizarded,
> Th'unworthiest shows as fairly in the mask.
> The heavens themselves, the planets, and this centre
> Observe degree, priority, and place,
> Insisture, course, proportion, season, form,
> Office, and custom, in all line of order.
> And therefore is the glorious planet Sol
> In noble eminence enthroned and sphered

Amidst the other; whose med'cinable eye
Corrects the ill aspects of planets evil,
And posts like the commandment of a king,
Sans check, to good and bad. But when the planets
In evil mixture to disorder wander,
What plagues and what portents, what mutiny,
What raging of the sea, shaking of earth,
Commotion in the winds, frights, changes, horrors,
Divert and crack, rend and deracinate
The unity and married calm of states
Quite from their fixture! O, when degree is shaked,
Which is the ladder to all high designs,
The enterprise is sick. How could communities,
Degrees in schools, and brotherhoods in cities,
Peaceful commerce from dividable shores,
The primogenitive and due of birth,
Prerogative of age, crowns, sceptres, laurels,
But by degree, stand in authentic place?
Take but degree away, untune that string,
And hark what discord follows!

Ulysses' lines offer opportunities for students to discuss both the nature of relationships in society (Is there a proper social order?), and whether Ulysses' views can be taken as being those of Shakespeare himself (Does Shakespeare put his own beliefs into the mouths of his characters?).

Change (metamorphosis)

In every play, characters change in some way. For some, the change is from life to death; for others, the development of new insights and increased compassion. Kings and tyrants fall from power, villains are unmasked. In *A Midsummer Night's Dream*, Nick Bottom is magically transformed into an ass. In *Twelfth Night*, a false letter tricks Malvolio into changing from an austere puritan steward to a foolish would-be lover. In some plays, the metamorphosis takes place in a special location: a wood, a storm-blasted heath, an island or a near-magical setting (Belmont, Ephesus). Time underlies the transformations of many plays: 'And thus the whirligig of time brings in his revenges'.

Themes are abstractions, but practical approaches can aid understanding. For example, groups of students can prepare and show a tableau (see page 192) of each of the four general themes: conflict, appearance and reality, order and disorder, and change. These frozen pictures are likely to be symbolic portrayals, not specific to any play. Students can also portray actual incidents from a play to illustrate particular themes. If the teacher selects particular themes for portrayal (say, from *Hamlet*) it may be appropriate to begin with a less abstract theme such as madness or revenge, then move on to a theme such as sin and salvation, or delay.

Levels

The four common themes work at three different levels in each play.

1. The individual level (psychological, personal). An individual might experience personal conflict, or mental and spiritual disorder; he or she might disguise his or her true feelings or identity; there might be changes in personality. Macbeth's false-faced treachery brings the agonies of conscience: 'the affliction of these terrible dreams/That shake us nightly'.

2. The social level (family, society, nation). The families of the Montagues and Capulets have been feuding for many years. Macbeth's Scotland is torn by tyranny and warfare. England goes to war with France, Rome with Egypt.

3. The natural level (cosmic, supernatural or nature). Storms, stars, witches, ghosts or nature itself express each theme. Disruptions and conflict in persons and society are mirrored by disruptions in nature. The storm is a potent symbol in *King Lear*, in *Macbeth* (on the night of Duncan's murder), in *Othello* (before the landing in Cyprus), in *Julius Caesar* (prefiguring Caesar's assassination), and in Hamlet's complex image, 'take arms against a sea of troubles'.

In active work, students can find ways to portray an example of each theme at each level. They usually find the social and natural levels more demanding than the individual level. Below is an example of how one group of students illustrated, at the three levels, the theme of appearance and reality in *Macbeth*.

1   Individual level: 'False face must hide what the false heart doth know' (a Janus-faced tableau).

2   Social level: 'This castle hath a pleasant seat' and the Banquet scene (a welcome party erupting into violence).

3   Natural level: 'Till Birnan Wood do come to Dunsinane' (a mime in which 'trees' eerily unfreeze into menacing soldiers).

Particular themes

Each play has its own distinctive themes, as some examples will illustrate.

1   *Macbeth*: ambition, evil, order and disorder, appearance and reality, violence and tyranny, guilt and conscience, man, equivocation, witchcraft and magic.

2   *Romeo and Juliet*: love and hate, fate and free will, life and death, youth against age, fortune (luck).

3   *The Tempest*: usurpation, nature *versus* nurture, imprisonment and freedom, colonialism, illusion and magic, forgiveness and reconciliation, sleep and dreams, transformation.

Racism in the plays?

All kinds of insulting and demeaning remarks about other races occur throughout the plays. 'Black' is often used as a symbol of evil or wrong-doing. In such language Shakespeare reflects the attitudes of his own times, but it is impossible to deduce his own personal views from the plays.

Othello and *The Merchant of Venice* clearly demand direct address to issues of racism and anti-semitism, and every play provides opportunities for students to discuss problems of bigotry and intolerance that still beset every society today.

4 *Hamlet*: procrastination (delay), madness, revenge, sin and salvation, poison, theatre and acting, corruption.

5 *Othello*: jealousy, racism, self-deception.

6 *King Lear*: justice, nature, sight and blindness, the tortured and broken body.

Fathers and daughters

Many fathers in Shakespeare's plays seek to dominate their daughters, and to control their choice of husbands. They forcibly express their displeasure when their daughters show signs of independence:

- Capulet in *Romeo and Juliet*
- Baptista in *The Taming of the Shrew*
- The Duke of Milan in *The Two Gentlemen of Verona*
- Egeus in *A Midsummer Night's Dream*
- Leonato in *Much Ado About Nothing*
- Polonius in *Hamlet*
- Lear in *King Lear*
- Brabantio in *Othello*
- Cymbeline in *Cymbeline*.

Even Portia's dead father in *The Merchant of Venice* seeks to control her choice of husband by imposing the casket trial for her suitors.

Acting and theatre

Shakespeare's fascination with his own profession provided him with a recurring theme: the world as a stage, with humankind, like actors, making brief, insignificant appearances, to play their parts. Imagery and the depiction of acting and theatre occur in many plays.

Macbeth compares life to:

> a walking shadow, a poor player
> That struts and frets his hour upon the stage
> And then is heard no more

King Lear speaks of 'This great stage of fools'. After the assassination of Julius Caesar, Cassius wonders:

> How many ages hence
> Shall this our lofty scene be acted over
> In states unborn and accents yet unknown!

In *As You Like It*, the progress of an individual life is compared to the different parts an actor plays on stage:

> All the world's a stage,
> And all the men and women merely players;
> They have their exits and their entrances,
> And one man in his time plays many parts,
> His Acts being seven ages. At first the infant,
> Mewling and puking in the nurse's arms.
> Then, the whining schoolboy, with his satchel
> And shining morning face, creeping like snail
> Unwillingly to school. And then the lover,
> Sighing like a furnace, with a woeful ballad
> Made to his mistress' eyebrow. Then, a soldier,
> Full of strange oaths, and bearded like the pard,
> Jealous in honour, sudden and quick in quarrel,
> Seeking the bubble reputation
> Even in the cannon's mouth. And then, the justice,
> In fair round belly, with good capon lined,
> With eyes severe, and beard of formal cut,
> Full of wise saws and modern instances,
> And so he plays his part. The sixth age shifts
> Into the lean and slippered pantaloon,
> With spectacles on nose and pouch on side,
> His youthful hose, well saved, a world too wide
> For his shrunk shank, and his big manly voice,
> Turning again towards childish treble, pipes
> And whistles in his sound. Last Scene of all,
> That ends this strange eventful history,
> Is second childishness, and mere oblivion,
> Sans teeth, sans eyes, sans taste, sans everything.

These 28 lines lend themselves to enactment by students. They also offer opportunities for students to write and perform their own parodies on 'the seven ages of woman', or 'students', and so on.

Dramatic effect

'All torment, trouble, wonder and amazement inhabits here'

Introduction

Shakespeare's theatre did not have the sophisticated technology that creates elaborate effects on modern stages. His dramatic effects were achieved through language. His basic resources were the human body, the bare stage of the Globe Theatre and above all, the human voice. Whereas Elizabethan audiences relied on the spoken word to carry them through a play, today's theatre and cinema audiences rely heavily on the visual aspects of the show.

Shakespeare's language provides actors with the means to create the dramatic effect of fear or joy, day or night, forest or tempest-racked sea, graveyards or open heath, battlefields or castle battlements:

> Give me a gash, put me to present pain,
> Lest this great sea of joys rushing upon me
> O'erbear the shores of my mortality,
> And drown me with their sweetness.

> A thousand fiends, a thousand hissing snakes,
> Ten thousand swelling toads, as many urchins,
> Would make such fearful and confusèd cries
> As any mortal body hearing it
> Should straight fall mad.

The audience's imagination was a vital ingredient in the creation of dramatic effect. In the prologue to *King Henry V*, Chorus apologises for the inadequacies of theatre in portraying realistic battles between the warring armies of England and France with only a few actors on a bare stage. The imagination of the audience must respond to the language of the play, creating in their minds battles between France and England:

> Think when we talk of horses that you see them
> Printing their proud hooves i'th'receiving earth.

Shakespeare's stagecraft assists the imagination of actors and audience alike. He contrasts scene with scene, character with character, silence with speech, in order to vary dramatic tension, sometimes intensifying, sometimes relaxing it. He uses subplots which mirror and add significance to the main plot: sons and fathers in *Hamlet* (Hamlet, Laertes, Fortinbras, Pyrrhus), Gloucester's family in *King Lear*, the multiple pairs of lovers in *As You Like It*. He intertwines tragedy with comedy, and as scene flows into scene, alters the emotional mood. The Porter in *Macbeth*, the Gravedigger in *Hamlet*, the Clown in *Antony and Cleopatra*, all hold up the action and, for a few minutes, change the climate of feeling.

Shakespeare's intention is to keep the audience constantly engaged. Conflict is always present. Episodes of dialogue or quiet reflection are balanced with dramatic spectacle: trial scenes, duels, dumb shows, battles, masques, love scenes, murders, banquets, witches, ghosts, the unmasking of disguised characters, shipwrecks and so on.

There are moments of electrifying dramatic intensity: Hamlet leaps into Ophelia's grave; Gloucester jumps from an imaginary cliff; the witches, Lady Macbeth and Macbeth, all, in different ways, invoke the powers of evil; Juliet awakes in the vault to find Romeo dead beside her; Lear rages against the storm; Shylock prepares to cut a pound of flesh from Antonio's breast. Every play contains such moments of high drama.

Stage directions

Every stage direction in Shakespeare's plays is an invitation to students' imagination to work out how it might be performed to greatest dramatic effect. Even the direction *Enter* is less simple than it might appear. Just how does a king enter? How does a servant with only one line enter?

The answers are different in every staging of each play. The way characters enter helps establish what they are like. How might students establish character and mood from the stage direction in *Hamlet*: *Enter two Gravediggers*?

Similarly, the seemingly simple direction *Exit* requires thought about how to leave the stage in a manner consistent with the dramatic nature of both the scene and the character. The more complex direction *Alarms and excursions* presents students with the problem of how to stage the sounds and comings and goings of battle. In Shakespeare's time, it may have been the cue for an extended period of stage action depicting a battle scene.

Certain stage directions have an instantly recognisable dramatic charge, as, most famously: *Exit, pursued by a bear*. Every new production of *The Winter's Tale* tries to find an exciting way of performing Shakespeare's best known stage direction. Among other ways, it has been performed:

- by an actor in a bear costume
- by a small actor dressed as a teddy bear, accompanied by the tune of *The Teddy Bears' Picnic*
- as an enormous shadow cast on the stage.

Enter Ghost

The entry of the Ghost of Hamlet's father is a thrilling moment in the theatre. Each new production attempts to ensure that the entry is as enthralling as possible. Students can prepare their own staging, experimenting with responses to a number of questions.

1 What does the Ghost look like?

2 How does the Ghost enter: slowly? suddenly? with particular gesture? any accompanying sound effects?

3 How might he leave the stage?

4 In some productions the Ghost does not physically appear. The audience has to imagine his presence through lighting, sound and the reactions of the other characters. How could students make this style of presenting the Ghost dramatically effective?

Longer directions make equal demands on students' imagination as they work out how to stage such directions in a particular space in their school or college:

> *Jupiter descends in thunder and lightning, sitting upon an eagle. He throws a thunderbolt. The ghosts fall on their knees. (Cymbeline)*

> *Thunder. Enter Third Apparition, a child crowned with a tree in his hand. (Macbeth)*

The dumb show, performed by the Players in *Hamlet*, is Shakespeare's longest stage direction. A dumb show is a mime of the action of the play that is to follow. The task for students is to find a dramatically effective way of performing it:

> *Enter a KING and a QUEEN, very lovingly, the Queen embracing him. She kneels and makes show of protestation unto him. He takes her up, and declines his head upon her neck. He lies him down upon a bank of flowers. She, seeing him asleep, leaves him. Anon comes in another man, takes off his crown, kisses it, pours poison in the sleeper's ears, and leaves him. The Queen returns, finds the King dead, and makes passionate action. The poisoner, with some two or three mutes, comes in again, seeming to condole with her. The dead body is carried away. The poisoner woos the Queen with gifts. She seems harsh awhile, but in the end accepts his love. Exeunt.*

The Tempest contains more stage directions than any other play. Some people think that it is because Shakespeare wrote the play after he had retired to Stratford. Knowing he would not be present in rehearsal, he added more explicit stage directions than usual. Students could enact some from four episodes in the play.

1   The shipwreck:

> *A tempestuous noise of thunder and lightning.*
> *Enter a Shipmaster, a Boatswain and Mariners.*

> *Enter Mariners, wet.*

2   The Banquet:

> *Solemn and strange music, and Prospero, on the top, invisible.*

Enter several strange shapes, bringing in a banquet, and dance about it with gentle actions of salutations, and inviting the King etc. to eat, they depart.

Thunder and lightning. Enter ARIEL, *like a Harpy, claps his wings upon the table, and with a quaint device the banquet vanishes.*

Ariel vanishes in thunder; then, to soft music, enter the shapes again, and dance, with mocks and mows, and then depart carrying out the table.

3   The hunting of Caliban, Stephano and Trinculo:

A noise of hunters heard. Enter diverse spirits in shape of dogs and hounds, hunting them about, PROSPERO *and* ARIEL *setting them on.*

4   The entry of the court:

Solemn music (Prospero traces out a circle on stage). Here enters ARIEL *before; then* ALONSO *with a frantic gesture, attended by* GONZALO; SEBASTIAN *and* ANTONIO *in like manner attended by* ADRIAN *and* FRANCISCO. *They all enter the circle which Prospero had made, and there stand charmed; which Prospero, observing, speaks.*

Critical incidents

Every moment in a Shakespeare play has a dramatic charge, but some episodes are climactic: the appearance of Banquo's Ghost, Mercutio's death, Ophelia's madness. Such episodes are not confined to tragedy. There are critically dramatic scenes in every play: in *A Midsummer Night's Dream*, the Pyramus and Thisbe play, the quarrel of Hermia and Helena, and the meeting of Oberon and Titania ('Ill met by moonlight'); in *Twelfth Night*, the gulling of Malvolio.

Some lines have an intensely high charge of dramatic potential because every character on stage has a particular interest in them. The line affects them in some way and they need to respond, even if that response is to conceal their true feelings with a show of indifference. Minor or non-speaking characters also recognise that what is being said is crucial and they would wish to see how major characters respond. For example, in *Macbeth*, after Duncan has been found murdered, Macbeth tells that he has killed Duncan's two bodyguards.

Macduff says, 'Wherefore did you so?' In the theatre it is an electric moment. How does Macduff speak? Are his words full of suspicion? Do they arouse suspicious thoughts in others? Do the other thanes look at Macbeth? How do Macbeth and Lady Macbeth respond? Does Macbeth somehow express guilt? Does Lady Macbeth look terrified that her plot is about to be discovered, or is she composed? Even the servants on stage will react to Macduff's question.

Using the critical incident technique described below, students can work in groups of eight to twelve or more. Each student steps into role as a character (critical incidents often occur when many named characters are on-stage, but other Lords and Ladies, guards and servants and so on can be added as appropriate). Students then discuss how their characters are likely to behave at that precise moment. Who looks at whom? Where is each character positioned in relation to the others? What facial expressions, gestures, body postures are appropriate? The aim is for each student to work out what his or her character is thinking and feeling as the line is uttered.

At least ten to fifteen minutes is needed for each group to prepare how it will present its critical incident. Some students have prepared a mime unfolding in slow motion, but the most favoured method is to present a tableau. Each group presents its frozen moment, holding still for one minute. Other students view, identifying characters. After unfreezing, it is helpful to have a discussion and put positive questions to characters, for example, 'Gertrude, why were you/weren't you looking at Hamlet? What were you thinking at that moment?'

Three critical incidents from *Hamlet*

> But now my cousin Hamlet, and my son

Everyone in the court will wish to see how Hamlet responds, and Hamlet, Gertrude and Claudius have their own very special interests in the line.

> Give me some light, Away!

Many people are on stage. How does each respond to Claudius' reaction to the play scene?

> The drink, the drink – I am poisoned!

Again, the stage is crowded with people. How does each react to hearing the Queen say she has been poisoned?

143

Creating atmosphere

In the eighteenth and nineteenth centuries, theatre productions often added a scene to show the funeral of Juliet. Students can work in large groups to stage Juliet's funeral procession as dramatically as possible. The mourning language at the discovery of the 'dead' Juliet is filled with a vocabulary that signifies grief at death (Act 4 Scene 5). The lines can be shared among students to speak, chant or sing.

Mourning lines from other plays have been used to great effect in this activity: about Ophelia (*Hamlet* Act 5 Scene 1), about Hero (*Much Ado about Nothing* Act 4 Scene 2), or Constance's lament for Arthur (*King John* Act 3 Scene 4). The dirge from *Cymbeline* has irresistible plangency as students, alone or in unison, speak pairs or single lines:

> Fear no more the heat of the sun
> Nor the furious winter's rages,
> Thou thy worldly task hast done,
> Home art gone and ta'en thy wages.
> Golden lads and girls all must,
> As chimney-sweepers, come to dust.
>
> Fear no more the frown o'th'great,
> Thou art past the tyrant's stroke.
> Care no more to clothe and eat,
> To thee the reed is as the oak.
> The sceptre, learning, physic, must,
> All follow this and come to dust.
>
> Fear no more the lightning-flash,
> Nor the all-dreaded thunder-stone.
> Fear not slander, censure rash,
> Thou has finished joy and moan.
> All lovers young, all lovers must,
> Consign to thee and come to dust.
>
> No exorciser harm thee!
> Nor no witchcraft charm thee!
> Ghost unlaid forbear thee!
> Nothing ill come near thee!
> Quiet consummation have,
> And renownèd be thy grave!

Another dramatically effective mourning activity leads up to a presentation in a blacked-out classroom or hall. The 'dead' Juliet lies in the centre of the room, lighted candles at her head and heels. Each student in turn approaches Juliet to deliver his or her line (chosen from Act 4 Scene 5) accompanied with some kind of gesture or tribute:

> Have I thought long to see this morning's face,
> And doth it give me such a sight as this?

> All things that we ordainèd festival,
> Turn from their office to black funeral

Opening scenes

As a playwright, Shakespeare knew that he must seize the interest and imagination of the audience right from the start of a play. Conflict must be introduced quickly, because conflict is at the heart of drama, the ingredient that keeps the audience on the edge of their seats, eager to know what happens next. Who will win the battles of war or love, jealousy or justice?

In the opening scene of every play, Shakespeare uses language and creates situations to catch audience interest. The seeds of conflict are directly evident, or very strongly implied. At the start of each history play, ambitious nobles scheme and quarrel, civil strife threatens or there is news of foreign wars. In the comedies, it is very soon obvious that the course of true love will not run smooth. Two comedies begin like tragedies: *The Comedy of Errors* with a threatened execution; *As You Like It* with an evil-intending brother.

Each tragedy opens with a scene that sows the seeds of the catastrophes that will follow: Iago plots against Othello; Antony rejects Rome for Cleopatra; Hamlet's father's ghost appears as Denmark prepares for war; Coriolanus reviles the citizens of Rome; King Lear rejects Cordelia and banishes Kent; the witches plan to meet Macbeth; the Montagues and Capulets bloodily brawl.

The four late plays (or Romances) all quickly ignite with furious action: Leontes' mad jealousy in *The Winter's Tale*; Antiochus' determination to kill Pericles; Cymbeline's rage at his daughter. Most dramatic of all, *The Tempest* begins with a realistic shipwreck.

The opening of any play is an invitation to students to work out how it might be staged to greatest dramatic effect. Shakespeare provides rich resources to feed students' imaginations. The language of the opening scene of every play helps students to create a charged atmosphere, establish a major theme, and predict what the play will be about.

The first scene of *The Tempest* takes place on a ship at sea during a terrible storm. Its first stage direction, *A tempestuous noise of thunder and lightning heard*, poses the challenge: just how can the shipwreck be staged to greatest dramatic effect? What simple props could suggest a ship? One production had only a large ship's wheel at the back of the stage; sailors struggled to turn it to keep the ship on course.

Students working in large groups (there are six speaking parts, and many sailors) can work out how the language helps create:

- the fury of the waves and wind
- the sense of fear and crisis
- the illusion of a ship caught in a tempest
- the challenge to traditional authority (the king and courtiers have to obey the Boatswain's orders)
- men desperately concerned to save their lives (do they panic, or are they well-disciplined?).

'We split, we split!' A Japanese staging of the shipwreck.

The first scene of *Macbeth* is filled with similar imaginative possibilities. Three witches vow to meet Macbeth after the battle. Their familiar spirits call to them. As they leave, they chant ominous words.

Thunder and lightning. Enter three WITCHES

FIRST WITCH When shall we three meet again?
    In thunder, lightning, or in rain?
SECOND WITCH When the hurly-burly's done,
    When the battle's lost, and won.
THIRD WITCH That will be ere the set of sun.
FIRST WITCH Where the place?
SECOND WITCH Upon the heath.
THIRD WITCH There to meet with Macbeth.
FIRST WITCH I come, Graymalkin.
SECOND WITCH Paddock calls.
THIRD WITCH Anon.
ALL Fair is foul, and foul is fair,
    Hover through the fog and filthy air.

Students can work in groups of three or more to learn the lines and act out the scene. Their aim should be to present the scene as dramatically as possible guided by their responses to some of the following questions.

1   How might sound effects be added: thunder, rain, battle sounds, cats, toads and so on?

2   How do the witches enter?

3   How do they move?

4   Are they old or young? Are they male or female? (In Shakespeare's time they would have been played by males; in one modern production they were spiderwomen on a giant cobweb overhanging the stage.)

5   Do they like each other or hate each other?

6   How is each witch different from the others?

7   How are they dressed? What are they carrying?

8   What do they do as they speak?

Hamlet, with its memorable first line 'Who's there?', presents another such an opportunity. It is midnight on a gun platform on the battlements of Elsinore castle. Francisco is on sentry duty. Barnardo comes to relieve him. Horatio and Marcellus arrive to join Barnardo. Every production of *Hamlet* aims to make the opening moments of the play as gripping and dramatic as possible. The actors know they must create a tense, urgent and ominous atmosphere using Shakespeare's words. Students face precisely the same challenge as they work out how to stage the opening nineteen lines:

Enter BARNARDO *and* FRANCISCO, *two sentinels*

BARNARDO Who's there?
FRANCISCO Nay, answer me. Stand and unfold yourself.
BARNARDO Long live the king!
FRANCISCO Barnardo?
BARNARDO He.
FRANCISCO You come most carefully upon your hour.
BARNARDO 'Tis now struck twelve, get thee to bed Francisco.
FRANCISCO For this relief much thanks, 'tis bitter cold
    And I am sick at heart.
BARNARDO Have you had quiet guard?
FRANCISCO   Not a mouse stirring.
BARNARDO Well, good night.
    If you do meet Horatio and Marcellus,
    The rivals of my watch, bid them make haste.
FRANCISCO I think I hear them.

Enter HORATIO *and* MARCELLUS

    Stand ho! Who is there?
HORATIO Friends to this ground.
MARCELLUS   And liegemen to the Dane.
FRANCISCO Give you good night.
MARCELLUS   Oh farewell honest soldier,
    Who hath relieved you?
FRANCISCO   Barnardo hath my place
    Give you good night.   *Exit Francisco.*
MARCELLUS   Holla, Barnardo!
BARNARDO   Say,
    What, is Horatio there?
HORATIO   A piece of him.

Students can explore answers to the following questions to help them heighten the dramatic effect.

1 What will be the first thing the audience sees?

2 Is Francisco on sentry duty, patrolling the stage, before the first members of the audience enter?

3 How long a pause before Barnardo speaks his first words?

4 Why does Barnardo, the newcomer, challenge Francisco, contrary to military practice? (Francisco should challenge him.)

5 How might you convince the audience that the night is bitterly cold?

6 What accent or speech-style does each character use?

7 In Shakespeare's time, the play would have been staged in broad daylight. Which words or phrases help create the impression of night and darkness?

8 What do the very short sentences suggest about the atmosphere?

Filming the opening

Hamlet has been filmed many times. The opening sequence of different films have shown:

- battle scenes between Denmark and Norway, and Hamlet's father wounded
- Hamlet's funeral procession
- flags unfurling on the walls of Elsinore castle to signify old King Hamlet's death
- a chef peeping around a curtain to see if the next course can be served at an Elsinore banquet (to signify the theme of spying)
- Queen Gertrude weeping over the tomb of King Hamlet.

In the 1996 film of *King Richard III* (set in the 1930s), the first words of the play 'Now is the winter of our discontent' were preceded by a five-minute sequence of war and victory celebrations. Orson Welles' film of *Othello* begins with Othello's funeral procession passing Iago suspended in an iron cage.

Knowing of such examples, students can plan the opening sequence of a film of a Shakespeare play. The sequence should be constructed to accompany the credits and lead up to the first line of the play.

Active methods

'Suit the action to the word, the word to the action'

Content

A student's view of Shakespeare in school or college is likely to be simple and direct: 'I'm doing *Macbeth*.' Teachers, however, need an organised framework within which to plan, teach and assess their students' Shakespeare courses. Most use a version of the simple categories employed throughout this book to discuss what 'doing *Macbeth*' involves. Thus, the content of any Shakespeare course in every type of school and college comprises five key elements:

- story
- character
- language
- themes
- dramatic effect.

How far other elements are included in students' Shakespeare experience is decided by the professional judgement and interests of each teacher. Such elements include matters of context (historical, social, intellectual, ideological, literary) and questions of sources, stage history and textual history. Decisions usually depend on the teacher's own view of Shakespeare and the needs, aptitudes and abilities of the students he or she teaches.

Each element is, of course, not as discrete as these categories imply: each is organically related to all others. Further, each can be understood and taught at very different levels. For example, some teachers will treat the context elements in a life and times course (see page 212), others may introduce context to their students as cultural materialism or literary theory (see pages 26–44).

The teacher's role

How does a teacher set about 'doing *Macbeth*'? Within the time available, each teacher decides how the play will be studied. Many spend a good deal of time on a limited number of what are judged to be key scenes or moments. Other scenes are covered by a variety of other methods: watching a video, students' private reading, teacher reading, brief summaries and so on.

The teacher's task is to organise the framework within which students work on the play. The responsibility for course structure, sequence and methods is necessarily the teacher's. Guided by his or her aims and the principles set out in Chapter 1, each teacher determines how time is to be used, organises the work for each lesson, chooses the section of the play to be covered and the methods by which students will work. Any plan will be flexible, ready to adapt to how students respond. In practice, students' interests or difficulties often result in what was originally planned as a single lesson stretching to two or three. Unexpected outcomes are a regular feature of Shakespeare teaching.

The school context necessarily influences any Shakespeare course. There are very obvious differences in teaching a class of twelve-year-olds studying a Shakespeare play for the first time, and a class of seventeen-year-olds studying it for an examination. Similarly, a course which comprises six one-hour lessons will be very different from a course of twenty lessons. Space is a crucial factor. A course which has access to a drama studio or hall, will be different from a course that does not have such opportunities and is taught entirely in a small classroom.

If a teacher feels strongly that *The Tempest* is a play centrally about colonialism, or that *Romeo and Juliet* is a play about patriarchy, the students will have different Shakespeare experiences from those whose teachers do not share those beliefs. But whatever a teacher's own views, all teachers take certain things into account as they plan a Shakespeare course for their students. Some of the following considerations are severely practical, others are matters of principle.

1   How much time is available? How many lessons can be planned?

2   Where will the lessons take place? Will all lessons be in the classroom, or can we also work in the drama studio or hall – or outside the building?

3   How well do I know this class? What do I think are their abilities, needs, aptitudes, expectations? What is their past curriculum experience of Shakespeare?

4   How well do I know the play? Do I have particular views on the play? How might these views affect my teaching?

5   Do I like this play? If the answer is an emphatic 'no', choose another. Even in examination syllabuses, there's usually an alternative.

6   What teaching methods shall I use? How much active work, with students up on their feet? What will be the balance of such active performance work, with discussion, written and other work?

7   Do I intend to cover the whole play in class time? That is, do I want every student to hear *in class* every word of the script?

8   Do I intend to focus on key scenes, moments, speeches, and actions, exploring these actively and in depth? Which scenes will be given detailed, sustained attention in class? How can I justify the selection of such scenes to myself and to others?

9   How will students cover parts of the play that I do not have time to teach actively and in detail? What is the place of summaries, or teacher readings, or video or audio recordings and so on? Are there parts of the play I expect students to read in private study or homework?

10 How will I organise the class? What will be the balance of working in pairs, groups, as a whole class?

11 Do I intend the course to culminate in some kind of performance? Will groups of students in the class make some kind of presentation to other students? to other audiences?

12 Do I 'get straight into the play', or do I use the first lesson or two for students to improvise on some of the themes of the play?

13 What use will I make of videos?

14 What written work do I expect from the students? In what form? What design and other expressive work?

15 Is a theatre visit possible? Are there 'visitors' such as Theatre in Education companies or outreach actors that I can invite in to work with the students?

16 How much account do I intend to take of 'Shakespeare's stage'? Should I do anything on Shakespeare's life and times, and conditions of performance on the Globe stage?

17 What is the place of criticism or theory in this course? Do I think that my students should know the names of certain critics, commentators, or directors?

18 How far do I see this course as being about, say, *Macbeth*, and how much about the play as a vehicle to deepen students' understanding of gender, race and social class issues?

19 How can I ensure that, whatever my own Shakespeare agenda as a teacher, my students have the right and opportunity to follow *their* interests and enthusiasms? How do I ensure they have meaningful choice, and that I'm not imposing my views, but am genuinely affording them opportunities to make up their own minds?

20 How do I ensure that every student has their own copy of a suitable edition of the play?

Teacher attitudes are crucial

Each of the following teacher attitudes contributes to successful school Shakespeare.

1 A recognition that one never finishes with Shakespeare – a willingness to go on learning.

2 An awareness that fresh insights can come from active work on the play in the classroom – the students can teach the teacher.

3   A concern to encourage students' personal responses – to help
    them see that learning about Shakespeare doesn't simply mean
    reading and reproducing other people's views, however
    prestigious those people might be.

4   A recognition that teachers' attitudes are crucial – teachers who
    are enthusiastic about their subject, and who teach in interesting
    ways, motivate their students to share that enthusiasm.

5   A concern to avoid bardolatry – students often react
    unfavourably to being told that Shakespeare is the greatest.

The teacher as performer

Some readers of this book will remember with mixed feelings a teacher
from their own schooldays who did all the reading, spoke all the parts.
It is, of course, important that in any classroom teachers should speak
and act Shakespeare's lines as part of the teaching process. But how
large a part should the teacher take in speaking and performing?
Answers to that question are decided by the circumstances. Every
teacher, every class of students is different.

Teachers must perforce take the lead in the organisation of lessons,
but will make their own judgement on how much of the language they
will speak themselves. What can be said with confidence is that it
would be as inappropriate for the teacher to speak all of the language
(the Bully Bottom option) as it would be for the teacher to speak none.
Sometimes it is entirely appropriate for a teacher to read aloud all or
part of a scene. This could be because of the constraint of time, or
because a video version has cut the scene, or as preparation for
students' active work.

Very obviously, each teacher should make use of his or her own
particular skills. Drama-trained teachers, and those experienced in
acting and performance bring uniquely valuable qualities to the
Shakespeare classroom. Such skills should be used to maximise students'
motivation. Students learn much from hearing the language spoken
well, and seeing their teacher's evident enjoyment of Shakespeare.
That enjoyment also helps other, less experienced, teachers to overcome
any initial lack of confidence in the resonance of their voice, and
uncertainty about their skill to act a Shakespeare part.

Two aspects of being a teacher

First, teachers should hold in suspension their recollections of studying Shakespeare at university or college. The one-hour lecture, heavy reliance on criticism, academic essays, and scholarly editions (written with university-level Shakespeare scholars very much in mind), are inappropriate to school Shakespeare. This is not to diminish the value of such experience, it is a reminder that the knowledge acquired from such experience needs to be mediated in appropriate forms for school students. Shakespeare is accessible to all students, but takes different forms for different groups: 'forget Shakespeare, think of Shakespeares'.

Second, teachers have almost certainly *seen* far more Shakespeare than their students. Those productions, on stage, or in film or video versions, will have been constant reminders of the fact that a play can be performed in many different ways. Some presentations may seem less appropriate than others according to taste, but teachers will know there is no 'one right way'.

The various productions are also reminders of how, in practice, directors and actors treat Shakespeare as a *script*, cutting it, rearranging it, interpreting it, and contesting previous interpretations. They show that any Shakespeare script is an invitation to staging, and that different stagings can take very different forms. For instance, *Macbeth* has been performed in traditional style with kilts and flaming torches; as a Chinese warlord struggle; as a Japanese Samurai epic; in a Second World War setting; as a Balinese spirit play; and even as a Marx Brothers production. Even traditional productions can present characters in different ways. They can give very different emphases to lines or moments or scenes. They can end in very different ways. Three different productions of *Macbeth* have ended respectively predicting future disruption, in celebratory triumph, and in exhausted stoicism.

Teachers' experiences of Shakespeare study and their own playgoing or screen viewing are intensely valuable resources; a source of knowledge that can be drawn upon, adapted, and modified to prepare suitable experiences for their own students.

Organising the classroom

Balance and variety are key principles of effective classroom organisation. A Shakespeare course usually contains the following elements.

1   Class work: examples include warm-ups or other active work in the drama studio or hall; teacher storytelling; debates; brainstorming; trials and Courts of Inquiry (see pages 205–6); newspaper offices (see page 207). Work on this scale is a useful preliminary and follow-up to many kinds of small group work. Some teachers find it valuable, where possible, to have the class sitting in a circle. Some activities can begin by reading around the circle, handing on at each punctuation mark (to gain initial familiarity with a speech or scene). The circle then turns into small groups for activities based on that reading.

2   Acting companies: here the class is divided into two groups, and lesson by lesson, the groups take turns to perform scenes in sequence. One lesson is used for preparation, one for presentation and discussion. A more typical practice, as a course proceeds, is for groups of 6–10 students to take responsibility for a scene or sequence of the play that they will present in the final lesson.

3   Group work: some scenes can be simply handed over to students to work on in groups. All the witches' scenes in *Macbeth* are obvious examples. Teachers can reduce their role to the briefest of scene-setting, to organising the students into groups, and to providing such help or questions as are felt necessary. But, as in all methods, the teacher should play an active, if unobtrusive, role in monitoring progress of groups and individuals.

4   Pair working: this is popular with students for a wide variety of tasks. An example is sharing a soliloquy as a conversation. This is a useful preliminary to a more detailed study of the language.

5   Individual work: this should be used in balance with the different sorts of group work. It is a key component of work on all aspects of Shakespeare.

However, many classrooms are ill-suited for active group work. The small size and the number of desks, chairs or tables make it impossible to have every student on their feet at the same time acting out the language. Many of the activities in this book can be adapted or scaled down so that students can undertake them in some form without leaving their seats. But even in small classrooms, teachers can use a variety of strategies for making a space.

Some teachers clear a space at the front or in the middle of the room. They take the lead in directing one or two groups in that space, ensuring that the seated students are also actively engaged (for example, as co-directors) and are learning from what they see and hear. The active work is a preliminary and stimulus to all students' work.

Small group or pair work can be undertaken by students pulling their chairs together. If possible, the groups should be arranged in a circle, leaving a space in the centre of the room for activities. The circular arrangement also facilitates group reporting when the teacher moves to whole class work.

Introduction to activities

Reading around the class can be an intensely boring experience for many students. Reading can be painfully slow, and when only a few students take part the attention of the others wanders. The usual root of the trouble is that Shakespeare is treated as a text for decipherment, rather than as a script for dramatic enactment.

The key to successful classroom Shakespeare lies in directly acknowledging the theatricality of the script. It means using active methods, rehearsal and performance techniques. Such methods encourage the students to experiment, explore, invent, discuss, dispute, practise and play with the language. It recognises that school Shakespeare does not stop at the Adam's apple, but involves the students in physical action.

The accounts that follow describe activities which increase students' participation. Some accounts may read a little like a recipe, but they are offered in the knowledge that teachers will adapt them to suit the particular circumstances of their own students.

Acting a scene

The teacher should select a scene or part of a scene with potential for striking dramatic enactment. Ideally there should be at least five or six characters (longer parts can be shared by two or more students). Experience suggests that first attempts at such performance activity should not involve more than 80–100 lines for a single one-hour lesson.

Some very short scenes or sequences are loaded with dramatic and imaginative possibilities. For example, the opening scene of *Macbeth* has only thirteen lines, but deserves a lesson of its own in which groups of students prepare and present their version of the witches. Many scenes contain more than 100 lines. Here, teachers can briefly explain the context, then choose an extract of around 80 lines, telling the class that 'like actors, and because of time, we'll concentrate on one section of the scene only'.

The lesson begins with the teacher saying something like:

Shakespeare wrote plays, not books. He wanted his plays to be acted on stage, not just read like any book. He wanted actors to turn his words into drama that audiences really wanted to watch. So we will treat Shakespeare as a play, as drama, as theatre!

This lesson will be something like how actors rehearse a play. We'll use some of the same techniques. The actors are aiming at a performance, and so will we. But don't worry, no-one's going to be embarrassed by being singled out to play Lady Macbeth on their own in front of the whole class! 'Performance' is all about working together, just as actors do in their rehearsals.

The first thing actors do is a read through. They sit down, take parts and read through the whole play to gain a first understanding of it. So we'll do the same with a scene.

Many actors will tell you that on the first reading they don't really understand what's going on. They find some of the words difficult or unfamiliar, and have to look up their meaning. But they know that turning the language into action will reveal meaning.

So we'll do what actors do. First of all, two fairly quick readings, with everyone having the chance to speak. Don't worry if you don't understand some words at first, and don't worry about the pronunciation. There isn't a 'right way' of saying Shakespeare's words, whatever anyone tells you.

The purpose of the first couple of readings is simply so that we can all get a first impression of the scene. Later you will get plenty of chance to choose the parts you want to play, but for this lesson, I'll just hand out the parts. So that more people can take part, I'll ask two or three of you to play one part.

The teacher then allocates parts for the first reading without worrying about cross-gender casting (it doesn't worry the students). There should be from six to ten students involved in the first read-through. No-one will speak a very large number of lines; everyone will speak at least one line. The teacher speaks any stage directions that may be included. Some teachers prepare large labels with the characters' names on, and hand them out to the students as the parts are allocated.

A character with a fairly large number of lines in a scene (for example, Bottom or Quince) can be shared between two or three students. It is vital that the students are quite clear about how the sharing out of speaking is to be done. For example, the teacher might say, 'John will speak Bottom's lines on page 19, Mary will play Bottom on page 21, and Jenny will speak his lines on page 23.' An alternative is for the students to take turns to speak successive speeches, but make sure the students are sitting next to each other.

After the first read through, which may be slow and uncertain, students should be praised for the helpful start they have made. The teacher then says that the second step is to do what actors do: go straight on to a second read through to get familiar with what's being said. Different students should be quickly cast as characters and the script is read through once again. If the scene is shorter than 30 lines, all students can work in groups to do their own read through.

After the second read through, the teacher tells the students that actors then discuss the scene using a simple set of questions – 'And we'll do the same!'

The class is then introduced to the W-structure. It helps to have it already prepared on the blackboard or on a large sheet of paper.

1   Who? Who are these characters? Briefly talk about your
    impression of each one – what's he or she like?

2   What? What's going on? Briefly discuss what you think is
    happening.

3   Where? Where is this taking place? Briefly describe what you think the setting might look like.

4   Why? Why do you think the characters say what they say, and behave as they do? What does each one *want*?

Some teachers run this part of the lesson as a whole class discussion; others prefer the students to discuss in small groups. If groups are used, the teacher should make sure that each group gets an opportunity to share its views with the whole class. If time is very short, each group could be asked to give its view of a particular character.

At the end of this fairly brief discussion, the teacher tells the students that there's one more very important question that actors ask, and that they spend the rest of their time actively working out on their feet:

5   How? How can we lift these words off the page to act out a performance that will really hold an audience?

The teacher again has a choice of options of how to address this question practically. The whole class can be kept together, with one group of students acting the parts and the others 'directing' from their chairs. Or the class could move into small groups, and each group work out its own version of the scene. But should they sit down to do so, or get up on their feet?

Some teachers may feel the classroom is far too small to have four groups on their feet working at the same time. Others think that the restricted space can be a positive advantage. The practical questions of furniture shifting in the normal classroom often decides the issue. It presents few problems for group discussion, but it often makes it extremely difficult for more than one group to do active work at a time. A possible solution, which depends on a teacher's level of trust and confidence in his or her students, is to send groups out of the classroom to other spaces to rehearse their version.

The advantage of having only one group performing, with the others watching and directing, is that the teacher can act as a kind of referee. The teacher ensures that everyone who wishes to do so gets a chance to offer their 'directing advice'. The teacher is also a prompter of questions, reminding the class of other questions that might be asked.

Many teachers provide a framework of questions that students can use in their own group explorations of how to stage the scene. The questions are put at points the teacher deems appropriate. Some teachers provide them as a typed list to each group as they begin rehearsing. Others leave them until the end of the lesson. Yet other teachers believe that many are quite unnecessary as the students intuitively address them in preparation. Such questions include the following selection.

1 Where is your audience?

2 How does each character get on stage?

3 Where is each character in relation to the others at the start of the scene? Where do they move to as the scene proceeds?

4 How does the speaking character behave? How do others react?

5 How does each character speak his or her lines? Details to be considered include tone of voice, pauses, emphasis, facial expression, gesture and movement and so on.

6 How do characters leave the stage?

The aim of this first lesson is to provide a framework which students can use in later lessons, enabling them to work independently in groups, preparing scenes for some kind of enactment. Some classes achieve that independence quickly, others need sustained help and guidance. The pace at which the teacher hands over full responsibility for independent group work to the students is a professional decision which each teacher takes in the light of the particularities of each class of students.

Some scenes for performance lessons

Line numbers are from the Cambridge School Shakespeare editions.

1 *Macbeth* Act 1 Scene 3 lines 1–86: meeting the witches. Five speaking characters: First Witch, Second Witch, Third Witch, Macbeth, Banquo.

2 *Romeo and Juliet* Act 1 Scene 1 lines 1–79: the brawl of the Montagues and Capulets. Eleven speaking characters (teacher reads the stage directions): Sampson, Gregory, Abram, Benvolio, Tybalt, Officers, Capulet, Lady Capulet, Montague, Lady Montague, Prince Escales.

3   *Romeo and Juliet* Act 1 Scene 5 in total: the first meeting of Romeo and Juliet. Ten speaking characters: four servants, Capulet, Cousin Capulet, Romeo, Tybalt, Juliet, Nurse.

This scene is 143 lines long, and has several distinct episodes:
- the four servants (lines 1–14)
- Capulet greets his guests (lines 15–39)
- Romeo first sees Juliet (lines 40–52)
- Tybalt is rebuked by Capulet (lines 53–91)
- Romeo and Juliet fall in love (lines 92–109)
- the lovers discover their identity (lines 110–43).

Student groups can take one or more of these episodes. If they play from Romeo's first words (line 40), there are 104 lines and six speaking parts.

4   *A Midsummer Night's Dream* Act 1 Scene 2 lines 1–88: the Mechanicals meet to cast the play. Six speaking characters (Bottom says most): Quince (share between 3 students), Bottom (share between 3 students), Flute, Snout, Starveling, Snug.

5   *Hamlet* Act 1 Scene 1 lines 1–69: the guard on the battlements at Elsinore. Four speaking characters (and the Ghost, who does not speak): Barnardo, Francisco, Horatio, Marcellus (the parts of Barnardo, Horatio and Marcellus could each be shared between two students).

6   *Macbeth* Act 3 Scene 3 in total (25 lines): the murder of Banquo. Four speaking characters (and Fleance, who enters but does not speak): First Murderer, Second Murderer, Third Murderer, Banquo.

The scene is the basic unit of construction of every Shakespeare play. Each scene is related in some way to those that precede it and to those that follow, juxtaposed by Shakespeare to intensify dramatic effect. Nonetheless, each scene has its own coherence, its own mood or moods. For students, a single scene can be an excellent teaching, learning and performing unit. Long scenes contain a number of distinctive units of action, each of which can be used for student performance within a lesson.

Beginning the play

In many plays, Shakespeare provides a gripping dramatic opening that invites active staging by groups of students. The openings are rich in follow-up activities of the speculative 'What happens next?' type, but the obvious first activity is one of staging (see pages 145–9).

1 *The Tempest*: how might students stage a storm at sea?

2 *Macbeth*: in groups of three, students prepare their own versions of the witches' 13 lines.

3 *Hamlet*: how might students create the tense, foreboding, atmosphere of the night guard on Elsinore's battlements?

4 *Romeo and Juliet*: here there is a choice of ways into the play.

In the case of *Romeo and Juliet*, students might stage the opening brawl between the Montagues and Capulets. Lines can be shared, and roles invented for citizens and followers of the two households. Movements can be choreographed, played in slow motion and fitted to lines (everyone should have the opportunity to experiment with gestures to accompany 'Do you bite your thumb at us, sir?').

Alternatively, students might work on the Prologue spoken by Chorus:

> Two households, both alike in dignity,
> In fair Verona (where we lay our scene),
> From ancient grudge break to new mutiny,
> Where civil blood makes civil hands unclean.
> From forth the fatal loins of these two foes
> A pair of star-crossed lovers take their life;
> Whose misadventured, piteous overthrows
> Doth with their death bury their parents' strife.
> The fearful passage of their death-marked love,
> And the continuance of their parents' rage,
> Which but their children's end nought could remove,
> Is now the two hours' traffic of our stage;
> The which if you with patient ears attend,
> What here shall miss, our toil shall strive to mend.

This fourteen-line summary of the play invites enactments which can be presented in different ways. For example, each group of students could take responsibility for the entire speech and as one person narrates each line, the others mime accompanying actions. Or, the lines might be shared among three or more groups of eight to twelve students.

The teacher says something like:

> We'll present the story of Romeo and Juliet as Shakespeare first narrates it, speaking the language and showing the actions. Every group will have two or three lines. The choice is yours of how to present each line. You might do it a word at a time, or as a mimed story, or...whatever.
>
> *Group 1:* Your first line is 'Two houses both alike in dignity'. You have to show the two families of Montagues and Capulets, both are very concerned about their dignity, their honour.
>
> *Group 2:* Your first line is 'In fair Verona (where we lay our scene)'. You'll show all Verona, the market traders, the jugglers, the shoppers, the thieves ...everything that's going on in the city.
>
> *Group 3:* Your first line is 'From ancient grudge break to new mutiny'. You'll prepare and show just what that ancient grudge, that old quarrel, is. How it festers and rankles, and finally erupts in yet another fight between the two families.
>
> *Group 4:* Your first line is 'Where civil blood makes civil hands unclean'. Your challenge is to show what the outbreak of fighting does to everyone. How can you show 'civil blood' making 'civil hands unclean'?

If there are only four groups, the teacher now returns to the first group to give them their next line to work on, continuing until all fourteen lines have been shared out. Each group thus has three or four lines to prepare and show. Each teacher will decide for him or herself the extent of hints given to students for performance. For example, 'You may choose to do it a word at a time, or as a little playlet. But all the words must be spoken, all actions shown.'

When the teacher feels the groups are ready, the class is invited to perform the whole story. Group after group speak their lines with accompanying actions (perhaps with a 'fast-forward' version as an encore). If there is time in the lesson (but there usually isn't), groups can discuss how they could adapt or extend their own, or another group's presentation. Or the teacher might choose to end by speaking the lines, pointing to each group in turn, silently inviting a brief recapitulation.

Some groups present a mime as a narrator speaks. Others have chosen quite different methods. One group of American students presented line 11 a word at a time:

Which	*a mime of witches*
but	*they slapped their buttocks vigorously*
their	*pointing*
children's	*mime of small children*
end	*more buttock-slapping*
nought	*circle made with finger and thumb*
could	*mime of cooking, as one student shook her head while tracing K in the air and then tracing D*
remove	*much picking-up and carrying away*

A purist might object, but such free-wheeling play with language catches something of the spirit of the play (think of Mercutio's constant wordplay, and of Shakespeare's enjoyment of language games).

It also goes without saying that students who present such imaginative re-workings are fully aware of the difference between 'which' and 'witch', and 'but' and 'butt'. What they demonstrate is a grasp of the possibilities of language that is so evident in every Shakespeare play: an alertness to ambiguity, a love of the protean quality of language as different meanings emerge from the same sounds.

Students do not have to begin a Shakespeare play with Act 1 Scene 1. Any particularly dramatic or imaginative moment can be a valuable first introduction, for example, Caliban's 'This island's mine', or Isabella's violent rejection of her brother Claudio in *Measure for Measure*, or part of the trial scene in *The Merchant of Venice*.

Students can dramatise the extract in some way, and then speculate about the context. What led up to this moment? What happens next?

Sense units

Many students are daunted by the appearance of a Shakespeare script. The language on the page seems to them to lie lifelessly: an impenetrable solid block of print, monolithic and uninviting. Students need help to lift those words into active dramatic life. Appropriate help enables them to find each 'sense unit': a section of language that comprises a thought, a coherent unit of dramatic language. Clearly, when students can identify the sense units within a stretch of language, their ability to understand, imagine, speak and enact it increases.

A range of active methods is available to help students conquer their fear. Using them, students realise that every speech is made up of thoughts, each making a unit of sense on its own. Each thought links together with others, revealing more and more of what the character is thinking and feeling. The following methods of working on a speech are complementary to the 'taking parts' style of techniques described elsewhere in this book. Their purpose is to enable students to identify their own preferred sense units in any speech, and to speak them confidently enough to communicate their meaning.

The teacher should select a long speech or soliloquy from the play being studied, and students can work through some of the following activities. Some teachers feel it appropriate to begin with a speech that has many end-stopped lines, where the sense unit is the line itself. In the early Shakespeare plays each line often makes sense on its own (see pages 66–8). However, many other teachers have found that their students can work successfully on almost any speech, for example these lines from *Hamlet*:

> Am I a coward?
> Who calls me villain, breaks my pate across,
> Plucks off my beard and blows it in my face,
> Tweaks me by th'nose, gives me the lie i'th'throat
> As deep as to the lungs? Who does me this?
> Ha, 'swounds, I should take it, for it cannot be
> But I am pigeon-livered, and lack gall
> To make oppression bitter, or ere this
> I should ha' fatted all the region kites
> With this slave's offal. Bloody, bawdy, villain!

Remorseless, treacherous, lecherous, kindless villain!
Oh, vengeance!
Why, what an ass am I! This is most brave,
That I, the son of the dear murderèd,
Prompted to my revenge by heaven and hell,
Must like a whore unpack my heart with words,
And fall a-cursing like a very drab,
A scullion!

Individual work

Walking the line
Students should walk around the room speaking a line at a time, making a sharp 90-degree turn at the end of each line.

If the teacher wishes the students to remain seated, the activity can be adapted. Students can turn their hands, or can speak each unit of meaning to a different part of the room, merely by turning their heads.

Walking the punctuation
Students should walk around the room speaking the script, but turning abruptly left or right at each punctuation mark. There can be two stages in this activity. Students read the same speech twice, but turn at different points in each reading:

• at every punctuation mark

• only at full stops.

Punctuation is a helpful guide to sense units, but no-one really knows how Shakespeare punctuated each speech. Much punctuation is the work of editors, and varies from edition to edition. But however the 'Who calls me villain' speech is punctuated, the many physical turns that students experience as they speak give them insight into Hamlet's disturbed state of mind and intensity of feeling. The purpose of this activity is to help students discover their own preferred length of sense unit, which is the focus of the next activity.

Walking *your* sense unit
Students should walk around the room speaking the speech. Each student makes a 90-degree turn at the end of each unit of speech that makes most sense to him or her. Different students can (and will) prefer smaller or larger units, and both will be right.

Working in pairs

Linked pairs
Students should link arms and attempt each of the walking activities described above. The activity in which students choose their own sense unit can have its dramatic results when one member of the pair decides to turn earlier than his or her partner! The physical disagreement results in close attention to the script and intense discussion over preferences for different units of meaning.

Following a partner
This is a highly motivating activity that can take different forms.

1   Hypnosis: one student holds the script in one hand and extends the other hand, palm upwards (or holding a pencil) towards the other student who fixes his or her eyes intently on the palm (or pencil). The first student then moves very slowly around the room, slowly speaking a short section of the speech and pausing between each sense unit. The second student follows, with eyes never moving from his or her partner's palm (or the pencil), and repeats each unit of speech. The hypnotic effect aids both co-operation and memory.

2   Eyes-closed leading: one student (the follower) keeps his or her eyes firmly closed and extends one arm, palm down. The other student (the leader), holds the script in one hand, and with a finger of the other hand lightly makes contact with the follower's palm. The leader guides the follower gently and safely around the room, speaking short sections of the script which the follower repeats.

3   Mirror-mime: students stand facing each other, but only one of them can see the script. The script might be pinned up in large type on the wall, or propped up between the two partners, or held by a third, or (if the student can manage it) held in his or her own hand. The student who can see the script speaks each small unit of meaning, accompanying it with a gentle, slowly performed movement or gesture which need not match the meaning. The other student repeats both the language and the movement or gesture. Some students try to turn this mirror-mime activity into a competition. By moving very fast, they seek

to defeat their partner's attempt to follow. Teachers should emphasise that this is a co-operative activity in which the objective is to help one's partner. But that doesn't prohibit setting demanding challenges of movements or gestures!

4   Back to back: partners stand closely back to back, arms linked. One person (who can see the script) speaks a speech, a small section at a time, pausing between each section. In each pause, the other repeats the spoken words. To add movement, the pairs can revolve very slowly as they speak.

5   Changing style: this involves one student repeating back a sense unit in a different style. Students face each other, one holding the script. The script-holding partner speaks each short section in a neutral tone and without emphases. The responding partner repeats everything back as a question (or an order, or a joke, or fearfully, or sadly and so on). Responders can also be asked to emphasise just one or two words as they reply.

6   Conversation: partners share the speech, alternately speaking small sense units as a kind of conversation. This activity works well with soliloquies, which are a kind of internal conversation (see pages 12–13).

7   Forgetful actor, helpful prompter: one student takes on the role of the actor who simply cannot remember his or her lines. The other plays the prompter and holds the script. The 'forgetful actor' leads: entering, bowing to the audience, preparing elaborately to begin to speak, then suddenly realising he or she has forgotten the lines – every word! The actor must appeal in some way to the prompter for a 'feed'. The prompter quietly gives the feed, the actor delivers it with great panache and much business, and is about to speak the next line when the same thing happens again – and another feed is required.

8   Puppet and puppet controller: one student, as puppet controller, speaks short sections of the script and operates imaginary strings to control the second student who moves and speaks as a puppet. Individual students have made intriguing adaptations of this activity, controlling a real or imagined puppet, and repeating each sense unit in a 'puppet voice'.

9   Nouns and verbs: one student works through the speech speaking only the nouns, the other then speaks only the verbs. Together, the pair work out a brief performance in which only nouns and verbs are spoken.

Further pair work using examples from *Hamlet*

Students can work in pairs to identify the sense units in the following speeches. They perform actions as suggested as they speak.

1   'To be or not to be…': sharing the speech as grave diggers, or as undertakers measuring a corpse and making a coffin.

2   'O what a rogue and peasant slave am I…': sharing the speech as scenery painters (imagine large brushes and a big bucket of paint).

3   'O my offence is rank…': as gardeners, sharing the speech while they weed a garden patch filled with difficult weeds.

4   'How all occasions…': as mountain climbers roped together and sharing the speech as they help each other up a vertical cliff face.

5   'O that this too too solid flesh…': fearfully whispering the speech as political prisoners chained together in a cell and forbidden to speak.

6   'O all you host of heaven…': as librarians sharing the speech while they stack books.

Good angel, bad angel

In this activity for three students, one student kneels, as if in prayer, script in hand. The two partners, as good angel and bad angel, stand behind the kneeling student who speaks a short section at a time. The bad angel repeats it malevolently, the good angel seraphically (teachers will, of course, choose their own appropriate vocabulary of 'good' and 'bad' as they set the task for students).

Performing an everyday action

In this activity for individuals or pairs, energy from one focused task seems to transfer to the language, often giving unexpected and thought-provoking insights. Students, pausing often, speak small units of a speech or scene as they perform some familiar action or simple every day task.

Individually

Suitable tasks for individual work are:

- putting on make-up
- painting a wall or ceiling
- cleaning shoes
- counting piles of money
- wrapping up a parcel
- hanging clothes on a washing line
- throwing horse shoes or playing bowls
- building a brick wall
- chopping wood
- practising throws at a basket ball net
- walking a tightrope (particularly suitable for 'To be or not to be...'.

In pairs

Suitable tasks for pair work are:

- throwing bricks to each other as building workers
- drinking in a bar and slowly getting drunk together
- carrying a very long plank
- sawing logs with a two handled saw
- paying for goods in a shop (the customer hands them over one at a time to the check-out assistant).

A presentation

After using some of the above sense unit activities to work on a particular speech, groups of students can devise a presentation of the speech to be enacted in some way by the whole group. The various experiences of line, punctuation, own sense unit, and so on will resource their preparation as students argue for the dramatic validity of longer (or shorter) units of thought to structure their enactment.

Size of sense units

A sense unit is a small section of language that make sense on its own; a thought that has internal coherence and meaning. It can be acted out in some way because it is intelligible in its own right.

It is advisable to urge students to identify small sense units: a phrase, line or short sentence that is clear and distinctive. However, different students prefer to work with different sizes of sense unit. For example, some students will take 'To be or not to be, that is the question' as a sense unit. Other students are happier to split the line into two sense units. Each preference is appropriate for the different students.

There is, of course, no such thing as *the* sense unit of a Shakespeare play. Each word, phrase, line, sentence, speech, Scene and Act has meaning and coherence. Each is related to all the others. The whole play is itself a sense unit, a totality that gives meaning to each of its parts. In practising reading by the line, punctuation, sentence and so on, students come to recognise the fluidity and inter-relatedness of sense units.

Speaking Shakespeare

> Speak the speech I pray you as I pronounced it to you,
> trippingly on the tongue; but if you mouth it as many of our
> players do, I had as lief the town-crier spoke my lines.

Hamlet probably had in mind the town-crier who merely bellowed every word. Such a way of speaking gives no thought to meaning, or to communicating that meaning by variation of tone, volume, inflection and so on. In contrast, an actor has to convince the audience that it *is* Hamlet, or Claudius or Ophelia they are seeing and hearing.

Are there rules about how Shakespeare should be spoken? Is there a correct way to speak the lines? Like everything else about Shakespeare, very different answers can be given to those questions. Some believe that the answer to each is 'yes', others answer with an equally firm 'no'. The two opposing views can be called 'form' and 'feeling'.

Those who believe in 'form' argue that everything must scan (that is, speaking should make clear the metrical structure of the verse). Each line should be spoken with five stresses and a pause (however short) at the end of each line. Learning about iambic pentameter should therefore be the first step in the study of Shakespeare's language.

The 'feeling' approach is more relaxed about rules. It argues that students should begin by speaking and acting out scenes or short extracts, to gain a sense of characters' emotions, thoughts and motivations. Students should experiment to find speaking styles appropriate to the particular dramatic situation. In this view, teaching iambic pentameter comes much later. Shakespeare may well have begun his career thinking in 'line units' (that is, a single line makes sense on its own), but he increasingly moved away from that practice, making thoughts run over line endings (sense units increasingly cease to match line units). To give each line five stresses becomes mechanical and unrealistic. For example, when Henry V wants to motivate his troops to attack Harfleur, the dramatic context makes it perfectly feasible that he gives his first line at least seven stresses (see page 67). Each teacher will decide what is suitable advice for his or her own students, but here are some commonsense suggestions.

1   Make sure you can be heard by your audience (who might be only one other student, a small group, the whole class, or a large audience watching a school production).

2   Accent is immaterial. Don't put on an artificial, false voice, but use your own natural voice. Shakespeare does not have to be spoken in the received pronunciation of the English upper middle classes. A Shakespearian king need not have any particular accent, but he usually speaks with the tone of authority.

3   Look for the sense units in the language. Sometimes they will be shorter than a line, sometimes longer, and sometimes the line itself. When you speak as a character, try to communicate his or her thoughts and feelings in an appropriate tone and style.

4   Pause or emphasise whenever you think it seems appropriate for dramatic effect, to give significance to what you are saying. Silence can be very powerful.

5   There is never one single right delivery: any speech may be spoken in many ways. The accepted style of speaking and performing Shakespeare changes from generation to generation.

What audiences at the Globe Theatre heard in Shakespeare's time would seem very strange today.

6   Remember that Shakespeare wrote plays, not recitation pieces. His language is an invitation to imaginative, dramatic enactment.

How to speak?

In *King John*, Constance, the mother of Arthur, believes that he should be the rightful king of England. She reacts sharply when Eleanor, Arthur's grandmother (who does not wish him to be king) calls Arthur to her:

ELEANOR Come to thy grandam, child.
CONSTANCE Do, child, go to it grandam, child.
          Give grandam kingdom, and it grandam will
          Give it a plum, a cherry, and a fig.
          There's a good grandam.

Constance's language is colloquial, short simple commands echoing Eleanor's words. The repetition of 'grandam' implies contempt. It is like a command to a very small child (in the play Arthur is about twelve years old), expressed in a childlike way. The huge contrast of 'kingdom' with 'plum', 'cherry', and 'fig' emphasises the irony and contempt. The final short sentence is a climax to the sarcasm.

Constance's meaning and intention are clear. Her words are heavily ironic, but how does she speak?

She can sneer the lines, snap them angrily, say them in exasperation, lay heavy or light emphasis on 'grandam', try to make a joke of it for others to laugh at, or heavily emphasise 'kingdom', 'plum', 'cherry', and 'fig'. She can load the verbs with sarcasm. She can speak very fast, or stretch the language out with extended contempt, or speak it like an exaggerated fairy tale spoken to a three-year-old. And, of course, she can add all kinds of accompanying business: movement, gestures, facial expressions.

What Constance's lines show is that it is easy to reach a firm understanding of what she says (meaning), and to infer strong reasons and intentions for why she ridicules Eleanor (motivation). But that still leaves students with many choices of how they might decide to have Constance speak the language.

Teacher leading

This follow-my-leader activity is a prelude to group work. The lesson begins with the teacher taking the lead very directly, as preparation for independent work by students. The teacher works with the whole class to demonstrate finding the sense unit.

Students can stand or sit. The teacher faces the students and speaks the script a short unit at a time, adding actions, gestures and expressions. The whole class repeats the phrase or line, together with the teacher's intonation and actions.

Some teachers like the students to have their own copy of the script in their hands, or on the desk in front of them. This enables the students to see just how the teacher is dividing up the speech. Other teachers prepare a transparency of the speech, to be shown on an overhead projector. They mark out each sense unit on the script with a vertical line so that students can see how the dividing up was done. A transparency script should be enlarged, so that it can be read easily by all students, even those at the very farthest point of the classroom or hall.

Every play has many passages containing action, imagery and description, that are suited to this activity. One example is the 'bloody sergeant' episode from *Macbeth*:

DUNCAN What bloody man is that? He can report
As seemeth by his plight, of the revolt
The newest state.

MALCOLM This is the sergeant
Who like a good and hardy soldier fought
'Gainst my captivity. Hail brave friend;
Say to the king, the knowledge of the broil
As thou didst leave it

CAPTAIN Doubtful it stood,
As two spent swimmers that do cling together
And choke their art. The merciless Macdonald –
Worthy to be a rebel, for to that
The multiplying villainies of nature
Do swarm upon him – from the Western Isles
Of kerns and galloglasses is supplied,

> And Fortune on his damnèd quarrel smiling,
> Showed like a rebel's whore. But all's too weak

down to

> But I am faint, my gashes cry for help.

Here is how this episode has been taught as a preliminary to small group work. The sense units spoken by the teacher are shown, with accompanying actions in italics (each teacher will, of course, use actions they think suitable). The whole class of students repeats each unit.

What bloody man is that? *vigorous pointing*

He can report *hand flaps near mouth*

As seemeth by his plight *fearful facial expression as hands indicate bleeding wounds on body*

of the revolt *hands, arms and face indicate fighting*

The newest state *cup hand to ear*

This is the sergeant *stand to attention, indicate stripes on sleeve*

Who like a good and hardy soldier *stiff salute*

fought 'gainst my captivity *fighting gestures and arms around body to show capture*

Hail brave friend *greeting gesture*

Say to the King *place imaginary crown on head*

the knowledge of the broil *tap head for knowledge, followed by fighting gestures*

As thou did'st leave it *freeze into running away posture*

Doubtful it stood *puzzled expression, finger on lips*

As two spent swimmers *weary swimming gestures*

that do cling together *embrace yourself*

And choke their art *many options here – literally drowning, or indicate both 'choke' and 'art'*

The merciless Macdonald *some teachers grit their teeth and do a little highland dance – others choke on a hamburger!*

Worthy to be a rebel   *shake fist defiantly*

for to that the multiplying villainies of nature   *again, a huge range of facial and bodily options*

Do swarm upon him   *'ugh' gestures as teacher scrapes off bees*

from the Western Isles   *invite the class to point: from where? – the result is usually hilarious, hands point on all directions!*

Of kerns and galloglasses is supplied   *few students are likely to know what 'kerns and galloglasses' are; it's usually best to simply say and demonstrate 'lightly armed and heavily armed soldiers'*

And Fortune   *toss coin, throw dice*

on his damnèd quarrel smiling   *fighting and grinning*

Showed like a rebel's whore   *the accompanying gestures and postures the teacher makes here will depend on his or her self-image, relationship with the class – and probably a host of other things!*

But all's too weak   *slump with exhaustion*

and so on down to

But I am faint   *hand on brow, stagger*

my gashes cry for help   *indicate wounds and appeal for assistance*

Enacting the speech in this way involves all the students, though some teachers feel uncomfortable with this very direct leading of the class. However, those teachers who do use the method report that students value and enjoy the activity and learn from it as a prelude to their own pair or small group work. It helps students to share the imaginative excitement that Shakespeare's language generates. Group follow-up work to this initial teacher leading activity includes the following five activities.

Questioning group responses

The class can be divided into four groups, one in each corner of the room. Each group in turn speaks and 'shows' a small unit of script. The teacher, in the centre of the room, highlights particular words or phrases by posing questions after the group has spoken and acted a unit:

First group (*With actions*) What bloody man is that?

Teacher What *what* man is that?

The students will call out 'bloody!', and the teacher can then ask them to *show* the word as well as speaking it. They demonstrate that the man is wounded. Similarly, following groups show, in response to the teacher's questions, actions for report, plight, revolt, and so on. Further questions might include:

This is the *who*? (students emphasise and show 'sergeant')

Fought 'gainst your *what*? (students physically explore how captivity might be signified).

Students enjoy such challenges and vigorously respond, verbally and physically. Recapitulations of 'the hare, the lion' and 'as sparrows, eagles' are always popular!

> At 'Or memorise another Golgotha', there is usually at least one student in the group who can put an action (crucifixion) to the phrase. The teacher should reward this with 'Good, yes, look at (student's name) – Christ crucified on the cross at Golgotha', and invite other students to imitate. If no student demonstrates the action, the teacher should perform it with the brief explanation. In this activity, it is unhelpful to pause for longer explanations.

Showing the actions in pairs

Students should work in pairs, at their own pace. In turn, each student speaks a short section, showing the other student a suitable action.

Echoes

Students should work in small groups. One student slowly speaks the lines, the others echo every word to do with war, fighting or armies. This activity helps students discover how Shakespeare creates atmosphere through language (see pages 47–9, 138–49).

Individual enactment

Students work in threes as Duncan, Malcolm and the Captain to act out the episode. The wounded soldier kneels or lies on the floor and gives his report to King Duncan. After the preparatory work, little reminder is needed that he's terribly wounded, possibly near to death, fighting for words as he struggles to tell his story. Each student takes turns to act out each of the three roles.

Writing home

The wounded captain has had his wounds dressed. He now has time to write home to tell his adventures. Here, he's not speaking to a king, but to his family, so he's likely to use a different language style. Students can write his letter based on lines 1–42 ('What bloody man... cry for help').

Five investigations

Teachers can fit this technique to the time available. It yields results in even a short lesson (on a single scene), but is particularly suited to a longer lesson or workshop on an Act or the whole play.

The class is divided into five groups. Each group is given one specific question (Who? What? Where? When? or Why?) and one 'shared' question (How?). Each group works on its two questions.

Group 1

1 Who are these characters?

2 How can we portray them?

The group identifies each character: their personalities, relationships, past experiences and so on. It then devises an active way of showing who's who – mime, play, 'family photograph' (tableau), and so on. The presentation can be closely tied to the play or completely free-wheeling. One energetic and committed student inquiry on *Hamlet* resulted in a tug-of-war between Hamlet and Claudius, with Gertrude as the agonised, stretched rope.

Group 2

1   What's going on?

2   How can we portray it?

The students identify what's happening in the extract, then devise an active way of showing it. They may act out the story using some of Shakespeare's language, or find some other mode of presentation: a series of newspaper headlines with accompanying 'photographs' (tableaux by the group); a kindergarten version; a party political broadcast, and so on. The aim of the group is to make some imaginative re-creation that gets to the heart of the story of the scene.

Group 3

1   Where does the scene take place?

2   How can we show it?

Some groups take a 'whole play' approach and find an active way of identifying the various locations of the play. This has been done as a television travel show, as a tourist agency 'living brochure', as a land and sea excursion, and by chalking a large circle on the floor within which the students 'journeyed' to different locations.

Other groups might take an 'individual scene' approach and concentrate on the details of the set, and on working out the moves for characters. When students have used their bodies to form castle battlements, trees in a wood, furniture in banqueting hall, and so on, the results have been both hilarious and insightful. Students have set scenes in pubs, supermarkets, cinemas and a host of other places.

Group 4

1   When does the action take place?

2   How can we portray those times?

Some groups take a historical approach: at what period of history does this play (or scene) take place? Could it be staged in modern dress? and so on. Other students have considered the timescale of the scene or play: does this action take place at night or in the day? How long does the action last? What are the major events in sequence? Students working on *Hamlet*, *Othello* and *Macbeth* have staged 'night/day' presentations to show how much of the significant action happens at night.

Group 5

1 Why do the characters behave as they do? (What causes the action of the scene or play?)

2 How can we portray those causes?

Students often concentrate on characters' motivations, staging a series of 'I want...' presentations (see pages 112, 158–61).

Other groups have chosen to present explanations based on social or supernatural factors: that the witches 'cause' Macbeth's tragedy, or that its roots lie in the feudal and military structure of medieval Scotland; or that *Romeo and Juliet* can be explained through the patriarchal society of Verona, or just by bad luck, or by fate (the influence of the stars), or even by love itself.

The How? activity here depends upon the time available. Students discuss possible ways of portrayal, then move into very practical, active work, exploring ways in which their answers might be staged.

Follow-up

Some groups have written up their investigations as 'Inquiry reports', sometimes on large sheets of paper for display in the classroom. Teachers can judge whether or not such writing and display will arise and follow on from the active work. Where it does, a wall display built up during the period of the Shakespeare course can prove to be a valuable visual aid to assist further work.

Sections and headlines

This activity is suitable for older students who have already gained some Shakespeare experience. It gives them choice and responsibility, and has been successfully used in groups of about eight to ten students.

The group should sit in a circle. The first reader (the teacher) begins to read slowly (speaking cues and all). Individual students call out 'section' whenever they think a change in subject or mood has taken place. Obviously, this is a matter of judgement, so the group discusses whether the 'section' identified by the caller is appropriate. If the group thinks the mood or direction has not changed, the reading continues until another student calls 'section'. This is also discussed, to find if the group generally agrees. When agreement is reached on a section, the group can decide on a newspaper headline to describe it. The headline must be brief and relevant, a few words only.

Another person then takes up the reading until the next section and headline are agreed. The process is continued until the end of the scene, by which time the group probably has between five and fifteen headlines. These headlines can be used for active work, such as the following four examples.

1   A mime can be enacted or series of tableaux built as the headlines are spoken by one or more students.

2   The headlines can become the basis of an improvisation, using students' own language.

3   The students can present a brief performance of the scene, using the headline and several of Shakespeare's lines in each section.

4   The headlines can be used to develop the story, told from memory, by group members. One student begins the story using the first headline and telling the first section from memory. The next student continues with the next section, and so on section by section, around the circle.

Student as director

The role of the director is one which enables students to work at their own level and challenges them to develop their potential. In any Shakespeare course, it is valuable to encourage students to think about, discuss, and take on the role of, the director. This is best done practically by preparing a scene for performance.

When a class of students works together on a scene for the very first time, the teacher will probably find himself or herself acting as director for the first lesson or two. However, the aim of a Shakespeare course using active methods is to enable students to work independently in self-directed groups. Taking on the role of director is a major step towards that aim.

When students work in groups or 'acting companies', each company or group takes responsibility for enacting part of a play. Each group can appoint a director, who takes on the special responsibilities involved. Students who are diffident or reluctant to act, are often highly motivated by the planning and co-ordinating aspects of the director's role.

The term 'director' is a nineteenth-century invention. As far as we know, in Shakespeare's time neither the term nor the role existed. It is highly likely that Shakespeare would have given advice to his fellow actors as they rehearsed for a performance on the Globe stage, or perhaps another actor 'took the lead'. Today, every production of a play has a director. He or she is someone who guides the performance, co-ordinates the actors and designers and everyone else involved, and is the major influence in all artistic decisions. A good director is a leader but not a dictator. He or she has a vision of how the play could be performed: its style, mood, setting and costumes, and so on. In rehearsals, the director helps actors to achieve performances that contribute to the success of the production.

A director doesn't simply tell actors what to do, treating them merely as puppets. He or she works with them, encouraging them to try out their own ideas and to help others who are involved in the scene. The professional director sees it as his or her task to release the unique creative energies of each actor in ways which contribute positively to the eventual live performance.

Some people are critical of what they call 'Directors' theatre'. By this they mean a production in which one person, the director, has imposed his or her own concept of the performance on the actors and determined every detail of the production. For example, a director might decide that *Hamlet* is 'really about' Hamlet suffering from an Oedipus complex. As a result, he or she tries to deliver a production that bears out that single psychological explanation. Such dictatorial views are rare, and in practice most directors are flexible in rehearsal. They believe that by encouraging actors to experiment, to try out their own ideas, a particular way of performing will emerge that releases, rather than restricts, creative energy and potential. Most teachers of Shakespeare share the same attitude in their own work with students.

Guidelines for student directors

1   A good director works by asking questions, rather than by ordering, and offers constructive advice and praise to the actors.

2   A good director leads by negotiation and encourages actors to experiment in rehearsal; he or she endeavours to build feelings of success and to eliminate fear of failure.

3   The director decides where and when the play will be set.

4   A good director gives an introductory talk to everyone involved in the production, setting out his or her views on the play, and describing what he or she hopes to achieve.

5   The director arranges and conducts rehearsals of every scene.

6   The director decides which parts of the script to cut or amend or rearrange; he or she might also include extracts from other plays or from the Sonnets.

7   The director works with the set and costume designer, the lighting director, and the voice and movement director (in small-scale or amateur productions, the director might undertake all these functions).

8   The director tries to achieve a performance that coherently matches his or her view of the play.

9   A good director reads the play over and over again – and reads widely around it: criticism, descriptions of past performances, and so on.

One introduction to the role of the director is to focus on Peter Quince in *A Midsummer Night's Dream*. He calls the actors together, hands out the parts, gives advice, conducts the rehearsal and seems to be generally in charge. Students can work in groups of six, reading and acting out Act 1 Scene 2 (or Act 3 Scene 1 lines 1–82).

They can experiment with playing Peter Quince in different ways, for example, as an impatient dictator or as a director who is very hesitant about giving other people advice and instruction.

Point of view: theory

Traditional 'point of view' activities can take account of recent theoretical writing (see Chapter 3). Students can stage a particular scene or episode from the play they are studying guided by one of the following interpretative standpoints:

- feminist (from a woman's perspective)
- cultural materialist (politics, wealth and power strongly influence every human relationship)
- psychoanalytic (childhood experience, unconscious or sexual motives underlie all adult behaviour)
- new historicist (the production shows the repressive conditions of Shakespeare's own time)
- poetic–aesthetic (the beauty of the language is what matters)
- liberal–humanist (freedom and human progress are the goals of life, and final reconciliation and harmony are possible).

Improvisations

Two kinds of improvisation are particularly useful in developing students' understanding. The first explores how characters might behave when they are not on stage. Students can step into role as particular characters and, in free-ranging, spontaneous enactments, play out conversations, meetings or happenings that do not occur in the play. All kinds of seemingly improbable situations can be improvised: Hamlet consults a doctor to request sleeping pills for his bad dreams; Claudius seeks help from Alcoholics Anonymous; Horatio recalls the day he first met Hamlet; Ophelia asks Polonius about her mother; Prospero first meets Ariel in the cloven pine, and they strike their bargain as master and servant; Macbeth and Lady Macbeth argue about which TV programmes to watch.

In the second type of improvisation, students explore a theme or situation of the play, but not as Shakespearian characters. For example, they might role-play an ambitious wife, determined to further her husband's career; or a group of businessmen who conspire to overthrow the chairman of the company; or a jealous husband whose suspicions are inflamed by a false friend; or a young man depressed by his mother's re-marriage.

Some teachers suspect both types of improvisation, seeing them as questionable in the context of Shakespearian studies. Other teachers find improvisations invaluable in developing student motivation and insight. Teachers will, of course, judge which student activities they consider to be genuine engagements with the script and which are evasions. Such judgements weigh particular improvisations in the context of the students' wider Shakespeare experience.

Warm-ups

For actors, warm-ups are short physical exercises that begin a workshop or rehearsal or precede a performance. For school students, warm-ups are introductory activities in workshops or active lessons. They need a large space where free movement is possible. Warm-ups relax inhibitions and self-consciousness, and create a sense of enjoyment and shared activity. By increasing blood-flow and energy, they prepare the students for further physical and verbal work on the script.

There are many kinds of warm-up, for example, passing a handclap at speed around the group, or games of tag and so on. The warm-ups below are more directly related to Shakespeare's language and characters.

Robots and robot controllers

This is an activity on characters' names. It is an unembarrassing way of helping students to practise pronunciation; some students are unsure how to pronounce names such as Tybalt or Mercutio if they have not heard the name spoken.

Students should work in pairs. The teacher begins with a demonstration, choosing a student as partner. The teacher stands behind the student, asks him or her to close their eyes and follow a simple set of commands:

- 'go' means 'walk forward slowly'
- 'stop' means 'stop'
- 'left' means 'turn left' (a quarter-turn)
- 'right' means 'turn right' (a quarter-turn).

The teacher then briefly demonstrates, giving orders as robot controller for the student robot to follow.

Next, the teacher tells the class, 'This isn't just learning robots – it's doing Shakespeare, so now I'll re-programme my robot':

- 'Romeo' means 'go'
- 'Juliet' means 'stop'
- 'Montague' means 'turn left'
- 'Capulet' means 'turn right'.

'Got it? Yes, of course you have! So, eyes tightly closed – let's go!' And away the teacher goes guiding the student robot on a very short journey around the room. Then, to get all students in the class working together actively, using some of Shakespeare's names, the teacher says something like:

> Work with your partner, one as robot, one as robot controller. The robot controller will programme the robot, then take him or her around to the four walls of the room, without bumping in to anyone else. Remember, robot controllers, your robot's safety is in your hands! You can use my programme, or you can use any of the names of the characters in the play.

At this point the teacher can show and read aloud the list of characters, either using an overhead projector transparency, or a hand-written list in large letters that are clearly visible all around the room.

Students of all ages enter enthusiastically into the activity. There'll be much laughter, and the teacher will probably need to remind robots to keep their eyes tightly closed, and trust their robot controllers!

This warm-up can be kept going as long as students enjoy it. All kinds of variations can be played upon it. For example:

- robots and robot controllers change roles
- students re-programme with different names
- students invent additional commands for the robot to perform (some students will do this on their own initiative before the teacher invites them to do so).

Students will choose their own level of difficulty at which to work, as they add additional commands to the initial four. In practice, student-invented commands will range from the simple (when I say 'Benvolio' it means 'walk backwards') to the fiendishly complex (when I say 'Mercutio', jump up and down three times, drop on your hands and knees, and crawl forwards saying 'a plague on both your houses'). Some students programme in 'slow motion' commands, but it is advisable on safety grounds to ban 'fast-forward'!

As students become more familiar with a play, they can use lines for robot commands and so on. The activity involves everyone in the class, is open to many adaptations and extensions, and enables students to work at their own level and pace. Importantly, it is non-threatening: no-one is put on the spot to perform in front of others.

Banquo's Ghost

Students find ghosts fascinating. A warm-up with Banquo's Ghost needs a number of extracts from Macbeth's language. Teachers can present these using an overhead projector transparency, or a list in large print on one or more large sheets of paper. The words should be in full view of everyone in the room. An alternative is to give each student Macbeth a sheet containing the words.

Students should work in pairs, each student taking turns to play Banquo's Ghost and Macbeth. Teachers set the scene in as much or little detail as they wish (the shorter, the better, is often advisable). For example:

> Macbeth has had Banquo murdered. At the banquet, Banquo's Ghost returns from death to haunt Macbeth. But, Macbeths, it's like a nightmare, and you can only move very slowly, as if you had a huge weight tied to your legs. You want to get away from the Ghost, but he keeps following you. Ghosts, follow him inexorably (here the teacher gives a two-second imitation of Banquo's Ghost). Let's do it with Macbeth all cheerful at first – then Ghosts – make your appearance!

The room fills with movement as a variety of ghosts slowly pursue each fearful Macbeth who speaks the lines, trying to escape:

Avaunt, and quit my sight!

Let the earth hide thee!

Thy bones are marrowless

Thy blood is cold

Thou hast no speculation in those eyes which thou dost glare with

What man dare, I dare

Approach thou like the rugged Russian bear

The armed rhinoceros

or the Hyrcan tiger

Take any shape but that, and my firm nerves shall never tremble

Hence, horrible shadow!

Unreal mockery, hence!

In brief follow-ups, students can tableau one or two phrases; or the teacher can ask for shows of marrowless ghosts, Hyrcan tigers and so on; or students can perform the activity from memory.

Finger-fencing

This very short energetic activity involves all students and gets the adrenaline flowing. It illustrates the theme of conflict and encourages line learning.

Students should work in pairs. The teacher demonstrates with a partner (who should be selected very carefully indeed!), and reminds the students that Shakespeare wrote drama – and all drama is about conflict: in love or war, in quarrels over power or land. In many Shakespeare plays there's a sword fight of some sort, so... 'Draw your sword!'

Here the teacher faces up to his or her partner, arm extended, telling students that the index finger is the point of the sword. The partner does likewise. Each person has only one vulnerable point – the small of the back. The object of the game is to touch the small of your opponent's back with your finger. The teacher reminds the students that: 'This is Shakespeare – so we've each got some language to say! Here's mine:'

Obey and go with me, for thou must die.

'And,' the teacher says to his or her opponent: 'Here's yours:'

Wilt thou provoke me? Then have at thee, boy!

The opponent repeats their line once or twice, then – into action!

My own experience is that I can only keep this up for ten or twenty seconds before my opponent taps me in the small of the back. But I ensure that the language is spoken often, and the class enjoys seeing the teacher get the worst of it!

After the demonstration, it's time for everyone to fence, but before they do, teachers should insist on some practice with the language, and stress the safety aspect. Each pair starts fencing on a given signal. After a short time, a halt should be called. However, students get carried away with the activity so a sharp 'stop now' sound such as a whistle or cymbal that everyone can hear and understand is needed.

Every play has 'conflict' words that can be used in this activity. The teacher can make them specific to characters or freely adapt them:

> Turn, hellhound, turn. My voice is in my sword.

> Lay on, Macduff,
> And damned be him that first cries, 'Hold enough!'

Statements and replies

For this activity, students should stand in a circle. One walks across the circle to another and says to him or her:

> I am afraid to think what I have done.

The other replies:

> Infirm of purpose! Give me the daggers.

The first student then takes the place in the circle of the second student who walks across the circle to another student and says:

> I am afraid to think what I have done.

Again the reply is:

> Infirm of purpose! Give me the daggers.

And the third student sets off to another student, and so on.

This simple activity, with only two lines to learn, generates a tense, dramatic climate as students vary how they speak and respond, and any movements they make. Other statements and replies that have worked effectively are:

> Some say the earth was feverous and did shake.
> 'Twas a rough night.

> Our royal master's murdered.
> Woe, alas. What, in our house?

> It will have blood they say, blood will have blood.
> You lack the season of all natures, sleep.

Your castle is surprised. Your wife and babes savagely
slaughtered.
What, all my pretty chickens and their dam at one fell
swoop?

A memory game

This game helps students with the vocabulary and subject matter of a
play. It can be adapted to be played by any number of students. The
following example is for *Macbeth*. The teacher writes each of the words
or phrases below on a separate slip of paper or card:

- a dagger
- a cauldron
- a cat
- a cannon
- a Norwegian banner
- ten thousand dollars
- a crown
- a pilot's thumb
- a drum
- a letter
- a serpent
- a flower
- Banquo's Ghost
- Birnam Wood
- a naked new-born babe
- a diamond
- a bell
- a painted devil
- the great Doom's image
- a trumpet
- an owl
- lots of dogs
- two murderers
- some scorpions
- a bat
- a toad
- a beetle
- a crow
- a horse
- a kite
- a rugged Russian bear
- an armed rhinoceros
- a Hyrcan tiger
- a chough
- a hedge-pig
- a fenny snake
- a newt
- a frog
- a lizard
- a dragon
- a wolf
- a shark
- a goat
- a tiger's stomach
- a baboon
- a wren
- an egg
- a candle.

Each student receives one slip. The first student begins by saying: 'I came back from Scotland with (word on card – a dagger).'

The next student repeats the sentence, but adds their own word, saying: 'I came back from Scotland with a dagger and (word on card – a cauldron).'

The third student repeats and adds his or her item and so on.

Some classes can achieve remarkable feats of memory: the sight of the succession of speakers is an aid.

The first time the class plays this memory game, the teacher may wish to restrict the list to familiar items such as insects, animals, birds, and so on. In preparing the slips, teachers will exercise their judgement about the level of difficulty involved in remembering the various items.

One variation of the game is for students to work in groups of six to eight, and for each student to have two, three or four items, contributing one each time his or her turn occurs. A valuable development is for students to take over the game, without teachers' prompt-cards. They can add their own favoured items from the play they are studying: 'a cream-faced loon', 'a shag-haired villain' and so on.

Tableaux

Tableau work can be undertaken in pairs or groups of any size. A tableau (from the French *tableau vivant*, a living statue) is like a sculpture or a still photograph. Students portray a moment frozen in time, catching the action at a precise instant. Each character is held fixed, displaying a particular gesture, expression or movement.

Tableau method has two very student-active components. Preparing their living sculpture stimulates students into valuable discussion of character motivation and relationships, themes and imagery. The tableau generates further discussion among the spectator students as they 'decode' the sculpture, questioning and commenting on what they see.

A good introductory tableau activity is to ask pairs of students to use whatever space is available to prepare a tableau of the Ghost's command to Hamlet, 'Revenge his foul and most unnatural murder', making it as dramatically striking as possible.

Each pair shows its tableau, staying perfectly still for one minute (a demanding discipline). It is often helpful in terms of time and potential embarrassment to have four or five pairs all showing their tableaux at the same time. Other students can walk into the 'sculpture park' so created, viewing each 'statue' from all angles.

An equally effective introduction is for students to work in groups to prepare a tableau of a line which involves more than two characters or a particularly striking image, for example:

> The triple pillar of the world transformed
> Into a strumpet's fool.

The students' task is to find a physical language for the presentation of their tableau. Discussion and analysis is finally embodied in a non-verbal, non-written form of bodily expression.

In the early stages of tableau work, as with all active methods, it is important not to judge what students produce, but to praise every effort. It is also valuable to encourage constructive discussion in which students can pick out what made some tableaux distinctive and impressive. Below are some variations on tableau work (see 'Critical incidents' pages 142–3).

Character tableaux

Each student can prepare a tableau of a character of their choice, showing that character in a typical pose, mood or gesture. Students can show their character tableaux in turn, or as small groups, for the other students to guess which characters are being portrayed.

Guess the line

This activity gives students choice and responsibility. The class is divided into pairs or groups, and each chooses a phrase or line from a scene and prepares a tableau. The tableau is held for one minute as other students 'read' the frozen pictures and pool their guesses as to the line portrayed.

This activity is suitable for early lessons of a Shakespeare course when only the scenes or episodes students have already covered are used. It also makes an excellent lesson at the end of a course when students are familiar with the whole play. Here students need plenty of time for their selection and planning (say 30–40 minutes for preparation in a one-hour lesson and the rest of the time for showing).

Start and end tableaux

The class is divided in half and the teacher lists about twelve characters that both groups have to portray (the actual number will depend on the size of the groups). Each group allocates parts, and prepares and presents two tableaux:

- tableau 1 shows the character relationships just before the start of the play
- tableau 2 shows the characters at the end of the play (some characters are not on-stage at the end, so the students must decide how to integrate such characters into this final tableau).

Each group presents its two tableaux to the other group whose task is to guess who's who! It is helpful to ask students to consider whether each student should play a different character in each tableau, or whether they should portray the same character in both.

Theme tableaux

Students can work in pairs or groups of any size. The teacher should list some of the major themes of the play and the students prepare a tableau of one or more of these themes. A helpful beginning is for all groups to work on the same theme, so that in the showing session, students can see the wide range of responses to the same challenge.

Genre tableaux

For this activity, students should work in groups to prepare and show tableaux of the endings of:

- a tragedy
- a history
- a comedy (teachers usually tell students that in Elizabethan theatre, a comedy was a play that ended in marriage).

For some students, it is a valuable variation on this activity to ask them to prepare tableaux for 'problem play', or 'romance' or 'late play' endings.

Relationship tableaux

There are many variations of this activity (see pages 124–5). The nature of the activity is clear from the following example.

One student strikes a pose as a character (say, Macbeth). A second comes forward, says the name of another character (say, Duncan) and the two students freeze into a tableau to show their relationship. After ten seconds or so, the second student unfreezes and departs as a third student comes forward declaring the name of another character (say, First Witch), and a new relationship tableau is struck. Students succeed each other in unfreezing and stepping out of frame to be replaced by another character.

Human emotions tableaux

Students can work singly, in pairs, or in groups to prepare tableaux depicting human emotions: hate, love, jealousy, happiness, guilt, fear, despair and so on.

Realistic or symbolic?

As students prepare a tableau they invariably find themselves facing the question 'How realistic should our frozen picture be?' It is a question best decided by the students themselves for each particular moment or line they have chosen. For example, when Claudio in *Measure for Measure* says to his sister Isabella, 'Death is a fearful thing', the students might choose to portray:

- a stage picture, showing the brother and sister at that moment
- a non-realist imaginative portrayal, with Death personified and its terrors represented in all kinds of different ways (for example, bodies in death throes, or fearsome creatures which serve Death)
- a mixture of both – the brother and sister in conversation and an expressionistic representation of the words behind or around them.

Choral speaking

There are many kinds of choral speaking activity. The aim of such activities is to enable every member of a group of students to contribute to a presentation of some of Shakespeare's lines. Some lines are spoken in unison by two or more voices, some are echoed or repeated or differently emphasised. Movement, gesture, sound effects, and music can be added along with any other effects that increase the imaginative impact of the presentation.

For students' first experience of choral speaking, it is often advisable to choose extracts from plays written early in Shakespeare's career. In these plays, the lines are frequently end-stopped, so that each line makes sense on its own. In later plays (for example, *Macbeth*), many lines run on, and individual lines do not make appropriate sense units for choral speaking. However, with a little practice students quickly identify sense units of different lengths.

Clarence's dream from *King Richard III* is rich in atmosphere, and can be delivered line by line. It offers many opportunities for follow-up work of creative writing or art and design (for example, a collage of pictures based on the lines). The whole speech contains two sections. The first is a twelve-line story of Clarence escaping from the Tower of London and taking ship across the English Channel. It is followed by the thirteen-line undersea experience:

> O Lord! Methought what pain it was to drown!
> What dreadful noise of waters in mine ears!
> What sights of ugly death within mine eyes!
> Methoughts I saw a thousand fearful wracks;
> A thousand men that fishes gnawed upon;
> Wedges of gold, great anchors, heaps of pearls
> Inestimable stones, unvalued jewels,
> All scattered in the bottom of the sea.
> Some lay in dead men's skulls and in the holes
> Where eyes did once inhabit, there were crept,
> As 'twere in scorn of eyes, reflecting gems,
> That wooed the slimy bottom of the deep
> And mocked the dead bones that lay scattered by.

Many speeches lend themselves to choral speaking. The following examples from *Romeo and Juliet* have been used successfully with school students.

1   The Prologue: the 'whole story' of the play.

2   Act 1 Scene 1: Prince Escales' rebuke.

3   Act 1 Scene 4: Mercutio's Queen Mab speech.

4   Act 3 Scene 2: Juliet's opening speech.

For older school and college students, these examples from *Measure for Measure* have been successful.

1   The Duke's speech 'Be absolute for death…' (music adds greatly to the atmosphere of this long speech, for example Faure's *Requiem*).

2   Claudio's speech 'Ay, but to go we know not where…'.

Insults

Students enjoy Shakespeare's richly inventive language of invective. The exchanges in *The Tempest* between Prospero and Caliban are always popular, as is Kent's diatribe against Oswald in *King Lear* (see page 12). A successful activity uses a few of the things that Prince Hal and Falstaff call each other in *King Henry IV Part 1*:

PRINCE Thou clay-brained guts
FALSTAFF You starveling
PRINCE Thou knotty-pated fool
FALSTAFF You elf-skin
PRINCE Thou whore-son obscene greasy tallow-catch
FALSTAFF You dried neat's-tongue
PRINCE Sanguine coward, bed-presser!
FALSTAFF You bull's pizzle
PRINCE Horse-back-breaker! Huge hill of flesh!
FALSTAFF You stock-fish!
PRINCE Bolting-hutch of beastliness, swollen parcel of dropsies
FALSTAFF O for a breath to utter what is like thee!
PRINCE Huge bombard of sack
FALSTAFF You tailor's-yard
PRINCE Stuffed cloak-bag of guts
FALSTAFF You sheath, you bow-case
PRINCE Roasted Manningtree Ox with the pudding in his belly
FALSTAFF You vile standing tuck
PRINCE Reverend vice, grey iniquity, father ruffian, vanity in years!
FALSTAFF You Prince of Wales
PRINCE Why, you whore-son round man, What's the matter?

For this activity, the teacher should prepare the list of insults on a sheet of paper. Each student has a copy, and for a few minutes students can walk around the room greeting each other with an insult chosen at random from the list. The teacher then divides the class in half. One group stands lined up against the wall at one side of the room, facing the other group lined up opposite.

The 'Prince' group speaks first, all together: 'Thou clay-brained guts'. The 'Falstaff' group replies with 'You starveling'. The two groups can verbally trade all the insults on the list. Alternatively, after four or five pairs of insults have been exchanged, the teacher could stop the activity and reminds the students of Hamlet's advice to the Players: 'suit the action to the word, the word to the action'. The two groups then re-start the insults, this time adding actions to show just what they mean!

An additional variation is to have the groups slowly advance towards each other, one step to accompany each insult. Here, teachers need to lay down a strict 'no touching' rule, otherwise when the two groups meet at the centre of the room, the action can become too physical! Another variation is to have students working in pairs, experimenting with a variety of ways of speaking the insults. For example, they can be whispered, said lovingly, or as if they were the funniest joke in the world and so on.

This activity can serve as an introduction to character work. Students often volunteer the observation that the gestures that they have made up for the insults directed at Prince Hal tend to be 'narrowing' actions, whereas the insults directed at Falstaff tend to produce wide and expansive actions: an example of Shakespeare matching language to character (see pages 115–16).

Insult generator

For this activity, the teacher should prepare enough copies of the insult generator for every student to have one. Insults are made up by choosing one word from column 1, one from column 2 and one from column 3. Students can individually stroll around the room exchanging insults. Alternatively, students can work with a partner and make up a conversation of insults. Every word is Shakespeare's!

Column 1	Column 2	Column 3
simpering	languageless	block
painted	wasp-stung	drone
notable	lack-brained	lubber
threadbare	mad-headed	patch
decayed	shotten-herring	fancy-monger
flattering	nimble-footed	shoulder-clapper
shallow	puppy-headed	fragment
capering	fell-lurking	varlet
embossed	marble-hearted	popinjay
revolted	glass-gazing	mad wag
superfluous	outward-sainted	promise-breaker
meddling	lascivious	pander
counterfeit	strangely visited	coxcomb
twangling	lily-livered	hilding
juggling	cream-faced	mountebank
viperous	super-servicable	puke-stocking
venomous	frosty-spirited	basilisk
wretched	egregious	ticklebrain
slovenly	smooth-faced	bubble
manifest	whore-son	whey-face
scurvy	all-changing	horse-drench
odoriferous	cony-catching	shrimp
abominable	hard-hearted	boggler
malicious	long tongued	time-pleaser
juggling	pigeon-livered	flibbertigibbet
unpolished	fustillarian	whoremonger
insinuating	hare-brained	bug
paltry	logger-headed	candle-maker
execrable	iron-witted	double-dealer
testy	foul-spoken	pantaloon
giddy	stretch-mouthed	boil

Using videos

The ever-increasing number of Shakespeare plays available on video provides an excellent teaching resource. Videos make it possible for students to engage in insightful performance study. In a theatre or cinema, the play or film unfolds inexorably with no opportunity for an audience member to hold up or review the action or words. If you miss a word or action, it is irretrievably gone. There is no time to study how a particular effect is achieved. But video provides students with excellent opportunities to 're-read' performances.

At the same time, film and video, like television, can be intimate media. They can concentrate on character and show close-ups quite naturally. In the theatre, an actor's whole body is in view, and the minute changes of expression that would fill the screen on film, are quite unseen by those in the gallery, or even a few rows back from the stage.

Teacher opinion on how videos should be used is, however, sharply divided. Every point of view is represented. A few teachers never use videos. Others (again few) restrict their students' experience of Shakespeare solely to a single lesson or two watching one video of a play. Between these extremes exists a vast range of practice and strongly held convictions. Some teachers are certain that 'it's best to show a video right at the start of the course, so that students gain a general understanding of the play, even before they see the script'. Others are equally passionately convinced that the video must not be shown until after substantial experience of reading or acting out the play. Some teachers claim to be 'experts of the fast-forward and freeze-frame buttons'. Others favour 'intensive viewing of segments with frequent rewind'.

Within this great variety of practice and belief, one essential principle governs the use of the video: *active, critical viewing*. This involves close study of particular scenes, actions or speeches. Student inquiry should focus on how a Shakespeare film has been constructed, how its meanings have been made, and whose interests are served by those meanings. It should identify the underlying values and ideology (or more simply, point of view), and the film techniques and forms of representation used.

Active critical viewing recognises that the director, through the camera, selects and dictates what must be watched, giving the illusion of a seamless performance. It asks how language is turned into visual images, noting, for example, how Polanski's *Macbeth* employs a recurring bear-baiting motif to illustrate such imagery in the play, and how the McKellen *King Richard III* makes similar use of boar images.

Wherever possible, one video version of a play should be compared and contrasted with another to find out how scenes are presented and juxtaposed, how speeches or lines are delivered. Students' analyses of contrasting versions of the same play graphically demonstrate that Shakespeare is open to multiple interpretations. Analysis can lead students to discover that there is no one definitive performance, and that each director constructs his or her own perspective on the play. For example, in these well known versions of *Hamlet*:

- Laurence Olivier's version virtually takes place inside Hamlet's mind
- Kozintzev's Russian version is a vibrantly social reading
- Zeffirelli's film with Mel Gibson as Hamlet gives full weight to *Hamlet* as a family drama with Gertrude at its centre
- Kenneth Branagh's four-hour version combines political and personal readings.

Similar contrasts emerge from comparisons of versions of *King Lear*:

- Kozintsev's is consciously political
- Jonathan Miller's BBC video is domestic and familial
- Peter Brook sets his production in a pitiless natural world
- Olivier's version centres on the fragile empathy-evoking character of Lear himself.

Comparison of the film techniques and forms of representation used for soliloquies can also be revealing. 'To be or not to be' in the BBC version with Derek Jacobi is filmed in one long single shot, always focused on the actor. In contrast the Zeffirelli film shows the soliloquy as an edited sequence of well over a dozen shots, each of which vividly illustrates the imagery. Similar comparisons can be made to highlight different portrayals of character. In Olivier's *Hamlet*, Hamlet thrusts a blazing torch into Claudius' face as he cries for light. In the BBC *Hamlet*, Claudius seizes a torch to threaten Hamlet.

Particularly interesting critical viewing opportunities exist in the two films of *King Henry V* by Kenneth Branagh (1989) and Laurence Olivier (1944). On first viewing the two versions appear radically different.

Olivier's film was made to boost morale for the imminent invasion of Europe on D-Day. It is dedicated to the men of the Commandos and Airborne forces, and comes over as a patriotic hymn, with Olivier as the model of all Christian princes, a view that J. H. Walter's Arden Shakespeare edition strongly echoes. Anything that questions Henry's nobleness is excised or altered. The bishops clown rather than conspire; the aristocratic conspirators disappear; Henry's blood-curdling threats before Harfleur are cut, as is Williams' awkward questioning.

Branagh's version appears to present the sharpest of contrasts. Olivier's chivalric Agincourt gives way to the blood, mud and sweat of Branagh's battle. Branagh's king is an honest man, beset by a troubled conscience over politics and personal friendships alike. Against flashbacks to the Boar's Head in Eastcheap, he is shown visibly grieving over Falstaff's death.

Students can inspect Branagh's film more closely on video. They can identify the cuts, alterations and emphases when it is compared with Shakespeare's script. What emerges are the striking *likenesses* between Branagh's and Olivier's films. By careful editing of the script and the film, Branagh also renders Henry as a 'good guy'. The Burgundy–Henry sexual innuendo disappears as does Henry's second highly dubious argument to Williams that many troops deserve their death. The facts of the parliamentary Bill are removed. The slow-motion battle is followed by a long tracking shot accompanied by an emotional *non nobis domine* as Henry carries a dead boy through the aftermath of battle. These are sequences reminiscent of a right-stuff, buddy–buddy Vietnam movie.

A detailed critical viewing reminds students that there is no such thing as *the* video, only *a* video that presents one particular vision of the play. It is helpfully accompanied by an activity which asks 'How would *you* do it?' Students can work out their own version of a scene or speech, comparing it with what they have seen on video.

Students will frequently adapt what they have seen. After watching Zeffirelli's *Romeo and Juliet*, many student Mercutios are likely to take a dip in Verona's fountain as part of their own enactment; after seeing Luhrmann's *William Shakespeare's Romeo + Juliet*, student Mercutios are likely to attend the Capulets' party in drag. In almost every case, the inspiration that the film provides will be adapted and extended, not precisely copied.

King Henry V on film: Although different in appearance, Laurence Olivier (left) and Kenneth Branagh (below) share recognisably similar interpretations of King Henry.

A technical vocabulary

Students need a simple set of terms to give precision and focus to their discussion of videos of Shakespeare's plays. Such terms help students to read a video, and include the following:

- tracking
- long shot
- zoom
- story-board
- shot
- close-up
- moving or stationary camera
- intercutting
- camera angle
- subtitles, credits
- editing
- cutting
- focus
- windows
- inserts
- frame
- wind-back
- freeze-frame
- montage
- fade
- voice-over
- panning
- soundtrack
- flashback
- camera position.

Every teacher will decide whether he or she wishes to devote a particular lesson to study of these techniques, or whether they are best introduced as required during study of a particular play. If students video their own performance of a scene, the vocabulary comes fully into active use.

Advantages and disadvantages of video Shakespeare

Advantages

1 Videos are easy to use under normal classroom conditions (no problem with daylight viewing).

2 Video is a user-friendly medium with which most students are already familiar.

3 The cassettes are comparatively cheap to purchase, and much cheaper than taking a class of students to a live performance.

4 The play can be viewed by teachers in advance of student viewing (an option usually not available in live theatre productions).

5 The nature of video provides opportunities for rewinding to review a particular movement or scene.

6 Viewing provokes discussion of costumes, sets, characters, properties and so on.

7 Close-ups of characters' faces can be especially revealing.

8 Videos can facilitate independent study: students can be in control of when to stop or fast forward the video. They can identify cuts, rearrangements and additions to Shakespeare's script (for example, Polanski's showing of the murder of Duncan).

9 Many plays are easily available. Some plays (notably *Macbeth*, *Hamlet*, and *King Lear*), are available as different productions on video, so making comparisons possible.

Disadvantages

1 The director's intentions are dominant and decide what the audience must watch. Students' gaze cannot rove to watch reactions, groupings, or a character who especially interests them.

2   The sense of occasion and of risk (things can go wrong!) that a
    live theatre performance evokes is missing, as is the unique
    audience–actor interaction of live theatre. The very familiarity of
    video can cause distancing, reducing students' feeling of
    heightened involvement.

3   The 'smoothness' of video, the illusion of effortless continuity,
    hides the amount of construction and editing that goes into any
    television production or film.

4   If the video is of a television production rather than of a film,
    long shots and general views are usually less well handled than
    close-ups.

5   Over-reliance on a video may fix an image of a particular
    character too firmly in students' minds.

6   Watching a video can be merely a passive activity, unexamined
    and undiscussed.

Trials and inquiries

Do characters get what they deserve in Shakespeare's plays? All kinds
of innocent people die: Romeo and Juliet, Cordelia, Duncan, Banquo,
Lady Macduff and her son, Desdemona. So, too, do characters with
blood on their hands: Macbeth, Lady Macbeth, Claudius, Edmond
and Richard III. A host of other characters whose morality is less clear
cut suffer the same fate: Hamlet, Polonius and Laertes, Mercutio,
Tybalt and Paris. Are these deaths justly deserved? Who is responsible
for each?

   Everyone knows how gripping courtroom drama can be. From the
trial in *The Merchant of Venice* to the many contemporary television
courtroom series, there is something about the judicial process that
seizes the imagination. The same involved fascination is at work when
students undertake such procedures in the classroom. Trials, or Courts
of Inquiry, set up towards the end of a Shakespeare course, can be an
excellent way of enabling students to review a play in fresh ways.

   In a trial, a specific character or characters is charged with
responsibility for a death, or deaths. A Court of Inquiry does not try an
individual, but calls witnesses to give their account of the story and to

be cross-questioned. Teachers will, of course, choose which form they adopt, weighing the advantages of each, and remembering the need for all students to be involved as fully and actively as possible.

In a trial, possible student roles are:

- defending or prosecuting lawyers
- judge or judges
- witnesses
- defendants.

In a Court of Inquiry, possible student roles are:

- members of the panel of assessors
- witnesses.

Both methods work well when the teacher sets up the initial framework and briefly defines the roles and procedures. Whichever method teachers choose, time management is vital and a limit should be set on how long each witness or defendant is allowed to speak. Formality of procedure aids rather than inhibits the activity: some student judges have appeared in gowns and wigs.

Trials

In a trial, a specific charge is made against a character or characters, for example, 'That you did cause the deaths of Romeo and Juliet.'

It is helpful to discuss with the whole class who might be charged, but it is advisable to restrict the number to two or three characters. Other main players in the tragedy should be available as witnesses, to be called and questioned by both prosecution and defence lawyers.

Courts of Inquiry

Here is an example of one teacher's initial preparation and briefing for a Court of Inquiry.

Title
An inquiry into the causes of the events in Scotland from the death of King Duncan to the accession of King Malcolm.

Members of the panel
Five assessors will hear evidence, question witnesses, and finally deliver their verdict.

Note for students: the five students who act as assessors have one lesson to prepare their questions before the Court meets in the following lesson.

Witnesses
The witnesses to be called can include both living and dead characters: Macbeth, Lady Macbeth, Banquo, Three Witches, Malcolm, Seyton, Lady Macbeth's gentlewoman, the Porter and so on.

Note for students: two, three or four students can take on the role of each character and have one lesson to prepare their view of events to present to the Inquiry.

Procedure
Each witness called will be asked to give an account of their knowledge of the events which took place. This account must not take more than five minutes and can be in any form the witness prefers (verbal testimony, mime, or whatever).

Witnesses will then be questioned by the Panel for up to ten minutes. (These times will depend on the time available for the Inquiry and the number of witnesses to be called.)

Preparation
At least one lesson is required for preparation in small groups. The Court of Inquiry will be formally conducted in the following lesson (one and a half hours long).

It is sometimes helpful if the teacher takes the role of Secretary to the Inquiry, in order to ensure time-keeping, but it is best if students manage everything by themselves.

Writing and design

Newspapers

Student-compiled newspapers such as *The Dunsinane Times* or *The Verona Gazette* are long-standing, familiar and motivating activities. It is possible to purchase ready-designed mast heads, but it is usually preferable for students to design their own. The following activity has proved very successful in many classrooms, partly because the whole class works together to achieve a common purpose and meet a deadline.

The classroom becomes a newspaper office – where time is always short. There are pressing deadlines. The aim is to produce a full edition of *The Verona Mail* in two hours, using as much of Shakespeare's language as possible. The teacher specifies the point in the play at which the paper is to be produced (if, say, it is immediately after the death of Mercutio, then many events in the play lie in the future, open to speculation). Students work in pairs and each pair takes responsibility for one or two sections of the paper, chosen from:

- News items
- Obituaries
- Advertisements
- For Sale and Wanted
- What's on?
- Weather
- Nature Notes
- Food and Drink
- Puzzle Corner
- Cartoons
- Crossword
- Readers' letters
- Leading article
- Sports page
- Business pages
- Property for sale
- Travel page
- News in brief
- International news
- Children's page
- Job vacancies
- Gossip column
- Science report
- Agony Aunt
- Engagements and weddings
- Horoscope
- Consumer page
- Law report
- Reviews: films, books, plays
- Births, marriages and deaths.

The activity works best in a two-hour session, but two separate one-hour sessions are feasible. In some classes, a student is appointed as Editor-in-chief, with a roving role to co-ordinate, assist, motivate and keep the writing flowing!

An interesting question for teachers is when such a newspaper activity should be set. Some teachers use it after the first few lessons (for example, after the initial brawl of the Montagues and Capulets, or after the second scene of *Macbeth* when victory is reported). Others place it near or at the end of the course when students are familiar with the whole play. It is usually advisable to set the publication day immediately after one of the climactic moments in the play, to provide a main lead story with eyewitness accounts and so on.

Diaries

Keeping a character's secret diary is an imaginative and productive activity. Many major characters do not have soliloquies in which they can directly reveal what is going on in their minds. Polonius or Gertrude (in *Hamlet*) might keep such a diary recording their thoughts and feelings at a series of precise moments in the play.

Even where a character has soliloquies, the diary technique is valuable. Students who have worked on *Hamlet* for some time, can write a series of diary entries recording Hamlet's changing moods and thoughts at particular points throughout the play.

Students' writing: some reminders

1 It is valuable to discuss with students the kind of writing they might do.

2 Give choice whenever possible.

3 Stress the importance of drafting and re-drafting, particularly for any published, displayed or assessed work.

4 Writing immediately after the intense experience of an activity can produce striking results.

5 Illustrations accompanying written work add to its appeal to both writer and reader. For example, students could write and illustrate their own (or Shakespeare's) spells, sonnets, poems, songs. Blake's *Songs of Innocence and Experience* invariably proves a stimulating model.

Write a missing scene

Students can write an imagined scene in the style and atmosphere of the play. For example, in *Macbeth*, such scenes might include:

• the thanes meeting in Council, after the murder of King Duncan, to elect a new King

• the coronation of Macbeth as king, with the thanes swearing loyalty

• the death of Lady Macbeth: does she say anything? does anyone witness her death?

Some students have written themselves into the play, inventing a friend from whom a major character seeks advice.

Preparing a production

Students should work in small groups and discuss the period and place in which they might set their play. For example, should *Romeo and Juliet* be set in medieval Italy, or in modern times in an actual city torn by conflict? How effective would a 'timeless' setting be? When the group has decided on a place and time, the students choose several of the following activities. Their finished assignment could be presented as a file of drawings, notes and suggestions for a production, or a showing of some kind.

1 Design the set: how can it be used for particular scenes?

2 Design the costumes: look at past examples, but invent anew.

3 Design the props – furnishings and hand props (swords, utensils for eating and drinking, and so on)

4 Design a lighting and sound programme for one or two scenes.

5 Design the publicity poster: make people want to see the play!

6 Design a flyer – a small handbill to advertise the production.

7 Write character notes for actors' guidance.

8 What major idea or ideas will guide the production?

9 Plan the advertising campaign for the production.

10 Work out a five-minute presentation to convince potential sponsors that the production deserves funding.

11 Prepare an audience survey to find out just what people liked or disliked about the production.

12 Design the programme: bear in mind the number of pages, the layout, and the content. Here are some suggestions for elements to be included in a programme for *Macbeth*: Lady Macbeth's diary; a psychiatrist's report on Lady Macbeth; notes on the costume design; stage design notes; a visiting professor writes about the play; an interview with an actor; an interview with the director.

Storyboards

Storyboards are a series of drawings prepared to assist the making of a film. Each picture shows a moment which the camera will capture, together with speech from the script. Many frames of a storyboard are prepared for each short sequence of film. For classroom Shakespeare, storyboarding is a popular activity with students. It works effectively with very short scenes or episodes (around 20–40 lines).

Marking up the script

Students can work individually or in pairs and step into role as directors about to put on a production. Each student is given a photocopy of around 40 lines of script. Their task is to 'mark it up' to show how they think each moment will be presented on stage. Students should annotate the lines to suggest:

- how the language is spoken
- what they envisage as accompanying gestures and movement
- blocking (positions on stage) of characters
- lighting
- use of props
- anything else they find relevant.

It is usually helpful to begin such a lesson by having a class discussion on the first two or three lines, to explore appropriate levels of attention to detail.

When the teacher thinks students have had sufficient time to finish (and the problem is they will all finish at different times!), he or she can ask them to join another student or pair to compare what they have done, and to talk about any differences.

Pick out a only a few lines for whole class discussion. Whole script discussion usually gets bogged down and risks losing student involvement. What is much more important is that marked-up scripts are exchanged, and pairs of students attempt to enact a swapped script following the director's notes!

Keeping a Shakespeare log or journal

Each student can keep a log or journal in which they write about their experience or thoughts in whatever manner they wish. Some teachers try to keep five minutes at the end of each lesson for such an activity, and encourage students to record their feelings. Just how did they feel about Puck, or Hamlet, or Lady Macbeth after this lesson? The entries are a valuable resource for future written work to be presented as coursework.

The journal entries can be notes on anything students felt relevant during the lesson. Students might record what they feel they have learned; vivid images that appeal; one or two lines, words or phrases that especially stick in the memory. They might note how they feel about the lesson itself: the most valuable part, the least interesting part (why?), the most difficult, least understood parts and so on. Entries might be hypotheses or predictions, or questions about something that puzzles the student. One teacher began some lessons by asking students to look back over what they had written, and ask any question to which they still hadn't been able to work out an answer.

Anything that goes in the journal belongs to the student. It won't be graded by the teacher. Some teachers promise they won't look at the journals at all. Others say they will do it by invitation. Others say they will look through them several times in order to see how to make the Shakespeare course more effective. But, whatever rules are agreed between students and teacher, stick to them!

Sequencing

For this activity, the teacher makes several photocopies of a speech, then cuts them into strips, line by line. Each set of strips is jumbled up and given to small groups of students to re-assemble in Shakespeare's original order: a sequence that makes emotional and dramatic sense. Students are urged to speak the lines and accompany them with actions to test out the dramatic effectiveness of their sequence.

For students' first introduction to sequencing, it is advisable to use only about ten lines so that the task is not too daunting. The first nine lines of Macbeth's soliloquy 'Is this a dagger which I see before me' (to 'As this which I now draw') is an appropriate beginning. Longer extracts can be tackled later in the Shakespeare course.

Shakespeare's life and times

Although Shakespeare's life and times is a popular subject with students, relatively little space is given here to the topic for two reasons. First, because the main endeavour of this book is to help teachers teach the plays. Second, because there is no shortage of publications already available on the life and times. Such publications typically cover:

- Shakespeare's family
- Stratford-upon-Avon
- schooldays
- marriage
- the 'lost years'
- London
- the Globe and other playhouses
- acting companies, playwrights, actors and audiences
- Elizabethan and Jacobean England (economy, religion, customs, dress, recreations, exploration, and so on)
- Queen Elizabeth and King James
- Shakespeare's increasing prosperity
- Shakespeare's return to Stratford.

Students usually undertake personal research into an aspect in which they are interested, and present their findings in a variety of attractive ways.

Younger students usually have 'the Tudors' firmly fixed in their imagination. It is a world of doublet and hose, ruffs, tall hats, swords, gallants in cloaks, and ladies in jewelled costumes and farthingales. The picture is of a 'Merrie England' that contains bear-baiting, hunting and hawking, public executions and horrible tortures, but which is essentially benign. Queen Elizabeth I, bejewelled, austere and remote, presides over a glittering court and a world of country houses set among fields and villages in which a contented peasantry and yeomanry happily cultivate the land.

How far teachers wish their students to challenge this perspective is a matter for individual decision. There is little doubt that many publications gloss over the harshness of life for most people in Elizabethan England. Maypole dancing and madrigals coexisted with the cruelties of bear-baiting and blood sports and the often savage intolerance and repression of political and religious dissent.

The many uncertainties and unknowns about Shakespeare provide excellent opportunities for students' speculation and imaginative exploration. What did he do in the 'lost years'? What explains his apparent unconcern for publishing his own plays? How were the plays rehearsed at the Globe? Where and how did he do his writing? How did he spend his time when he retired to Stratford? Why did he insert that 'second best bed' clause in his will? What were his relationships with his family? (He seems to have disliked his younger daughter's husband.)

William Shakespeare can be hot-seated, just like the characters in his plays. Students can work in small groups to prepare their answers to questions like the ones below.

1 What did you like most about growing up in Stratford? What did you like least?

2 What was school like?

3 What *did* you do in the 'lost years'?

4 How did you develop your interest in plays?

5 What did you do in you first year in London?

6 Tell us about how you worked at the Globe. Did you direct rehearsals, alter plays on advice from the actors, write parts with particular actors in mind?

7 Why didn't you publish your plays yourself?

8 Why did you leave your wife your second best bed?

9 What happened to all the books you owned?

10 Do you have a favourite play? character? line?

11 What do you think about school students studying Shakespeare today?

Theatre visits

A visit to a live production is a vital part of any Shakespeare course. The sights and sounds of theatre are far more appealing to most students than classroom discussion of metaphor, imagery and rhetoric. Shakespeare wrote his plays to be acted, watched and enjoyed, and a theatre visit confirms that intention. Students experience the words brought to life on stage by the actors, costumes, movement, music and lighting. Here are daggers and ghosts, Macbeth appalled at his bloody hands, Capulet storming at Juliet. The experience is unique: here, now, at this never-to-be-repeated moment, before this particular audience. The live actors are performing specially for *you*.

Whenever possible, theatre visits should be an integral part of

Visits to Stratford-upon-Avon and to the Globe Theatre on London's Bankside enrich Shakespeare courses for students of any age. In and around Stratford, the Shakespeare Birthplace Trust opens six properties, including the Birthplace pictured above. In London, thanks to the vision and energy of the American actor, Sam Wanamaker, the reconstructed Globe beside the Thames gives students a unique experience of Shakespeare's theatre.

students' Shakespeare experience. Their value in the context of active approaches to Shakespeare in the classroom is enormous. Students who have acted out characters, scenes, lines are acutely alert to how 'their' character, scene or line is performed. The sense of ownership is palpable. Some teachers have had to warn their students *not* to speak Lady Macbeth's lines with her as she sleepwalks on stage!

Preparation and follow-up enriches the value of any theatre visit. It is important for students to share their perceptions of a performance. Initial teacher structuring of discussion by setting particular topics, is often helpful. The following are activities that have been used successfully, and can be adapted by teachers to suit the nature of their own students.

Preparation

Characters and incidents
Each student can choose a character (or an incident or scene) to watch especially closely. Before the visit, students should write down their expectations of how that character (or episode) is likely to be performed. After the visit, each student reports back to the class on how their expectations were fulfilled or challenged. For example, did characters differ from those on the video the class watched?

Lines
Each student can choose a favourite line from the play. They listen carefully to how it is spoken on stage. Did the delivery add to their understanding of the line?

Reviews
The teacher can collect several published reviews of the production, and discuss with students whether they should read the reviews before or after they see the play: each student makes their own decision. After the visit, students discuss how far they agree or disagree with the reviews. Those who read the reviews before the visit can tell how, if at all, the review affected their response to the production.

Follow-up

Reviews
Students can write their own reviews. It helps to give them a few simple guidelines on extent and content:

- number of words
- the review should report what you personally saw and heard (sets, acting style, costumes, atmosphere and so on)
- were parts of the script omitted or rearranged?
- your feelings about the production, with reasons for some of your judgements.

Topic discussion

Students can work in pairs or threes to briefly discuss a given topic such as 'What did the costumes signify to you?' After a few minutes, a new topic is given. Teachers can ask students to move round to form a new pair or threesome for each new topic (some classes enjoy this change of partner, others don't). These brief discussions are a good preliminary to whole class discussion.

Brainstorming

To begin with, a topic such as 'What was your response to how Lady Macbeth was played?' is given to the whole class. Students call out their responses as single words or short phrases and the teacher quickly writes each on the board. Students should then work in pairs or threes. Their task is to use the brainstormed list to identify one or two responses with which they most agree and one or two with which they least agree. A whole class discussion can follow, or students can move into three or four large groups to compare their responses.

Memorable moments

For this activity, students first work alone, briefly writing down their answers to questions from the teacher.

1 What did you find the most exciting moment or scene?
2 What was the saddest moment?
3 What was the most boring moment?
4 What did you think was the most surprising moment?
5 What was the most horrific moment?
6 What was the most difficult moment to understand?
7 What did you find the most memorable moment?

The writing activity is a preliminary to small-group discussion or a class discussion. Students can begin by declaring to the group, with reasons, some of their memorable moments.

Guess the moment

This is a variation on the memorable moments technique. In small groups, students work out a tableau of a chosen moment in the production. Each group presents its tableau to the other groups whose task is to guess what moment in the play is shown.

The annual Shakespeare play

This book is mainly concerned with classroom Shakespeare, taught as part of the English and drama curriculum. Its purpose is to help teachers enable all their students to inhabit actively and with enjoyment the imaginative worlds of Shakespeare's plays. The enthusiasm and vitality generated by such classroom work often results in the students sharing their experience with other classes, or with students in other schools and colleges (see 'Shakespeare festivals' below).

In addition to such shared events, many schools and colleges have established a tradition of 'The Shakespeare Play'. This is an annual, full-length production of two to three hours including an interval, played to a paying audience over three to five nights.

The goal of public performance affects attitudes and commitment very positively. It is an opportunity for individual students to show excellence in achievement. The self-esteem derived from public performance is immense. The performance also provides a wide range of opportunities for many students other than the few playing the major roles. A large number of students can contribute to the production's success, on and off stage.

Practice varies greatly. For example, one school regularly mounts a production involving all one hundred and fifty of its ten- and eleven-year-olds (see page 232). In another school, open auditions take place to select a cast of not more than twenty. In yet another school, students are nominated by teachers without audition.

Here is a checklist of questions for teachers planning to mount a public performance of a Shakespeare play.

1   How full a performance of the script is it to be? What cuts of lines or characters?

2   How are students to be selected for parts?

3 How many students will be engaged in performance roles? How can student participation, control, and initiative be maximised?

4 How can the production involve teachers and students throughout the school or college? There are many possibilities: costumes, set, stage crew, lighting, publicity, box office, front-of-house, prop-making, make-up, refreshments and so on.

5 How can English, drama and other subjects contribute to the play as a normal part of the curriculum?

6 How many performances should there be? When? Does the Shakespeare play have a 'natural' place in the school or college calendar?

7 Who are the target audience?

8 Should teachers act in the production?

9 What kind of production is envisaged: proscenium arch? in the round? promenade?

10 What are the criteria by which to judge the success of the production?

11 When should rehearsals start?

Some teachers have reservations about an annual Shakespeare play, seeing it as elitist, selective, and teacher-directed. These critics argue that such performances involve only a small number of students who act out a teacher's version of the play. They claim that such performances are much concerned with the reputation and image of the school or college.

But there is no reason why the Shakespeare play should not take its full place in the rich variety of methods by which school students experience and enjoy Shakespeare. It is yet another opportunity for students to develop and display their talent.

Shakespeare festivals

A Shakespeare festival is an occasion when quite large numbers of students come together to celebrate their Shakespeare work. The scale of the enterprise can vary. A single school or college may organise its own festival, in which each class stages its own contribution. Or several schools or colleges might join together to share some of their Shakespeare experience. Festivals are often whole day events, but they can be shorter or longer.

Festivals (or celebrations or bardathons) have proved increasingly popular with students and teachers alike. They provide an opportunity to see and participate in a wide range of different approaches to Shakespeare. The different types of public performance contribute to the students' self-development and give pleasure and understanding to others. However, like all such large events, careful planning is necessary. What follows is a list of practical points which teachers thinking of organising a festival need to consider – and agree upon!

1   Who will participate: which classes, colleges, schools? In practice, separate festivals for older and younger students work more effectively than those which attempt to span widely different age ranges.

2   Is there a clear timetable for the day? Everyone taking part should know precisely when they will show their prepared piece.

3   Are teacher responsibilities clearly specified? For example, some festivals have a Master or Mistress of Ceremonies who introduces and links the presentations.

4   What requirements need to be made clear to participants? For example, whether or not performances should be in costume; whether or not each school should bring a banner showing play title, school name, emblem and so on.

5   Where will the stagings take place? Details of stage, audience placing, and any promenades need to be clear.

6   How long is each presentation? Experience suggests that between 15–25 minutes is appropriate.

7   How many schools and colleges, classes or groups can attend? The presentation time limit (see previous item) determines the maximum number of groups that can participate.

8   How will the Festival open? How will it close? Teachers should

decide what degree of ceremony they feel is appropriate to each occasion.

9 Is the choice of play and style of performance completely open to the participants' own choice?

10 Do students arrive in costume and stay in costume all day? Are changing facilities available?

11 What is the basis of participation: a whole class, or a selected group of students, or something else? Whole-class presentations are strongly recommended whenever possible, but much depends on the scale of the festival. Individual students will be in role, but ways should be found to enable every student in the class to participate actively in some way.

12 Should the presentations be entirely in Shakespeare's own language? Most festivals allow students' own language where appropriate, and sometimes it is highly desirable that this should be so. Cutting, choral speaking, speech sharing, re-arrangement of the script of a play should be permitted and encouraged. Lines should be memorised, but prompters (incorporated into the presentation) allowed.

13 Will there be linking activities between performances? These might be interludes provided by teachers, or professional actors, or older students in which all students can join (dancing, singing, games and so on).

14 Can a skill be taught to all students during the course of the day? Some festivals have taught a dance to over two hundred students; others have taught greetings and farewells. Even swordplay has been taught – without swords for anyone except the two demonstrating teachers!

15 Does every student get some kind of award or memento to record their participation? Festivals are non-competitive, but often an award or certificate is given to everyone who participates.

16 Food and lavatories? Essential items to plan in every organised event!

Researching the classics

As a schoolboy in Stratford-upon-Avon, Shakespeare's dramatic imagination was fired by the Roman poet Ovid (43 BC to AD 18). Ovid's *Metamorphoses* (from the Greek meaning 'change of form') was a huge collection of stories, drawn from Greek mythology, telling of human beings changing into animals or birds or trees or some other form. Shakespeare drew heavily upon Ovid in his two long poems *Venus and Adonis* and *The Rape of Lucrece*, in the Sonnets, and in every one of his plays.

Every play contains examples of change. Women dress as young men, villains conceal their nature behind a mask of honesty. Nick Bottom is transformed into an ass. In *Twelfth Night*, Orsino imagines himself turned into a hart (a male deer), pursued to death by hunters:

> That instant was I turned into a hart,
> And my desires, like fell and cruel hounds
> E'er since pursue me.

Orsino is thinking of Ovid's story of Actaeon, the hunter. Actaeon watched Diana (Artemis), the goddess of chastity, bathing. For his offence, she changed him into stag, and he was pursued and torn to pieces by his own hounds.

Contemporary comments

In 1598, Francis Meres wrote 'the sweet witty soul of Ovid lives in mellifluous and honey tongued Shakespeare, witness his Venus and Adonis, his Lucrece, his sugared Sonnets among his private friends etc.'

In *The Return from Parnassus Part 2* (a play acted in Cambridge in 1601), Will Kemp, a comic character, complains that University dramatists 'smell too much of that writer Ovid, and that writer *Metamorphosis*, and talk too much of *Proserpina and Jupiter*. Why, here's our fellow Shakespeare puts them all down.'

Today's students are less familiar with classical mythology than students of Shakespeare's own time. But such knowledge can deepen appreciation and understanding, because each mythological allusion illustrates some aspect of character, story or theme. In the play they are studying, students can research some of the classical stories that Shakespeare uses and suggest how each is relevant to the play at the point it is used. For example, when Hamlet speaks of Gertrude as being 'like Niobe, all tears', he is thinking of Niobe, Queen of Thebes who wept for her dead children even when she was turned to stone. This image of everlasting sorrow ironically comments on Gertrude's short-lived grief for her dead husband.

Other resources

Preceding pages have detailed all kinds of resources for teaching Shakespeare. What other resources exist? In active approaches to Shakespeare there is no need for elaborate equipment or props. Allied to Shakespeare's language, a simple paper crown, a mask, or even a chair can act as a major stimulus to students' imagination.

However, students do need an attractively presented edition of the play, for example from the Cambridge School Shakespeare series, that has been specially edited for students, and which is committed to active methods. The school or college library should possess a range of reference books which facilitate students' individual research projects.

Developments in information technology make it possible for students to use school facilities to present their written and design work in a range of styles and with graphics. CD-ROM versions exist of some plays; sometimes these have interactive opportunities. They usually include a range of information on language, themes, Shakespeare's theatre, critical commentaries and so on, and lend themselves to individual rather than group work.

The use of the camcorder increases motivation, because students enjoy and learn from making a video of their work. Such videos can also be used in assessment (see page 243).

Visitors are a major resource, particularly actors from a Theatre in Education or outreach company. Students gain enormously from working actively with theatre professionals.

Residential courses also have great value. A weekend at a centre away from the school or college, wholly devoted to Shakespeare, provides excellent opportunities for long exploratory sessions.

Shakespeare for
younger students

*'Those that do teach young babes
Do it with gentle means and easy tasks'*

Introduction

Teaching Shakespeare to younger students (seven to twelve years old) is an exhilarating experience. The stories and characters have instant appeal, and the powerful imaginative charge of the language makes much of it accessible. Many teachers have successfully challenged the depressing claim that the language is far beyond the reading levels of these younger students. Those teachers have shown that the freshness of approach and eagerness of engagement of their young students results in quite startling levels of achievement, motivation and expression. High expectations produce high standards.

A Midsummer Night's Dream is probably the play most often chosen by teachers of younger students, but many others are successfully taught: *Hamlet, Twelfth Night, Macbeth*. Teachers frequently base their students' Shakespeare work on particular qualities: the Cinderella-like nature of *King Lear*, and the excitement, heroism and bold storytelling of the histories. The magical realism of the romances holds special attraction. The exotic settings and stories of *The Winter's Tale*, *Pericles* and *The Tempest* have enabled teachers to create Shakespearian drama in suitable forms for their younger students who delight in the miraculous 'lost and found' aspects of the plays.

Shakespeare's language and younger students

How much of Shakespeare's language can be used with younger students? Don't underestimate their capability. Many teachers have found that younger students can cope with far more of Shakespeare's language than the teachers originally thought possible. They experience their students speaking the language not just as 'recitation', but with expression and feeling that shows understanding of the dramatic context.

Younger students have an uninhibited grasp of the physical aspects of language, taking delight in words, rhythm, rhyme, structure, sound. The very non-everydayness of the language catches their imagination: 'The multitudinous seas incarnadine', 'incharitable dog', 'Blow winds, and crack your cheeks'.

Much depends on the nature of the class and the attitude of the teacher. What is essential is that in every lesson, students should directly experience Shakespeare's language, and speak *some* of it, even if for many students it is only a line or two which they share in some kind of dramatic enactment.

Teachers can take advantage of the fact that, stripped to their barest outline, Shakespeare's plots have the mythical, folk-tale quality that so appeals to younger students:

- the brave soldier, corrupted by the witches' prophecy, who kills a king, but a menacing forest moves towards him…
- the sad prince who is told by his father's ghost that he must avenge a murder…
- a shipwreck, a remote island ruled by a powerful magician…

The key to making any play succeed with younger students is the teacher's enthusiasm. When a teacher enjoys a play and is committed to making it accessible in some form to the students, admirable outcomes are achieved. Plays which may seem unsuited to younger students have been adapted successfully by a few teachers: *Titus Andronicus*, *Measure for Measure*, *Antony and Cleopatra*.

What does a teacher of younger students need to teach Shakespeare successfully?

1   Some knowledge of the play (but that does not mean the specialised knowledge of a Shakespeare 'expert').

2   A personal enjoyment of Shakespeare, and a commitment to enable students to share similar enjoyment.

3   A delight in words and a belief that all students can also delight in the vivacity and imaginative power of Shakespeare's language.

4   A belief in the students. A conviction that they *can* enter Shakespeare's imaginative and linguistic worlds with understanding and feeling.

5   A willingness to use a wide variety of methods which always include dramatic experience of enacting the language, characters and stories.

6   A willingness to adapt Shakespeare to the needs, aptitudes and abilities of the students.

Short versions of the plays are available on video, notably the *Animated Tales* series in which a dozen of Shakespeare's plays are each imaginatively performed in 30-minute abridgements. Such shortened versions can give students a helpful introduction to story, characters and language.

Younger students respond positively to working in a wide variety of ways:

- drama
- all forms of creative expression
- art
- craft
- role-play
- music
- dance
- movement
- costume
- make-up
- puppet plays
- choral speaking
- reading
- writing of all kinds (from creative work to various word games).

Most teachers use a mixture of such methods within one or more of three major approaches to introducing their students to Shakespeare:

- Shakespeare's life and times
- storytelling
- dramatic storytelling.

Shakespeare's life and times

This approach is described on pages 212–14. Within the context of Elizabethan England, the focus is on Shakespeare the man, Stratford-upon-Avon, and London and the Globe.

Storytelling

Telling the story of a play celebrates children's natural delight in both play and storytelling. Younger students are readily willing to suspend their disbelief and to enter wholeheartedly into the imaginative world of the play. They revel in the larger than life characters and the twists and turns of the plot, and in Shakespeare's unfamiliar but inviting vocabulary and rhythms.

Some teachers tell their own story of the play. However, many teachers of younger students understandably feel some diffidence about the demands they see this method making upon them. Probably the most common method is reading to the class from one of the numerous 'Stories from Shakespeare' collections that are in publication. Lambs' *Tales* have largely fallen out of use. Their formal style and traditional attitudes are uncongenial to many students and teachers today. Modern re-tellings are much livelier or quirkier, and more aware of children's interests.

Storytelling a play can often be completed in a single lesson. Although some published stories take over an hour to read, many teachers report that they hold students' attention. But it is worth noting two drawbacks in the use of such stories.

1   Students' responses are often re-tellings of a prose re-telling, rather than a direct response to Shakespeare's own language.

2   The power of Shakespeare's language may be weakened or lost. One well known re-telling of *Hamlet* turns 'But look where sadly the poor wretch comes reading' into 'I see Hamlet coming now. How sad he looks!'

Dramatic storytelling

In dramatic storytelling, teachers give students direct access to Shakespeare's language: students speak it, enact it, improvise with it. The teacher leads by narrating the story, introducing the characters, and locating problems for students to solve. In each lesson, students imaginatively construct the world of the play inspired by what they have heard. In small groups, the students invent their own actions for imagined roles, speaking some of Shakespeare's language, individually or chorally.

Teachers using this method tend to alternate drama sessions with writing and creative art work: students express their response to their active, dramatic work in written or visual form. They write poems, songs, diaries, explorers' accounts. They paint or draw, make models, maps, collages, props, sets, and so on. Dramatic storytelling can take many forms. The following examples have all been successfully used with younger students.

The teacher as presenter

The teacher, script in hand, tells the story to the class, reading and acting selected extracts. The class become the audience at Shakespeare's Globe, waiting for the performance to begin. Students can be brought into the performance at particular points.

Hamlet
To present this play to a class of young children, one teacher spoke as both Hamlet and Ophelia (inserting 'and she says to me' as appropriate). Children, as Claudius and Polonius, watched from behind a curtain. The teacher sometimes moved close to the curtains, for example to shout 'Where's your father?' Other children knelt and prayed as Claudius, and the teacher dramatically acted out 'Now might I do it, pat…'.

Mini-scenes: the whole story

In this activity the teacher divides the play into a number of key episodes, and the story is told as a serial narrative. The class experience the story unfolding scene by scene, not knowing what happens next. All kinds of dramatic activity are employed: speaking individually and chorally, mime, movement, gesture, and so on. In each lesson, every student should speak at least one line of Shakespeare, in some they will speak and enact many more. As the story progresses, props, costumes and musical instruments accumulate and can be used by students to contribute their own special effects.

The teacher acts as director, actor-manager and teacher, organising group work, sometimes playing a character, sometimes leading the class who imitate words and actions, sometimes directing a scene as several students speak and others play non-speaking roles. Always the teacher is teacher: keeping order, ensuring that students are 'on task', judging when rehearsal should flow into performance. Physical activity is later followed by written work.

Here are two examples of mini-scenes, showing how the technique was used in two different classes.

Macbeth

The teacher of a class of seven- to ten-year-olds divided *Macbeth* into sixteen key scenes each of which was to be the basis of a lesson. The initial witches scene is only thirteen lines and was kept intact, but the other scenes were reduced to not more than 30 lines each. Some scenes were invented: the murder of Duncan, the coronation of the Macbeths, the burial of Duncan at Colmkill.

The subsequent lessons each involved all the children in some way. For example, there were multiple witches, and much choral speaking and echoing. Groups of students were servants at Inverness or Dunsinane castle, thanes at the coronation and banquet, soldiers in the armies of Macbeth and Malcolm. The advance of Birnam Wood on Dunsinane produced a fund of imaginative responses. Battle action and drill activities were greatly enjoyed.

The Tempest

The teacher of a class of ten-year-olds devised an eight-lesson course for this play. The eight sessions (each of one and a half hours) comprised:

- the voyage and the tempest
- exploring the island and finding clues
- Prospero: the magician
- Caliban's story
- Ariel's story

- the court: the magic banquet
- the masque: preparing for the marriage of Ferdinand and Miranda
- Prospero regains his dukedom.

In the first session, King Alonso and his court embarked from Tunis after the wedding of his daughter Claribel. The ship sailed off with sailors busily at work: hoisting sail, weighing anchor, heaving on ropes, climbing rigging, and helmsman at the wheel, with the Master and Bosun inspecting and so on. Then the tempest struck: 'We split! We split!'

In each of the eight lessons the students created a bustling world, based on characters and events in the play, and using lines from the play chosen by the teacher.

Using a character's story

This method, which constructs a drama from a character's story, aims to release the creative powers of younger students with free-wheeling but linked approaches to a play or a theme. It uses drama games and a host of co-operative activities. The teacher acts in role as a character from a play. Here is an example of how this method was employed by two teachers working together with their two classes of eight-year-olds.

The Winter's Tale
The course began with the two classes creating a storm at sea. One teacher orchestrated the children's movement as lightning flashes, whistling winds and tumbling waves. As the storm subsided, the other teacher appeared as an old shepherd. He told the story of a shipwreck with all the sailors lost, and on land an old gentleman torn to pieces and eaten by a bear.

The shepherd then discovered a casket in which was a baby (a doll) and a letter. He involved the children with questions. Who was the baby? Where had she come from? Why was she left on this desolate shore? The children offered their own answers, and put together and acted out their own story of the jealous king, the abandoned child, and the king's sorrow beside his wife's grave.

In each following lesson the children were invited to ask questions of one or two characters (the teachers in role telling their view of what happened). From what they learned from each character, the children constructed and enacted their own story of Perdita's sixteenth birthday party; the comic trader who sold songs and trinkets to the party-goers; the angry father who pursued two young people across the sea; happy reconciliations, and the statue of Hermione that came to life.

The teacher's storytelling role

In dramatic storytelling teachers have a choice. They can tell the story as an outside narrator, or they can become one of the characters in the play and, in role, present the story. The character can be actual (Peter Quince has been used with striking success) or invented (a servant or courtier who speaks as an insider in the play). Although in-role work might seem daunting, many teachers with no special dramatic training but with much commitment and enthusiasm, have undertaken it very successfully.

The teacher should identify the Shakespearian language he or she will use, and the language the students will learn and enact. This might be single lines or phrases, whole speeches, or dialogue. Within a single lesson, short extracts are usually appropriate, but given suitable preparation time, a ten-year-old can learn a remarkable number of lines and speak them with fluency, feeling and understanding.

It is vital that in every lesson some of Shakespeare's language is spoken. For example, a lesson on the shipwreck scene from *The Tempest* can include all the sailors' words from Act 1 Scene 1, and students can leap overboard crying Ferdinand's 'Hell is empty, and all the devils are here!'

The teacher should also prepare some prompts for students, inviting them to speculate about the story they are hearing and the world they will create. The prompts are intended to elicit concrete but open-ended and imaginative responses. Each prompt is a particular version (using the names and circumstances of the scene being studied) of the following generalised questions:

1   Who are these characters?
2   What do they look like?
3   What are they feeling?
4   What are they doing?
5   How do they move and speak?
6   How do they feel about each other?
7   What might happen to them?

> ## Two language lessons
>
> Short extracts from the plays can provide excellent opportunities for expressive and creative work.
>
> *The Tempest*: students shared the nine lines of Caliban's 'Be not afeared, the isle is full of noises...'. They created noises, sweet airs, a thousand twangling instruments, voices. The lesson included both choral and individual speaking of the speech. Students later illustrated their maps of the island and added quotations from the lines.
>
> *A Midsummer Night's Dream*: students physically experienced Titania's 'These are the forgeries of jealousy...'. The students heaved vainly at the yoke, lost their sweat with the ploughman, fatted themselves as crows with the murrion flock, and hopped through the nine-men's-morris.

A co-ordinated approach across the curriculum

This approach involves one or more whole-year groups and most curriculum subjects. One play is selected and all the teachers contribute in some way to the students' Shakespeare experience. Classes are often combined for drama and other active work, and teachers work together to share their strengths, skills, expertise, and knowledge.

Here is a description of how one school used this technique for five classes of nine- to eleven-year-olds, working for a whole term on *The Tempest*. The different teachers each took responsibility for one of the five areas of the curriculum to be explored through the play: language, history, geography, science and mathematics. One teacher also acted as co-ordinator, arranging regular teachers' meetings to plan, report and review progress.

Within the co-ordinated framework, the approach combined storytelling and expressive arts work. The term culminated in a spectacular production in which every student took part, most in costumes designed as part of the course. Three evening performances for parents and others were given.

The action unfolded on a centre stage, with two choruses – each of 60 students – sitting one on each side of the stage. The choruses accompanied the action with songs, echoes, sound effects, choral speaking and music played on a variety of instruments. Sometimes groups of twenty or more members of a chorus moved on stage to perform a dance, create an effect or enact a crowd scene woven into the developing story: the embarkation and voyage of Claribel's wedding guests, sailors caught in a tempest, strange shapes with the banquet, Ariel's spirits tormenting Caliban, dancers and singers in the masque, and the departure from the island.

A Shakespeare term

These activities were set by one school for its ten- to eleven-year-olds during their term's work (twelve weeks) on *A Midsummer Night's Dream*. A variety of approaches were used, and a two-day visit to Stratford-upon-Avon was included. Three kinds of task were set: performance, design, and writing. Students had to attempt one task from each of the three areas.

Performance tasks

1   In a group, choose a scene or part of a scene. Rehearse it and perform it. Your performance should be 10–15 minutes long.

2   Learn a speech or a sonnet to be spoken to the whole class.

3   Make puppets of any kind and use them to present a scene or extract from the play.

4   As a character, write and perform your own story of the part you played in the play.

5   In a group, learn, rehearse and present 'Ye spotted snakes…'. Use movement and musical instruments to accompany the song.

Design tasks

1   Make a costume for yourself (or for a doll) as a Shakespeare character.

2   Design a theatre programme of at least eight pages for a Shakespeare play.

3   Paint a picture of either a scene from a Shakespeare play, or of life in London or Stratford in Shakespeare's time.

4   Make a model of the Globe Theatre. Its stage should show characters from a play.

5   Make a list of objects or events you would see in London or Stratford during Shakespeare's time. Illustrate at least six items from your list (for example, as paintings, drawings, lino cuts, and so on).

6   Make a set of at least six props for use in *A Midsummer Night's Dream*.

Writing tasks

1   Write and illustrate your account of your visit to Stratford (or London). Present it in an attractive way.

2   You are an apprentice working in London in 1605. It is your day off and you are going with a group of friends across the River Thames to the Globe Theatre to see a performance of *A Midsummer Night's Dream*. Write a full account of your day telling your thoughts and feelings about all you saw and did.

3   Imagine you are William Shakespeare. Write your story of what you do during one week in London.

The three worlds of *A Midsummer Night's Dream*

One of the many features of this play that makes it so popular with younger students, and so suitable for active work, are the three distinct worlds of the play. This structure offers a teacher the opportunity to divide the class into three groups, each of which creates its own world. As the storytelling proceeds, the three worlds can collide with tremendous imaginative force.

1   *The fairy world:* Oberon, Titania, Puck and the fairies.

2   *The Mechanicals:* students create their own work activities, in groups as weavers, tinkers, joiners and so on.

3   *The Court:* Theseus, Hippolyta, the four lovers, Egeus the angry father and a host of courtiers.

---

4   Imagine you can travel back in time to the year 1600. You find yourself in Stratford-upon-Avon and you then make a journey to London. Write up the story of your adventures.

5   Inspired by what you did during the term, write either a sonnet or a short play. Whichever you choose, your style should be Shakespearian.

A puppet *Macbeth*

A teacher of a class of nine- to eleven-year-olds spent a term working on *Macbeth*. He first read his students two different versions of the story. This produced animated discussion and adventurous written work on the characters. One afternoon, the classroom was turned into a banqueting hall with the teacher acting the role of a servant to the children as guests. The class then discussed how the play might be staged in school (How could Birnam Wood come to Dunsinane?) and the idea of a puppet play emerged.

The students made puppets of the characters and the teacher chose nine scenes for improvisation:

- on the moor
- the King's castle
- Macbeth and Lady Macbeth plot
- the banquet and the dagger
- Duncan's murder
- Banquo's murder
- Banquo's Ghost
- the Witches
- Macbeth's castle.

As teachers of younger students know, the opportunity to 'speak through' a puppet can produce surprisingly fluent and confident language (and ready learning of verse lines) from students who in other circumstances appear less accomplished. A thirty-minute play resulted, with most characters included, and with sets and props constructed. The play was performed at the end of term for parents, other schools and the local teacher-training college.

Assessment

'What's aught but as 'tis valued?'

Process or product?

Assessment is a necessary part of any teaching. For a teacher to think about how to assess students following a Shakespeare course is to sharpen his or her perception of the nature, purposes and methods of teaching Shakespeare. It is to question what constitutes appropriate assessment, and to be concerned that assessment does not dominate and drive the teaching and learning that takes place.

Assessing Shakespeare work sets every teacher two major assessment puzzles that have to be resolved practically. First, what should be the balance between individual and group assessment? Shakespeare is drama, and drama is at heart a group experience, social and participatory, but assessment in school and college is almost entirely of the individual student.

Second, what is to be assessed? Any Shakespeare course comprises both product and process (analogous to actors' performance and rehearsal). Product is some kind of final presentation. It can take many forms: an actual staged performance, a folder of design work, a traditional essay and so on. Process is everything that precedes the presentation: discussion; improvisations; explorations; all kinds of exploratory, rehearsal-type work; free-wheeling imaginative activity; sketches; notes; and so on. Nearly all such work is transient, ephemeral, unrecorded. What is an appropriate balance between the assessment of product and process?

The assessment of staged performance is notoriously difficult and contested. Evidence of this can be seen every week in reviews of plays by theatre critics. The same production or actor can receive wildly different appraisals from different critics. Those critics will have sat beside each other on the same night watching exactly the same performance. They will claim to judge by the same criteria. But their reviews reveal that they see different things, and evaluate them quite differently. In this area, what applies to professional theatre applies similarly to schools.

If product is difficult to assess, so is process. Just how does a teacher keep track of the quality of activity in a number of small groups? All will be working at different levels and speeds as they experiment with the varied rehearsal techniques that precede performance. An active Shakespeare lesson is necessarily quite different from one in which each student sits at his or her desk, working individually on a task set by the teacher.

Such process work is intrinsic to students' Shakespeare experience. Some teachers argue that process is more central to Shakespeare learning than performance or presentation and should, therefore, weigh more heavily in any assessment than product. But it poses many problems. Such difficulties do not mean that assessment is impossible or merely subjective. Continuing reflection on practice, using appropriate criteria, helps to ensure reliable and valid ratings.

All kinds of criteria can be adduced by which both product and process are assessed, but judgement is at the heart of assessment. It is not a mechanical process, a matter of ticking a checklist, but a process involving the teacher's professional knowledge, skills and judgement. That judgement is not some ultimately mysterious pronouncement, but an appraisal for which reasons and evidence can be offered in support and justification.

Two approaches to assessment criteria can be discerned. One is of target setting, specifying precise objectives in advance. The second is intuitive, where assessment is governed by a general 'feel' of quality. Both approaches have obvious drawbacks. The first can be reductive and pseudo-scientific, falsely claiming to quantify the unquantifiable, and assuming that the only worthwhile objectives are those specified. The second can be vague and unjustified, dependent on the teacher's personal preferences.

Assessing in context: fitness for purpose

Students' Shakespeare learning has to be assessed in its appropriate context. If a lesson is devoted to Shakespeare's similes and metaphors, the success of students' learning is largely judged by how well students can recognise, understand, use, interpret and portray Shakespearian examples of metaphor and simile (and create their own examples).

If the lesson is an active session in which four or five groups work on and stage their own versions of *Macbeth* Act 1 Scene 1 (the witches), assessment is a more complex affair. It involves judgements on how fully the students have entered into Shakespeare's imaginative world: how they have taken possession of the script and been possessed by it; how far they have committed themselves to experiencing, exploring and realising some kind of performance of the scene which engages their audience, the other students.

In a 'show and share' lesson, part of the learning is the experience of being an audience. How appropriately do students respond to their peers' performance? Is there a willingness to help, to criticise constructively, and to recognise and acknowledge the achievements of their fellow-students?

Principles

There are a number of principles that should be borne in mind when assessing students' work on Shakespeare.

1 Assessment, like teaching methods, should be characterised by variety.

2 Assessment should be suited to what is being assessed and to the teaching methods used. All kinds of learning go on in a Shakespeare classroom, and assessment should balance knowledge and appreciation of content with personal and social skills: everything involved in treating Shakespeare as a script.

3 Assessment should judge by appropriate standards. Students should not be assessed as if they were professional actors or future literary critics.

4   Students should be involved in discussion of assessment criteria and procedures. They are entitled to know the criteria against which their work is judged, what will be assessed, and how and when it will be assessed.

5   Assessment tasks should be open-ended, enabling students to display thought, imagination and invention in active response. Such tasks should avoid the 'single right answer' attitude which treats the plays simply as opportunities to set comprehension exercises that show no awareness of a play's dramatic quality. Tasks should also acknowledge the instability of the script: language, character, plot, theme can all be rendered in different performances with different emphasis, different significance.

6   Assessment should acknowledge that Shakespeare wrote plays. The plays should be taught as plays; understood, experienced and responded to as plays rather than as novels or poems or moral essays. Assessment of Shakespeare concerns itself with how story, character, theme and language are treated dramatically.

7   Assessment can never be fully objective. Active methods which encourage multiplicity of interpretation are often the most difficult to assess.

8   Assessment should acknowledge that learning rarely takes place in a neat, linear progress. It is frequently marked by gaps, reversals, hesitations, forgettings, giant leaps, small steps and unexpected transfers, divergences, spin-offs, serendipities. Progress is uneven. Understanding of character, plot, language can proceed at a very different pace. It is usually mistaken to attempt to push students through a predetermined programme of stages of difficulty. To assume that students cannot understand, and imaginatively inhabit Shakespeare's imagery before they have mastered metaphor and simile or the iambic pentameter is simply mistaken.

9   Assessment procedures should be regularly reviewed, and revised where necessary. Discussion of criteria using past and present examples of students' work is helpful.

10 Where criteria are specified by Examination Boards or other

public bodies, students studying for such examinations should be made fully aware of them. The courses the students follow should aim at enabling them to achieve well when assessed by such criteria.

11 If assessment generates a mountain of paperwork, it is bound to be inappropriate. Beware the assessment tail wagging the learning dog!

Telling *versus* showing

Students (like everybody else) know far more than they can say. Many ten-year-olds cannot define 'balm of hurt minds'. But asking them to show it as a mime as part of Macbeth's 'sleep' speech enables them to demonstrate, physically, that they possess sharp insight into the imagery.

Student self-assessment

Some element of student self-assessment is crucial to Shakespeare courses. The following simple framework has been adapted in different forms by a number of schools and colleges.

1 Which part of the session did you enjoy most? Why?

2 Which part did you not enjoy? Why?

3 What did you learn?

4 How do you rate your own contribution to the session?

5 How do you rate the session as a whole?

6 What do you feel you need to do next session?

Assessment should take account of the questions that students wish to ask about a play, rather than simply having to answer other people's questions. Most teachers achieve this through coursework in which students set their own research and inquiry tasks, formulate their own questions and conduct their own inquiries into *their* questions about the things that really interest them about a play.

Assessment of performance

Where assessment is to be conducted by teacher-set criteria, individual teachers will, of course, determine the degree of complexity of criteria and rating scales they deem to be appropriate. For example, some teachers carefully list expected outcomes, divide those performance objectives into levels, list outcomes for each level, and compile a checklist with numerical marks for each. Other teachers reject such detail, and assess holistically. Any numerical or literal grades (if awarded) should always be supported by particular criteria.

Whichever method is used, teachers attempt to judge whether or not the performance shows that the students understand what they are saying, have feeling for the characters and the scene, and are trying to express those understandings and feelings appropriately in performance. Most teachers take the following questions into account in some way for both groups and individuals.

1 Do students know their lines?

2 Do students give a sense of having genuinely entered into the character, expressing his or her thoughts and emotions with conviction and feeling?

3 Do students participate fully in the performance even when they are not themselves speaking? Does each actor relate appropriately to others?

4 Does the performance feel convincing? Is it done with sincerity and conviction? Is it somehow truthful to the context in which it is set?

5 Is the performance sustained, without slack moments? Does it give the impression of having been thought through?

6 Was there a sense of the group working together to support each other's performances?

7 Does a sense of what this scene is about come over clearly?

8 Was a convincing atmosphere or mood created?

9 Was every member of the group fully involved in some way?

10 Does the performance suggest that students have undertaken sustained appropriate preparation?

11 Do they enter and exit, begin and end, appropriately?

12 Did the performance engage the audience? If fellow students act as audience for such 'show and share' activities, it seems sensible that they too should be involved in assessment.

13 Will assessment be made of props, sets, lighting, costumes, music, sound effects?

Essays

Critical essays have long been the dominant form of required student response in school and college examinations. Not to put too fine a point upon it, they ape the traditional form of essays and lectures by Shakespeare scholars and critics. The watered-down form of such essays, which many students are still required to write, encourages name–dropping and the veneer of scholarship rather than genuine and informed personal response.

Students' essays show increasing levels of imaginative involvement, beginning with straightforward re-tellings in which students recapitulate events in their own words. Deeper involvement is evidenced in judgmental or evaluative responses in which students express and justify opinions on themes, characters, and actions. A deeper level still is that of empathetic identification in which the student enters into the feelings and thoughts of a character, experiencing their perplexities or emotions of joy, love or jealousy with felt engagement. Some students fuse dramatic and linguistic response, writing in forms appropriate to the Shakespearian context: for example, writing in verse where vocabulary, syntax, and imagery echo Shakespeare's own.

In addition to traditional essays, all kinds of other written work representing the student's personal research can contribute to both process and product assessment. A file of work might include designs of all kinds (sets, costume, lighting, programmes, cast lists, posters); in-role poems, stories, letters, diaries; director's notes justifying cuts, blockings, stage directions, exits and entrances, and justifying ideas that will inform a production.

Other possibilities include sonnets, soliloquies or speeches written by the student; logs and diaries in which the student describes, comments on and evaluates his or her own work. Character analyses might tell how the student has prepared for a part: personality, motives, relation to other characters and so on. Reports of theatre visits and reviews of performances might take account of interpretations by others: critics, other performances on stage or screen, and so on.

A media essay is a video or audio tape, with accompanying material, of a student's investigation of a character or an issue in the play. The student might, for example, present the tape in the form of a radio or television documentary. The supporting material might include an account of decisions taken as the tape was planned and recorded, a shooting script, student evaluation of the tape and so on. Assessment would give credit for the technical skill displayed in the presented tape, but would be primarily concerned with the quality of the enquiry itself.

Assessment tasks

These tasks should be interesting and imaginative and allow students to draw on their experience and resources. For example, a class of thirteen-year-olds spent a term on *The Merchant of Venice*, covering the whole play in class, and in small groups each selecting, rehearsing and presenting a scene. During the final three weeks, their teacher set the following assessment task to be worked on by each student.

You wish to put on a production of *The Merchant of Venice* but need financial backing. A wealthy woman has offered the money, but she found Shakespeare really boring at school! She wants you to present a proposal to convince her that the play, and your production of it, deserve support. Your proposal should include item number 1 and at least three others from the following list.

1   An explanation of why you wish to stage the play: what are its qualities that make it worth staging.

2   Two hand-written and illustrated speeches that you like, together with an explanation of what makes the language passionate and dramatic.

3   Notes on how Jessica will be played in the final scene.

4   An eye-catching poster with an intriguing quotation from the play.

5   Designs for costumes for Shylock, Antonio, Bassanio, Portia and Jessica. Each design must be accompanied by an appropriate quotation, relevant to the character.

6   Designs for the three caskets.

Examinations

Examiners are sometimes seen as sinister figures, but contrary to stereotype, most are refreshingly positive about students' personal responses. They hope for writing that makes them pause in their reading, surprised or delighted by a fresh, surprising insight. Of course, they require students to show a good knowledge and understanding of plot and character, together with the ability to develop an argument. But most of all, they value the essay which conveys a sense of direct personal engagement with the script. They welcome evidence that the student is genuinely trying to record an authentic response, intellectually, emotionally and imaginatively, to his or her experience of the play, seeing it as a play.

Again contrary to stereotype, examiners do not have a set of expected right answers. What they do expect is that any interpretation or judgement is grounded in the script. Some examiners are themselves struggling to break free of the concept embodied in the term 'text' (which treats Shakespeare as revered literature), and to acknowledge his dramatic qualities through the use of the term 'script'. To acknowledge that the plays were written for performance is to be open to a wider variety of justified interpretation than can be realised in treating Shakespeare as a literary text.

Here is one teacher's advice to her students on the subject of examination answers.

1   Answer the question set! If you disagree with the question, construct an argument, grounded in the script, to support your challenge.

2   Examiners don't set trick questions. They want you to display

what you know, how you feel about these characters, in this situation, using this language. They are not trying to catch you out.

3　You are expected to quote, but quotations should be short and illustrative, genuinely supporting the point you are making.

4　The point of reading criticism is to develop your own thinking about the play, not to swallow other people's judgements. Name-dropping doesn't impress examiners. They want *your* response. Beware of critics who use 'we' and 'us' (as in 'we feel…, makes us see…', and so on) – they are assuming that everyone feels or thinks as they do.

5　You don't get good grades by merely recapping the story.

6　Show that you are aware that your own views can be challenged, that other interpretations are possible. There's never one single right answer to any examination question on Shakespeare.

Evaluating a lesson

In any lesson, the teacher will have in mind a series of questions which inform his or her evaluation of the lesson's success in enabling students to take ownership of the script. Did the students enjoy it? Did they take responsibility for their own work? Were they 'on task' throughout and interested in what they did? Did they work well together?

Such questions about the climate of the lesson are accompanied by others about method and content. Were the students clear about the task? Did they explore, hypothesise, speculate about possible interpretations, performance styles? How engaged and animated was discussion and experiment? How much enactment of the script took place in some way? What did the students learn? Was it what you intended them to learn?

The answers to such questions confirm the principles that underlie successful Shakespeare teaching. Treating Shakespeare as a script involves imagination, understanding, and feeling. Approaches in which students speak and physically enact Shakespeare's language increase enjoyment, appreciation, and understanding.

Quotations used in the text

This index provides line references for each quotation in the body of the text. The references are listed by page number (given on the left), and all quotations are listed in the order in which they appear on the page.

All references are to the New Cambridge/Cambridge School Shakespeare edition, with the exception of *As You Like It*, *Love's Labour's Lost*, *Coriolanus*, *Richard III*, and *Troilus and Cressida*.

53 *King John* 3.4.93–4; *Macbeth*
4.3.39–41; *Hamlet* 5.2.315–16;
King John 2.1.352–4; *Richard
II* 3.2.161–2; *Twelfth Night*
2.4.107–11

54 *Hamlet* 3.1.56; *Richard II*
3.3.183; *Dream* 1.1.199;
Measure for Measure 3.1.42;
Hamlet 1.2.12; *Romeo and Juliet*
1.5.134; *Coriolanus* 1.1.166–7

55 *Coriolanus* 1.1.168–75; *Hamlet*
3.1.56, 1.2.129; *Richard III*
1.2.215–16, 4.4.92–6

56 *Shrew* 2.1.178–86; *King Lear*
5.3.281–2; *Measure for Measure*
5.1.25; *Hamlet* 1.5.80; *Richard
III* 4.1.91–2

57 *Richard III* 4.1.93; *Richard II*
4.1.206–9; *Winter's Tale*
1.2.284–96; *Dream* 5.1.167–8

58 *Dream* 5.1.169–74; *Twelfth
Night* 3.4.120; *King John*
5.2.117; *Macbeth* 1.3.33–4; *King
Lear* 4.5.20–1; *Dream* 5.1.145–6

59 *Much Ado* 5.2.28–31; *Dream*
5.1.401–2; *Macbeth* 2.1.63–4

60 *Macbeth* 2.4.40–1; *Dream*
5.1.306–29

61 *Romeo and Juliet* 3.5.35–6;
Macbeth 4.1.1–15

62 *Macbeth* 4.1.16–21; *Richard III*
4.4.169–72; *Merchant of Venice*
3.1.46–50; *Henry V* 4.8.84–90;
Richard II 2.1.40–5

63 *Richard II* 2.1.46–51; *Comedy
of Errors* 1.2.97–102; *Hamlet*
3.1.144, 4.5.174; *King Lear*
4.3.2–6; *Much Ado* 2.1.199–204

64 *Much Ado* 5.1.190–7; *Macbeth*
4.3.57–60

65 *Macbeth* 1.4.35, 2.2.39–43,
3.1.1, 3.1.92–3, 3.4.24,
3.4.100–1, 3.4.125, 4.1.51–9,
4.2.34–5

66 *Macbeth* 4.3.4–6, 4.3.92–4,
5.3.25; *Romeo and Juliet* 2.2.2

67 *Henry V* 3.1.1; *Titus Andronicus*
5.2.186–9

68 *Macbeth* 5.3.22–3; *Henry IV
Part 1* 1.1.1

69 *Tempest* 1.2.396–7; *Romeo and
Juliet* 2.2.2–6, 4.3.30–58;
Twelfth Night 1.1.1–15;
Hamlet 3.1.144–55

70 *Antony and Cleopatra* 4.4.4–11;
King John 3.3.66

71 *Comedy of Errors* 4.4.29–33

72 *Comedy of Errors* 4.4.33–4;
Hamlet 2.2.280–92

73 *Macbeth* 2.3.23–30; *King Lear*
5.3.231; *Henry V* 3.1.1;
Macbeth 1.7.49

74 *Comedy of Errors* 2.2.105–6;
Merchant of Venice 5.1.1–20;
Richard III 4.4.102; *Macbeth*
2.3.56; *Othello* 5.2.7; *Love's
Labour's Lost* 1.1.77

75 *Hamlet* 2.2.95; *Henry IV Part 1*
2.4.319; *Macbeth* 1.7.1–19

76 *Macbeth* 1.7.20–8; *Henry IV
Part 1* 3.1.21; *Dream* 1.2.24–7;
Hamlet 5.1.236–7

77 *Hamlet* 5.1.238–51;
Henry IV Part 1 2.4.202;
Othello 5.2.277–8; *Antony and
Cleopatra* 1.1.35–6; *Love's
Labour's Lost* 5.2.407, 4.3.310

78 *Merchant of Venice* 3.2.115–16;
Julius Caesar 3.2.65–91;
Macbeth 3.1.29; *Richard III*
3.1.111; *Macbeth* 1.4.13–14,
1.6.1

79 *Twelfth Night* 3.1.126; *Othello*
1.1.66; *Tempest* 5.1.182–4;
Romeo and Juliet 2.2.184

80 *Romeo and Juliet* 1.1.166–72,
3.2.73–9

81 *Love's Labour's Lost* 5.2.686–7;
Hamlet 3.2.91–3; *Romeo and
Juliet* 3.1.89–90; *Macbeth*
2.2.58–60

82 *Much Ado* 3.5.13, 4.2.1,
4.2.61–2; *Measure for Measure*
2.1.63

83 *Hamlet* 3.1.56; *Twelfth Night*
3.1.126; *Macbeth* 1.7.82; *King
Lear* 4.6.42; *Twelfth Night*
3.2.35–6

84 *Two Gentlemen of Verona*
4.2.85–97; *Tempest* 5.1.188–91

85 *Romeo and Juliet* 5.3.231–64

86 *Tempest* 2.2.158

87 *All's Well* 4.1.52–3; *King Lear*
3.6.62; *Antony and Cleopatra*
2.5.65

89 *Macbeth* 2.3.63–6

90 *As You Like It* 5.1.46–55

91 *Henry VI Part 1* 4.9.60; *Antony
and Cleopatra* 5.2.322

93 *Hamlet* 1.5.15–16

95 *Romeo and Juliet* 1.1.65, 2.2.2,
2.2.33

96 *Romeo and Juliet* 3.1.98,
3.1.115, 3.5.160, 4.3.58,
5.3.119–20, 5.3.168–70,
5.3.309–10

100 *Macbeth* 1.1.48, 1.6.63–4,
2.1.33, 2.3.56, 68, 3.2.36,
3.3.19–21, 3.4.92, 4.1.10–11,
4.2.80–1, 5.1.30, 42, 5.8.33–4

101 *Romeo and Juliet* 1.5.30;
Macbeth 1.4.5–11

102 *Hamlet* 5.2.360–4, 1.5.25

103 *Titus Andronicus* 5.1.62–6;
Macbeth 5.1.27–58

105 *Tempest* 1.2.187–205

106 *Tempest* 1.2.205–15

107 *Tempest* 1.2.187–8, 214–15

108 *Julius Caesar* 3.1.113

109 *Dream* 1.2.17; *Comedy of Errors*
5.1.238–42; *Romeo and Juliet*
1.3.2–4

113 *Romeo and Juliet* 1.1.57–63

114 *Hamlet* 1.2.129, 3.2.351,
2.2.532–5, 2.2.286–8, 5.2.10–11,
5.2.337

115 *King Lear* 1.1.29, 31, 80–5,
100–6

116 *King Lear* 1.1.107–10

117 *Romeo and Juliet* 1.2.71

120 *Hamlet* 1.2.1, 3.3.36, 4.5.74

122 *Othello* 1.2.59, 4.1.40–1

126 *Twelfth Night* 3.1.126; *Merry
Wives* 3.1.68, 71–2

128 *Hamlet* 3.2.34

130 *Macbeth* 1.5.63–4; *Dream*
1.1.134

131 *Merchant of Venice* 2.7.65;
Othello 1.1.66; *Macbeth* 1.1.12,
1.7.82; *Hamlet* 1.5.106;
Macbeth 2.3.133; *Julius Caesar*
4.1.50–1; *Henry VI Part 3*
3.2.182; *Measure for Measure*
5.1.231; *Hamlet* 1.5.108

Index